The
LANGUAGE of SYMBOLISM

The
LANGUAGE of SYMBOLISM

Biblical Theology, Semantics, and Exegesis

Pierre Grelot

Translated by Christopher R. Smith

HENDRICKSON
PUBLISHERS

The Language of Symbolism: Biblical Theology, Semantics, and Exegesis
English translation copyright © 2006 by Hendrickson Publishers, Inc.
P.O. Box 3473
Peabody, Massachusetts 01961-3473

ISBN-13: 978-1-56563-989-8
ISBN-10: 1-56563-989-8

Translated from *Le Langage symbolique dans la Bible* © 2001, Les Éditions du Cerf, Paris, France.

Printed in the United States of America

First printing — May 2006

Cover Art: Margret Utbult, Hönö, Sweden. Used with permission.

Library of Congress Cataloging-in-Publication Data

Grelot, Pierre, 1917–
[Langage symbolique dans la Bible. English]
The language of symbolism : biblical theology, semantics, and exegesis / Pierre Grelot ; translated by Christopher R. Smith.
p. cm.
Includes bibliographical references and index.
ISBN-13: 978-1-56563-989-8 (alk. paper)
ISBN-10: 1-56563-989-8 (alk. paper)
1. Bible—Language, style. 2. Symbolism in the Bible. I. Title.
BS537.G7413 2006
2260.6′4—dc22
2006003638

Contents

Abbreviations

ET	English translation
LXX	Septuagint
MT	Masoretic Text
NRSV	New Revised Standard Version

AnBib	Analecta biblica
BETL	Bibliotheca ephemeridum theologicarum lovaniensium
CaESup	Suppléments au Cahiers évangile
DBSup	*Dictionnaire de la Bible: Supplément.* Edited by L. Pirot and A. Robert. Paris, 1928–
DEB	*Dictionnaire encyclopédique de la Bible.* Edited by P.-M. Bogaert et al. Turnhout: Brepols, 1987
DR	*Dictionnaire des religions.* Edited by P. Poupard. 3d ed. 2 vols. Paris: Presses Universitaires de France, 1993
EDNT	*Exegetical Dictionary of the New Testament.* Edited by H. Balz and G. Schneider. ET. 3 vols. Grand Rapids: Eerdmans, 1990–1993
HTB	Histoire du texte biblique. Lausanne, 1996–
LAPO	Littératures anciennes du Proche-Orient
LD	Lectio divina
NRTh	*La nouvelle revue théologique*

PL	Patrologia latina [= Patrologiae cursus completes: Series latina]. Edited by J.-P. Migne. 217 vols. Paris, 1844–1864
RHR	*Revue de l'histoire des religions*
RSR	*Recherches de science religieuse*
SB	Sources bibliques
Sem	*Semitica*
StudHel	Studia hellenistica
TDNT	*Theological Dictionary of the New Testament.* Edited by G. Kittel and G. Friedrich. Translated by G. W. Bromiley. 10 vols. Grand Rapids: Eerdmans, 1964–1976
TDOT	*Theological Dictionary of the Old Testament.* Edited by G. J. Botterweck, H. Ringgren, and Heinz-Joseph Fabry. Translated by J. T. Willis, G. W. Bromiley, D. E. Green, and Douglas W. Scott. 14 vols. Grand Rapids: Eerdmans, 1974–
ThWAT	*Theologisches Wörterbuch zum Alten Testament.* Edited by G. J. Botterweck and H. Ringgren. Stuttgart, 1970–
Transeu	*Transeuphratène*
TWNT	*Theologische Wörterbuch zum Neuen Testament.* Edited by G. Kittel and G. Friedrich. 10 vols. in 12. Stuttgart, 1932–1979
VTB	*Vocabulaire de théologie biblique.* Edited by X. Léon-Dufour et al. 2d ed. Paris: Cerf, 1970

Introduction

How can we speak of God? Since we have no direct perception of God, the real question is this: What language can we use to evoke God's presence? Every language uses speech that reflects the various aspects of human experience, primarily sensory experience. Our interior experience therefore expresses itself by using words whose content derives initially from sensory experience. By this means we are able to articulate abstract concepts in our intellectual reflections. Faith experience, however, is different. God is not an abstract concept; God is a living presence with whom we are in relationship. How, then, can we describe this relationship in intelligible language so that we can evoke the "presence" of the one who is an absolute "Thou" to us, but is invisible?

"Evoke" is the right word. Properly speaking, God cannot be defined; God's presence is beyond definition. In the words of Gregory of Nazianzus's familiar prayer, "O thou who art above all . . ."! This is precisely the expression, purely negative: it insists that God cannot be compared to anyone or anything else. Nevertheless, the language of the Christian faith is used to trace this indefinable presence so that it can be felt as a mysterious reality with which the believer is in personal relationship. This immediately poses the problem of religious language within Christianity.

The same problem must be posed for Buddhism. Born within the cultural and religious context of India, its essential objective is to offer people a way of deliverance by which they can escape *samsara,* the cycle of transmigrations, and reach *nirvana*, the negative pole of existence. Does this mean that Buddhism, the path of wisdom, is an atheistic religion? No, because atheism would be just another way of being trapped in the web of *samsara*. We rather should describe Buddhism as an agnostic religion, from which any idea or representation of God or the divine is absent.

Besides the monotheistic faiths that are more or less closely connected with the biblical tradition, there are other religions that have attributed, and still attribute, a transcendent value to cosmic or social realities. To evoke them in a way that speaks to the imagination and the emotions, these religions personify the powers that animate these realities, imputing to them feelings analogous to those of humans. Thus is born a "religious symbolism" that is easy to spot in all such circles. It has produced prolific mythologies, but still it is unable to speak of the Unique One, who cannot be the object of any direct perception unless he takes the initiative and reveals himself. And even then the questions remain of how this self-revelation is achieved, and to whom it is made, and how it can be translated into a language that was created to speak of another sort of experience.

Scientific language is inadequate; all it does is describe, in more or less detail, the thing that constitutes the object of sensory or psychological experience. Philosophical language abstracts certain concepts from experience, but in the process it strips them of their emotional and imaginary resonance. I once came across this statement in a book on "the encounter of God and science": "What theologian has not dreamed of demonstrating the existence of God mathematically?"[1] What an absurd concept! On the cultural level alone, religious language, by virtue of its very object, is of a different order than the theorems that are demonstrated in mathematics. It is also of a different order than that of the natural sciences and the humanities. We must not mix things together that belong on different planes. Neither the study of the natural world around us nor even the study of the mechanisms at work in the ego poses the ultimate questions on which the meaning and truth of our existence hang. God is located *above* everything, above the natural world that surrounds us, and above ourselves in our relationships with other people.

---

[1] Claude Allègre, *Dieu face à la science* (Paris: Fayard, 1997), 251.

So how, then, can we speak of God? The more precise our language tries to be in this realm, where we have no direct view, the more it stammers when it tries to appeal to clear concepts. This is because it is at the limits of the human condition. Nevertheless, we need to be able to speak of these things.

How, indeed, has the revelation on which our Christian faith depends succeeded in speaking to us of God, of God's action in the world and in history, of the person of Jesus and of the mystery that was hidden within him, and of his "transhistorical" work that has achieved our salvation? Given that these, taken together, are the essential aspects of our faith, what kind of language does the biblical revelation rely on to establish this faith and to fix its object? This is the essential question to which the present inquiry seeks an answer. Revelation stems from a historical source whose content flows through the books of the Bible. Therefore we will be investigating what kind of language is used in the Bible. Of course, we do not place our faith primarily in books, in texts, or in words; our faith is in God, by the mediation of a person whose life story we have sufficient documentation to trace: Jesus of Nazareth, in whom our faith recognizes the decisive manifestation of God in human history. But Jesus himself came at the end of a process in which the word of God had been brought to people within a particular human community: Israel. This community was descended from the Hebrew patriarchs and survived in the Jewish people throughout the time of the great Middle Eastern empires right down to the period of Roman domination. Jesus himself wrote nothing, but he embodied in his person the heritage of all those who had brought the word of God before him, and he bequeathed his own words and the memory of his actions to those who witnessed his public life.

Jesus proclaimed to his contemporaries in Galilee and Judea the "good news of the reign of God." "Good news" here translates the Greek root *euangelion,* from which comes the English "evangel." Those who heard Jesus recognized in these words a clear allusion to a text from Isaiah: "How beautiful upon the mountains are the feet of the messenger who announces peace, who brings good news [the evangelist], who announces salvation, who says to Zion, 'Your God reigns'" (Isa 52:7). The evangel, or "gospel," that Jesus announced is therefore presented as the fulfillment of the promises made to the people of Israel by a series of messengers from God. But what does the expression "the reign of God" mean? It uses royal traits to represent the one God revealed to the patriarchs, to Moses, and to the prophets. How are we to understand such an image? What kind of language is this, introduced so long before in the biblical revelation?

To inaugurate the reign of God among humans, Jesus did not make himself king in any way. It is a widely known fact, attested even by the Roman historian Tacitus, that Jesus' sojourn here below ended in defeat—his death on a cross. Tacitus even gives the name of the Roman prefect, Pilate, who ordered Jesus' execution, in keeping with what Christians themselves have always claimed. But Jesus' death on a cross had a transhistorical sequel: his resurrection from the dead and his entrance into the glory of God, and subsequently his mediation of a salvation extended from there to all people. This is the Christian credo. How are we to speak of these mysterious realities, which in this case go beyond all sensory experience?

This brings us to the characteristic trait of the language developed to transcribe the biblical revelation, a language suited to speak of the invisible God, of Christ in glory, of his mediation of salvation to every person through the paradoxical event of his cross, and the fact—humanly unverifiable—of his entry into glory and his salvific mediation. As we have noted, all religious languages rely on symbols to express the interactions between humans and the invisible powers that they sense behind the elements of this world. The biblical texts into which the revelation of the living God has flowed renounce the mythologies of these other religious languages, but these texts nevertheless rely to just as great an extent on a veritable flowering of symbols to give us a glimpse of who God is and of what God has done within human history to realize a purpose for humanity. The goal of this study is to understand the way in which this language, woven together of symbols, was formed in the course of the development of the two Testaments, first in Israel and Judaism, and then in the books in which the legacy of Jesus Christ has crystallized.

I need to make a confession at the outset of this long methodological study. In my notes I very frequently cite articles and books that I have published over the past forty years. There is a simple, objective reason for this: circumstances have required me to work at some distance from any libraries, even the one where my own books have been deposited, except for a few that I am still able to consult. I do not attach particular importance to my own publications, but I am at least able to consult them and thereby observe that since 1958 my research has developed in a logical fashion that, frankly, I cannot argue with. My continuing study in the sacred books has led me to re-present in the year 2000, in a more critical form, the principles that I proposed from a theological perspective in 1961 in my book *Sens chrétien de l'Ancien Testament* ("The Christian Meaning of the Old Testament"). When I study the biblical texts, even if I must use biblical criticism to see clearly, I seek nothing less than a correct understanding of the sacred Scriptures. The work of the critic is necessary, but it is not an end in itself. The end that we should pursue is a living relationship with the Holy God revealed definitively in Jesus Christ. The research that I have devoted to the symbolic language of the Bible has had a single purpose: to reveal something of this relationship, which is offered to every one of us. It then falls to each seeker of God to respond, by the grace that God gives even before we act. As Pascal has Jesus say in his meditation on "the mystery of Jesus," "You would not be looking for me if you had not already found me."[2]

---

[2] Blaise Pascal, *Pensées* (ed. Philippe Sellier; Paris: Mercure de France, 1976), no. 751.

I

The Language
of Biblical
Revelation

Religious sentiments are a universal phenomenon. Atheists are fooling themselves. They substitute equivalents for the God, or gods, they reject, and integrate these into their ideologies. They are prone to imposing their "religion" by force if they come to dominate a society. The twentieth century has provided some striking examples of this.[1] Here, however, we are looking into a different kind of question. We are taking it as a given that we believe in the revelation of the one true God, the living God, in a specific place and

---

[1] Within Christendom, distantly descended from the laws by which the emperor Theodosius II made Christianity the official religion of the Roman Empire, monarchies were given religious sanction in this way: James I of England expounded the theory of the "divine right of kings." In the eighteenth century, rationalist ideology issued paradoxically, during the French Revolution, in the cult of the goddess Reason. In the nineteenth century, the atheistic ideology of Karl Marx conferred an absolute value on its fundamental concepts. The states founded on this ideology canonized it by threatening all who opposed it with death (a situation that persists in some places). Hitler's national-socialist regime in Germany forcibly imposed a "myth of the twentieth century" (in Rosenberg's phrase) that represented something of a revival of German paganism. The worshipers of the true God must themselves be on guard against the temptation of totalitarianism, which would impose by force the cult of their God and the rules of the community that is dedicated to him. Examples of this, past and present, are not difficult to find. The true God is thereby misrepresented by social authorities that claim to have faith in him.

time, within a particular human community, within a people and a culture chosen by God in keeping with a secret design that God does not have to explain to us, and supremely in the person of Jesus of Nazareth, heir of this community's tradition.

That God chose this people, and that God directed its history, leaving signs that permit his presence and action to be recognized, are mysterious realities that can be recognized only by faith. This is not to say that the religious instinct that has manifested itself at all times and in every culture has not sketched out paths to lead people toward God, paths that have a measure of authenticity and that God himself has inspired in a certain way.[2] But God's revelation in its entirety has only come once, in Jesus, who was, paradoxically, rejected and put to death by humans, but who became for them the mediator of salvation by his resurrection from the dead. This ultimate reality—as mysterious as God himself—cannot be recognized except by faith. The problem being posed here is this: What language is capable of translating this faith in order to give people a glimpse into the mystery of God and the salvation that is theirs in Jesus Christ?

The language capable of translating this faith is that of the Bible, which was born in the course of a certain history and within the framework of a certain culture. Under what conditions was it written? What characteristics did it receive from its immersion in that history and that culture that made it capable of "speaking God"—that is, translating the mystery of God to which we owe our salvation? These are questions of capital importance for those of faith who are seeking understanding. We will examine two aspects of these questions: (1) In what culture(s) and in what languages(s) did the sovereign action of God take up human speech in order to make that speech a bearer of its own revelation? (2) What traits must

---

[2] This is what makes the Christian attitude toward the followers of other religions problematic. Their inward sentiments, their representations of the divine or of the problems posed by human existence, their ideas of morality and of life in community, may contain aspects that derive from a valid interior intuition to which the grace of God is no stranger. This is why, for example, the church fathers did not reject the precise intuitions of Stoic morality. Should not this insight guide our responses today to the religious traditions of India or of Buddhism?

human speech exhibit in order to be capable of translating the inexpressible mystery of this action and of God himself?

CULTURES AND LANGUAGES

The Bible is inseparable from the cultural framework within which it took shape. We might imagine that for its self-revelation Divine Providence would have chosen one of the great cultures characterized by advanced social development, political power, and a flourishing literature: in the ancient Near East, those of Sumer and Akkadia; or that of Egypt, whose abundant literature we have recovered; or in the Far East, those of China, India, or Japan. The cultures of the ancient Near East nourished those that developed on their ruins, while those of the Far East have left us their ancient masterpieces, and their religious traditions have passed their values on down to the present day. These cultural and religious values—those of the past that have now disappeared in the dust of time and those of the present that the biblical and Christian revelation has not yet profoundly penetrated—should not be condemned, even though their limitations become clearly apparent when they are confronted with the gospel.

Nevertheless, to reveal itself to people, and to make itself a part of humanity through the incarnation of Jesus Christ, Divine Providence in fact chose a humble human community undistinguished by either political power or cultural resources: the people of Israel, who were the source of the Judaism into which Jesus was born. Israel, a humble nation amidst the small Canaanite states that surrounded it, was distinguished from them by the continuity of a prophetic ministry that was responsible for the development of monotheistic faith, a phenomenon unparalleled in the history of religion. It contained, of course, beliefs, customs, and cultic rituals inherited from ancient times in a Semitic milieu that was strongly attached to its traditions. The cult of the true God was not imposed in a single day in its fully evolved form; on the contrary, it had to be continually reasserted. It was deepened through difficulties and crises, thanks to the inspired persons who transmitted the divine message in a way faithful to its original revelation. We need not retrace this whole story here.

This message, which culminated in the gospel of Jesus Christ, took form in texts that successively made use of different languages. The first was Hebrew, a Canaanite dialect like Edomite and Ammonite, Phoenician, and, even earlier, Ugaritic. Then, after the national disasters of the destruction of Jerusalem in 587 B.C.E., the Babylonian captivity, and the exile and dispersion of the Jews, Aramaic (a Semitic relative of Hebrew) came to dominate as the spoken language.[3] Finally came Greek, into which the ancient texts were translated.

This is not the place to review this entire history. The important observation here is that those persons whom God inspired to deliver and to deepen the divine revelation took up these languages in order to make them vehicles of the word of God. "The word of God"—that is the very expression that they themselves used to describe their actions and their message. It was not the fruit of human philosophical reflection, as took place in Greece and in Hellenistic civilization, but rather a message directly from God, which these persons brought at great risk to their own lives. What kind of speech did they find to transmit the message with which they were entrusted, and to designate the One who had entrusted it to their care?

THE DESIGNATION OF GOD

The Word "God" in the Bible

Those who transmitted the revelation did not begin by inventing a special word to designate the One whose messengers they were. They simply took up the existing name of the power that reigned

---

[3] In actual Jewish usage Aramaic supplanted Hebrew progressively. This is already observable in the fifth century B.C.E. (see Neh 13:24). Starting in the third century B.C.E., many pseudepigraphical books were written in Aramaic, as is seen in the manuscripts discovered at Qumran (*Enoch, Testament of Levi,* other fragments). Five manuscripts of the book of Tobit were recovered there, four in Aramaic and only one in Hebrew. The oldest chapters of the book of Daniel (Dan 2–7) are in Aramaic. The Aramaic portions of the book of Ezra (4:7–22; 5:6–6:12) are diplomatic documents dating from the sixth or fifth century B.C.E. in the Persian Empire.

over the Semitic pantheon. The Hebrew *'El* and the Aramaic *'Elah* (corresponding to the Hebrew *'Eloah*) represent a common word attested in both East Semitic[4] (*Ilu* in Akkadian texts) and West Semitic languages (*'El* in Ugaritic, taken into biblical Hebrew). The root appears in Arabic as *'Ilah: 'Allah* = *'al-'Ilah,* "*the* God." Before Islam there was a feminine divinity *'Allat* (= *'al-'Ilat,* "the Goddess"). This name, common to all divinities, sometimes was used in Hebrew in the plural to designate "divine beings" (Ps 58:1 [58:2 MT], metaphorically). But the biblical tradition prefers to use the plural *'Elohim*[5] with a singular meaning. It is a matter not of a plurality of the divine, but of its intensity in its own instruments. The root of the word seems to be the Semitic radical *'yl,* which designates vigor or force—hence its use for animals, *'ayil,* "ram," and *'ayyal,* "stag," and for a "great tree," *'elon.* This connotation also accounts for the associations of the word, in a construct state, in descriptive expressions such as "God of faithfulness" (Ps 31:5 [31:6 MT]), "God of eternity" (Gen 21:33 [= "the eternal God"]), or "God of vengeance" (i.e., of a justice that visits evil upon those who perpetrate it); in allusions to places where God has been revealed—for example, "God of Bethel" (a word that already signifies "house of God," *beyt-'el*); and with the name of the people whom God protects: "God of Israel" (frequently).

The recognition of God's uniqueness developed over time, beginning with a practical monotheism that first excluded the worship of any other divinities. The source of this exclusion was not philosophical reflection; it came from a concrete experience of being in relationship with God, an experience that Israelite tradition traced all the way back to the nation's ancestors, the patriarchs. God was the "God of Abraham, Isaac, and Jacob," the "God of our fathers" (as in, e.g., Gen 26:24; 28:13; Exod 3:6). God's absolute uniqueness is affirmed clearly in Deuteronomy (Deut 32:39) and in the "Message of Consolation" contained within the book of Isaiah (Isa 43:10; 44:6; 48:12). The matter is clear in Psalms, where the creator God (cf. Gen 1:1–2:4) is recognized as the God of the interior

---

[4] See F. M. Cross, "אֵל *'ēl,*" *TDOT* 1:242–61, a philological study of this root that takes Semitic parallels into account.

[5] See H. Ringgren, "אֱלֹהִים *'ĕlōhîm,*" *TDOT* 1:267–84.

life, as "my God" (Ps 42:6 [42:7 MT]) or "our God" (Ps 66:8). This is not metaphysical speculation; the people of the Bible were not inclined to abstraction. But God nevertheless constitutes the essential aspect of an original spiritual experience that deepens as the biblical revelation develops. Under these conditions the rejection and negation of other gods is automatic, without the need for any abstract reflection on God's nature. There are sufficient indications of how God acts in the world and in the lives of people to recognize that God is the Unique One, the Creator, the One to whose initiative people must respond by entering into relationship.

The Name of God

Within the biblical revelation there is a specific revelation of the "name" of God—that is, of God's original designation—within narrative texts, prayers, and prophetic discourses. In two important passages in the book of Exodus, which come from different sources (Exod 3:1–14; 6:1–9), God describes himself by revealing his name. How should we understand this name, which expresses the "nature" of God, as every name in the Hebrew language does, describing the reality that it designates? It is likely that there was an older designation that has been preserved in proper names: *Yaho* or *Yahu* or *Yah*. This designation, whose origin is uncertain,[6] is preceded by the account of the "burning bush,"[7] in which Moses interrogates the One who calls himself "the God of your father, the God of Abraham, the God of Isaac, and the God of Jacob" (Exod 3:6), and asks

---

[6] See D. N. Freedman, P. O'Connor, and H. Ringgren, "יהוה YHWH," *TDOT* 5:500–21. An excellent clarification is provided by H. Cazelles, "Yahwisme, ou Yahvé et son peuple," in *Études d'histoire religieuse et de philologie biblique* (SB; Paris: Gabalda, 1996), 35–47. It is interesting that among the Aramaic-speaking Jews who lived at Elephantine in the fifth century B.C.E., the divine name was written as *YHW* (*Yaho* or *Yahu*).

[7] The literary genre of the account must be recognized. It is not "history" in the modern sense of that word; rather, it evokes artistically the origin and meaning of the name that the Israelite tradition gave to God, connecting it with Moses and the Sinai covenant. But the image of the burning bush that is not consumed, symbolic of the eternal God, whom no death can ever overtake, is without parallel in the pagan environment within which the religion of Israel grew up.

by what name he should identify him to his fellow Israelites. In the parallel account from the Priestly tradition God takes the initiative in declaring, "I appeared to Abraham, Isaac, and Jacob as *'El Shadday*," a problematic designation whose meaning has not been fully elucidated.[8] The answer that God gives in the first dialogue, when interrogated by Moses, is difficult to translate into our language.

This answer depends on a play on words using the verb "to be," *hayah,* which must be understood in the sense of presence ("being there," "being present"), not in the abstract sense of existence, as in Greek speculative thought. But the "presence" of the One who "is there" certainly implies that this One exists. Moses poses the question "If . . . they ask me, 'What is his name?' what shall I say to them?" (Exod 3:13). God answers in Hebrew, *'ehyeh 'asher 'ehyeh* (Exod 3:14a). The repetition of the verb *hayah* requires the use of the first person in the expression introduced by the relative pronoun; this is a grammatical convention. But the verb has one nuance in the principal proposition, "I am," and a different one in the subordinate clause, which defines what the subject who speaks is. It is difficult for our language to express the relationship: "I am Who is" would be an unacceptable solecism. The Greek version translates the phrase as "I am the Being" (*ho ōn*), speculatively drawing out the existential value of the verb *einai.* All things considered, we could paraphrase by translating, "I am the one who I AM [spoken of oneself]." Indeed, as the account continues, it depicts God as saying, "Thus you shall say to the Israelites, 'I AM has sent me to you'" (Exod 3:14b). But in what sense should we understand the verb "to be" in this context? Certainly it includes an allusion to existence, but the verb should be understood primarily in the sense of presence: "I am-there," "I am-with-you." It is the living God who speaks.

---

[8] The current discussion of the origin and meaning of this name is very well presented by H. Niehr and G. Steins in "שַׁדַּי *šadday,*" *TDOT* 14:418–46. The article, written in 1993, contains two full columns of bibliographic references. Parallel terms in other Semitic languages are discussed by H. Niehr, who includes a corresponding bibliography (cols. 1080–83). The closest parallel is the mention of gods called *shaddayin* alongside the *'elahin* in an eighth-century B.C.E. Aramaic inscription from Deir 'Alla. Nevertheless, the meaning of the word remains obscure.

As for the name "YHWH," a third-person conjugation of a root related to the attested Aramaic verb *hawah*, "to be," how was it pronounced? The later cultic tradition, out of respect for the mystery of God, allowed only the Jewish high priest to proclaim it, inside the holy of holies on the Day of Atonement. Judging from certain Greek transcriptions of magical texts, we can presume that the word was originally pronounced *Yahweh* (since it was transcribed into Greek as *Iaoue*). The consonants would have had an early vocalization in texts of the prophets and the psalms, but eventually they were given the vowels of the word *Adonay*, "Lord," by the Masoretes, not out of fear, but out of respect. This is the source of the faulty transcription found in modern languages, *Jehovah*. In the Hebrew manuscripts from Qumran, which are not vocalized, the tetragram "YHWH" often is replaced by four dots or by the pronoun *hu'*, "he." In Greek manuscripts copied by Christian hands the divine name has most generally been replaced by *Kyrios*, "Lord," a practice bequeathed to the texts of the New Testament.[9] But in the Gospels and other books the word *kyrios* is generalized in order to be applied to Jesus. We will examine this point in detail below.

How the name of God would be designated was thus firmly established, and qualifiers began to accumulate to indicate God's interior dispositions toward humanity as well as God's acts in creation and in the history of the chosen people and of other nations. By this means, God's power, goodness, mercy, and interventions in the world to subdue the elements and to send people on religious and political missions were underscored. Each of these things will be examined in detail as we take up the language that refers to them. The essential thing to note here is the concrete character of this language, which nearly always avoids abstraction, until the Greek language begins to be used. We therefore do find abstract language in the New Testament, where God is revealed through the mediation of the person of Jesus, his words and his acts in history. But when the proclamation of the good news and the reflection that unveils the meaning of Jesus' acts transmit the legacy of the First Testament,

---

[9] In Greek texts of both Testaments the word *kyrios* preceded by the article should be translated as "the Lord," but the absence of the article indicates a proper name that may correspond to the tetragram "YHWH."

the texts then generally take up the concrete language of the Bible as a whole. As a result, we find the language of both Testaments making use of symbols.

THE NEED FOR, AND FUNCTION OF, SYMBOLIC LANGUAGE

Ordinary Language and Symbolic Language

God, the only true God, is not accessible to our senses. We have been given a direct perception of God, but we cannot use it to designate and describe him. Yes, God is present and active, but what is this presence? The prophets of the First Testament evoked God's presence only by communicating God's word; but how did they themselves receive this word, and how were they able to communicate it in intelligible language? In the Christian faith Jesus is the one who revealed this word definitively, by his own words, by his actions, by his life and even his death, and ultimately by his resurrection from the dead. But did he ever *define* God? For that matter, how could God be defined other than by the simple affirmation of his existence? Thomas Aquinas, in one article of his *Summa theologica,* poses the question of whether God's essence and existence are identical. He answers, "We cannot know what the *esse* of God is [God's existence], any more than we can know God's essence [what God is]. . . . What we do know is that the proposition we form with regard to God when we say 'God exists' is a true proposition: we know this by the effects of this existence."[10]

In other words, even if by faith we know with certainty that God exists, we still have no direct view or clear definition of this existence. The "mystery" of God is *above* what we are able to say about it. In that case, what language must we use to speak of God?

The same question must be posed regarding Jesus Christ, but not regarding his existence and his activity on earth right up to his death; on that point, we may conduct historical inquiries, drawing

---

[10] Aquinas, *Summa theologica* Ia, q. 3, a. 4. The text has been lightly paraphrased to make its very dense Latin more intelligible.

on witnesses who speak of him and allow our inquiry to take place within the purview of rational understanding.[11] Critical discussions of the texts that speak of Jesus would be meaningless if they did not rest upon the same kind of facts that would be adduced for any other person in human history. His entrance into the glory of God by his resurrection, however, is a matter for another kind of understanding.

Thus these questions are raised: How are we to speak of Christ in glory? How does his present admission into the glory of God retrospectively clarify what his human condition was, and what his relationship was to God during his life on earth? In short, how does it clarify the reality of the mystery of his person, the meaning of his deeds and of his death, his decisive role in the salvation of humanity, and so forth? The New Testament is centered on these mysterious realities, which are beyond any historical inquiry.[12] But how can it speak of them, since their existence also belongs to the invisible domain where the reality of God is hidden? What language does the New Testament use to speak of these things?

We can point to many places in the New Testament itself that demonstrate the inability of ordinary language to describe realities that are inaccessible to our senses. In his first letter to the Corinthians the apostle Paul must correct the ideas that his correspondents hold regarding the Christian hope, which ultimately is oriented toward the resurrection. He takes up a question that the Corinthians have posed, a question that they have formed in keeping with Greek thought: What can the resurrection of the body possibly mean?

---

[11] Nevertheless, it must be observed that if we seek at all costs to achieve an *exact* historical understanding of Jesus, we risk imposing an undue restraint on the truth of the texts that evoke his person. When it comes to the facts of his life and to his words, these witnesses can present a true understanding of him, even if they remain vague as to what his exact deeds and words were, in keeping with the accepted conventions of the time in which they were written and the development that the interpretation of his memory experienced as the gospel was proclaimed.

[12] I touch on these questions in chs. 20–25 of my book *Jésus de Nazareth, Christ et Seigneur: Une lecture de l'Evangile* (2 vols.; LD; Paris: Cerf, 1997–1998), 2:347–522. I treated the chapters of Luke and Matthew that evoke the birth and infancy of Jesus in this section of my book because they are told in light of his resurrection.

"How are the dead raised? With what kind of body do they come?" (1 Cor 15:35). After drawing on some simple analogies that are not in any way demonstrative (1 Cor 15:36–41), Paul comes to define the condition of resurrected bodies negatively: "What is sown is perishable, what is raised is imperishable" (1 Cor 15:42 [repeated in vv. 50, 52–53]). Then, in 1 Cor 15:53, another contrast appears, between "being mortal" and "immortality." Paul thus contrasts *phthartos* and *aphtharsia,* then *thnētos* and *athanasia.* These words in no way describe the condition of resurrected bodies; they simply say *what they are not,* by contrast with the condition of the body during life on earth.

The state of resurrected bodies in the "world to come"—to borrow an expression from Jewish eschatology—is identical to the condition of the resurrected Christ, even if, in his appearances to the witnesses chosen by God to attest to his resurrection (Acts 10:40–41), he took a concrete form that enabled them to recognize who he was. Therefore, in order to speak of his current presence and of his activity in bringing about our salvation, we must renounce all pretensions to description. No one knows what his entry into the "glory of God" consisted of, because God is beyond any possibility of description.[13] This mystery of Christ in glory, in intimate relation with God, reflects back upon the intimacy that he enjoyed when he was active down here in our midst: it was, from the beginning, the background of his historical existence and activity. The Gospel texts give us a glimpse of it from time to time, particularly when they evoke his relationship with "the Father." Here we meet in the New Testament the same difficulty in speaking of God that we observed in the First Testament.

---

[13] The fact of the resurrection is not described in any way by the canonical Gospels, but the presence of angelic messengers in the resurrection accounts shows that they depart from historical facts that could be verified by any observer. They manifest, on the narrative plane, the presence of the "world above" in this earthly world. Only an apocryphal Gospel from the middle of the second century C.E., the *Gospel of Peter,* shows the sky opening and the guards at the tomb witnessing the scene of Jesus' resurrection and his ascension into heaven. The text is available in François Bovon and Pierre Geoltrain, eds., *Écrits apocryphes chrétiens* (vol. 1; Paris: Gallimard, 1997), 251–52.

The Role of Symbolic Language

It is here that the role of symbolic language intervenes. A symbol does not describe the reality that it envisions and of which it gives a glimpse beyond the limits of natural understanding; rather, it evokes certain aspects of it, leaving the spirit to construct representations that, by intuition, will grasp something of the mystery evoked. In the literature of every religion literary genres exist that situate themselves immediately on the symbolic plane: parables, fables, myths, legends, and so on. The essential thing is to understand what the authors who make use of these genres are trying to say through them. However, a symbol, in itself, does not constitute a particular literary genre.[14] It is a kind of developed metaphor that suggests realities inscribed in the understanding of faith. Faith itself is intuitive and global, but diffuse in terms of its object, which it does not permit to be defined in clear terms. Thus the enumeration of God's "perfections" only acquires full resonance when it is grafted onto a general perception that has already put the human person in concrete relationship with God. A symbolic evocation of God's presence is needed to inaugurate this relationship, and so reflection on the perfections of God only sharpens what a prior intuition has already sensed.

By beginning with a collection of symbolic expressions to evoke the presence of God, of the "world to come," and of the resurrected Christ in action, human language acquires the ability to make us sense the mysterious realities that it has in view, using veiled words, even if it cannot give clear definitions of these realities. The Scrip-

---

[14] See J. Vidal, "Symbole," *DR* 2:1937–42, followed by applications to different religious systems. Vidal's bibliography (p. 1942) documents the study of this problem since 1952. Naturally, a "symbol" as such has a wider application than its use in religious language. The verses of Baudelaire are well known: "Nature is a temple in which living pillars / sometimes let out confused words; / Man walks through forests of symbols / that observe him, wearing familiar expressions" ("Correspondances," in *Les fleurs du mal*). The "correspondences" that nature contains remain vague. When religious language takes them up, it projects onto them specific meanings that are in keeping with the beliefs it has in view. Christian faith, which is closely tied to biblical revelation, turns spontaneously to symbolic language to envision those things that, in themselves, cannot be defined clearly.

tures of the two Testaments are able to make their distinctive affirmations by putting them in this form of expression: the uniqueness
of God as revealed within the framework of the Scriptures, and
nowhere else in as authentic a way; the choice of a historical community to be God's people, with a vocation unlike any other; the
successive transformations of that community in anticipation of salvation; the uniqueness of the salvation that Jesus of Nazareth
brought about, as a manifestation of God himself in a person whom
faith recognizes as "God's Son" (eminently symbolic language!).
Thus the role that God's messengers played within history, a role
taken up after the return of Christ Jesus to the Father by those
whom he sent into the world as heralds of the gospel, reaches its
culmination.

This is the framework within which we must situate the character of the symbolic language through which the revelation of God
has been transmitted to humanity. To be sure, symbolic language is
present in all religions. In the specific case of the biblical writings,
however, it is essential to identify with precision the different categories of symbols that are to evoke all aspects of God's revelation.[15]
Some types may also be found elsewhere, in the language of other
religions, but their selection and their internal correlations are decisive for determining their exact significance and meaning within the
Bible. We will see later that a certain category of symbols has no
counterpart in other religions, because it reflects an aspect of biblical
revelation that is unique in its kind. I will develop this point carefully because it is essential for an exact understanding of the
Christian revelation.

The Categories of Symbols in the Language of the Scriptures

We will not be working here with abstract classifications, but
rather examining the two Testaments to see how their authors constructed symbols that corresponded to their faith experience, in order
to evoke diverse aspects of the mystery of God in his relationship

---

[15] This interpretation of symbols is crucial for an exact understanding
of the texts in which they appear. Their correlation constitutes a system
that distinctively characterizes the language of the Bible in the midst of all
the religious traditions that use this form of expression.

with humanity and of the mystery of Christ as the ultimate and definitive realization of this relationship. To create a suitable language, the various biblical writers, and before them those who proclaimed the word of God in the oral tradition of the two Testaments, depended to a certain extent on the symbolic language used within the religious contexts that preceded them. However, they transformed this language according to the specific experience of faith that they had. For an entire range of experience that has no counterpart in other religions of the ancient East, they created a new symbolism that plays an essential role in the language of the New Testament. We can identify four categories of symbols,[16] to which I assign specific names: analogical, mythical, figurative, existential (using this last term for lack of a better one). These categories will serve as a guide for examining in detail the use of symbolic language in the biblical texts.

Analogical Symbols

These symbols are the simplest, and they can be observed at use in every religious language to speak of the relationship between a divinity and humans. But within the Christian faith this symbolism is grounded in an essential point of revelation: if we can speak of God in the image of humanity, it is because humans are created "in the image of God" (Gen 1:27). As a result, it is possible to draw an analogy between the realm of people's relationships with one another and that of their relationship with God, presented directly in the First Testament and continued in the New Testament thanks to the mediation of Jesus Christ. Two realms of relationships among people can provide a starting point for such analogical symbols: that of human families, and that of human society as it functioned insti-

---

[16] I have briefly presented this classification of symbols in the language of the biblical writings elsewhere: "Le langage symbolique dans la Bible: Note méthodologique," in *Kecharitomene: Mélanges René Laurentin* (Paris: Desclée, 1990), 43–69. I used this classification again to present "Un examen critique du langage symbolique" ("a critical examination of symbolic language") in my *Réponse à Eugen Drewermann* (Théologies: Apologiques; Paris: Cerf, 1994), 56–70. In that response I sought to critique the "archetypal" interpretation of the biblical language that Drewermann derived from Jungian psychoanalytic theory.

tutionally during the times when the Bible was written. I will make this general observation more precise as we examine the symbols found in the biblical texts, since not every form of family or social organization actually provides materials suitable for symbolic use in biblical language.

Mythical Symbols

The words "myth" and "mythical" are not used here in the sense of the imaginary constructions that have led to the elaboration of mythologies within religious cults that are strangers to the monotheistic revelation of the two Testaments.[17] These words are used simply to describe cases where the language of the Bible has had to construct imagery that evokes two domains that are radically inaccessible to human experience, or at least to clear definitions of the realities they contain.

In the first place, human experience sets each person between two poles that certainly exist but are impossible to describe; the only way to speak of them is by constructing imagery that suggests their opposing characteristics: on the one hand, the "world of God," to which every experience of goodness, joy, and life pertains; on the other hand, the "world of evil," where we locate everything that we sense as bad, whether it be physical (sickness, death) or moral (human failings and those faults that religion describes as "sin"). God, in mystery, is the source of everything good, and our imagination instinctively locates God's "place" above, in an inaccessible "heaven" where light reigns. By contrast, the ultimate source of evil cannot be defined, because of its absolute obscurity. It can only be

---

[17]Nor am I taking the words "myth" and "mythic" in the sense that R. Bultmann gave to the words "mythology" and "mythological" to promote the "demythologization" of the New Testament texts in order to bring out an "existential" interpretation. These words had an extensive significance for him, which he regarded as normative. See, for example, the long article "Nouveau Testament et mythologie" in the anthology *L'Interprétation du Nouveau Testament* (ed. O. Laffoucrière; Les religions II; Paris: Aubier, 1955), 139–83. Rather than "demythization" (*Entmythisierung*), we should speak of "demythologization" (*Entmytholigisierung*)— that is, the "interpretation of myth" rather than the "exclusion of myth" after the manner of nineteenth-century theological liberalism. But I am using the word "myth" here in a purely literary sense.

located "below," in an infernal domain that our imagination populates with nefarious personalities: Satan and his demons—that is, the spirit of evil and his minions, subjects of imaginative portrayal in every culture and in every religion. Here, the religion of the true God must be careful to moderate the representations that it generates of these infernal realities, ensuring that they are subordinated to God himself.

In the second place, the historical experience of humanity unfolds between two equally inaccessible poles of time. Unable to represent them objectively, the human spirit wonders about the "beginning" and the "ending" between which its present experience unfolds. More than one mythology has projected onto this unfolding of time the image of the cycles that, in nature, perpetually renew themselves in an "eternal return." Biblical revelation reacts against this "eternal return," which would lower humanity to the level of nature around it. Faith in the true God and in God's design within human history instead situates the unfolding of time between an inaccessible beginning and an equally inaccessible ending. When it comes to the beginning of time, to origins, biblical revelation demonstrates great sobriety, reacting against the prolific myths of origin that developed within a polytheistic framework in Mesopotamia and Egypt, in which the elements of the world were elevated to divine status. A few demythologized images, derived from Canaanite sources, still remain, but the rest of the Bible's images of origin are parabolic or didactic constructions transformed into poetic imagery. We will examine their specific features below. When the Bible evokes the end of time, which is equally inaccessible to direct comprehension, it mixes mythological images with historical reminiscences that have been transformed by a figurative interpretation, as we will also see.[18]

We should be clear about the Bible's use of symbolic representations that can be considered "mythological": even when it uses

---

[18] In the biblical books human history culminates in the realization of God's design. However, when the prophets evoke this "end," this is not an exercise in "futurology" (if I may use that word). It is only in the third century B.C.E. that this endpoint of time begins to be evoked as "the last days," in the strong sense of the word (*to eschaton*), allowing us to apply the term "eschatology" in its literal sense.

them, it remains strictly within the bounds of a revelation that breaks deliberately with earlier mythologies, and it subordinates the imagery in its language to clear affirmations of faith in the true God.

Figurative Symbols

Symbols in this category are not to be found in any other religious language. This is because it is only within biblical revelation that the unfolding of human history is valued positively as the realization of God's design.[19] However, it is necessary to take a step back from historical events in order to recognize their deeper meanings, which we can see God's messengers doing when they speak of events that have taken place within the history of the "people of God."

We must first understand how Israel can be described as the "people of God." The events at Sinai made them the "people of the covenant." As a result, the events of their history had meaning on two levels. Fortunate events, right up to the establishment of David's kingdom and the construction of the temple in Jerusalem, were manifestations of God's benevolent intentions. The defeats they suffered were, on the other hand, the result of God's judgments on his unfaithful people, right up to the final defeat that put an end to their national life with the destruction of Jerusalem in 587 B.C.E., the deportation of their elites to Babylon, and the subsequent dispersion of the Jews. However, at the same time, the prophets who announced these events as signs of God's judgment also offered visions of the future that depended on a figurative interpretation of past experiences: a new covenant with God's law written on the people's hearts, a new nation governed by an ideal king, a new temple with purified worship, and so forth. The details of this figurative interpretation of past history will be explored below. We will see that the role of the suffering and death of the righteous was not unappreciated within this reflection on past expectation, but it was not yet connected with the promises of a new covenant and the Messiah.

---

[19] The principles of this figurative interpretation of First Testament history and the texts that relate to it are presented in detail in the chapter devoted to them. For the moment it suffices to note the general principles behind this interpretation.

In the New Testament the essential fact of the mystery of Christ Jesus, the reality of the Word made flesh, and the details of his life are presented as something absolutely new. Nevertheless, as these things are interpreted in light of God's design, appeal to figurative passages in the prophets plays a dominant role, first in the thinking of Jesus and in his own words, and then in the apostolic faith that is founded on his resurrection. The essential language of Christology takes shape thanks to this figurative rereading of prophetic texts that significantly predate the Christian hope. We will have to go over this third category of symbols with the greatest care.

Existential Symbols

This category refers to cases in which various aspects of common human experience, whether in our perception of the world (the feel of the wind, light, etc.) or in our interpersonal relationships, are transposed metaphorically onto the plane of relationship with God. The identification of symbols of this type will become straightforward once we have examined a few significant examples. The category under consideration here will serve as guide for examining in detail the uses of symbolic language in the biblical texts.

2
Analogical Symbols

To speak of God or of Christ Jesus, the books of the two Testaments make use of analogical symbols that are based on metaphorical images. These symbols evoke, in their own way, certain aspects of the living God, or for Christ certain of his activities in the realization of the divine plan. They are applied not to the earthly life of Jesus, which is accessible to historical inquiry, but rather to the mysterious aspects of his person, which were always present in the background of his activity throughout his sojourn here on earth.

We must recall a fact here that is essential for a proper understanding of the Gospel texts that evoke Jesus' words and his actions: all of the Gospel texts that were written, as well as the tradition from which they developed, took shape only *after* his resurrection from the dead. Thus their authors and editors did not hesitate to project the light of his ultimate glorification retrospectively onto his earlier words and deeds. As a result, the words used to evoke his earthly life may have been chosen in keeping with faith in the glorified Christ, or they may carry overtones of this faith. For example, it is his resurrection that has elevated him to the rank of "Lord and Messiah" (Acts 2:36). Several times in the accounts of his earthly life his disciples address him by the title "Lord" (*Kyrios*), and the narrator may also call him "the Lord" when speaking of him (e.g., Luke 7:13). It is true that in the vocative the word can have the simple meaning "sir." This is the case, for example, when the Samaritan woman speaks to Jesus in John 4:11. Nevertheless, when reread within that Gospel as a whole, the word certainly carries the sense "Lord." Indeed, the Gospel texts are always a "rereading" of the words and deeds of Jesus, carried out in faith. It therefore is necessary to interpret them as having this specific resonance.

METAPHORICAL DESIGNATIONS OF
GOD AND/OR CHRIST

Is the word "metaphorical" truly suitable for the category of symbols we are studying here? Yes, but it must be limited to cases in which the evocation of God or of Christ in glory—eventually reflected back onto Jesus in his earthly life—is not related to family or societal functions. In those two cases, the use of a symbolic vocabulary belongs to another, "figurative" category that we will examine further below. Here we will take up some of the other cases that relate to God and to Christ.

Anthropomorphic Representations of God

An older study by F. Michaeli has already blazed the trail here.[1] Not surprisingly, its author observes[2] that ancient mythologies made use of the same procedure to represent their own divinities. However, there is a radical difference between the multiform gods that appear in mythologies and the Holy God of the Bible. The society of gods and goddesses is a carbon copy of human societies, with all of their negative aspects: their internal contradictions, wars, vices, and so forth. The progressive revelation, on the other hand, pushes all of these defects far away from the Holy God. This revelation emerged, it is true, within a cultural framework where "divine" was not understood in terms of *being*, as in Greek thought, but rather in terms of *power*, energy, force. This is why the various pagan cultures of the

---

[1] F. Michaeli, *Dieu à l'image de l'homme: Etude de la notion anthropomorphique de Dieu dans l'Ancien Testament* (Bibliothèque théologique; Neuchatel: Delachaux et Niestlé, 1950). The subtitle specifies the object of the study: "a study of the anthropomorphic notion of God in the Old Testament."

[2] Michaeli, *Dieu à l'image de l'homme*, 135–53: "Le Dieu saint et les dieux de la mythologie." See especially pp. 135–47.

Middle East divinized all of the powers at work in the universe, from the stars, which they represented as animate beings, to the forces that controlled animal and human fertility and fecundity, to the evil forces that make people on earth their victims and drag them off to their deaths.

Biblical revelation does not reject a representation of God in terms of power; it even calls God the "All-Powerful." However, it concentrates on God everything that belongs to what Greek philosophy regarded as the realm of the good, the true, and the beautiful (to use these "universal" terms from its logical classification), and it excludes their contraries, which are seen as enemies of humanity. Over against death, which people dread above everything else, God is the Living One par excellence. Numerous passages may be cited in which God is described this way, both in the First Testament (Josh 3:10; 1 Sam 17:26, 36; 2 Kgs 19:4, 16 [= Isa 37:4, 17]; Jer 10:10; 12:16; 16:14; Ps 42:2; 84:2; Dan 4:34; 6:26; Tob 13:1; 2 Macc 15:4) and in the New Testament (Matt 16:16; John 6:57; 2 Cor 6:16; 1 Thess 1:9; Heb 3:12; 9:14; 10:31; 1 Pet 1:23). This description is also associated with the eternity of God (cf. Gen 21:33): God is the "everlasting rock" (Isa 26:4) and is "king forever" (Ps 29:10), appeal being made here to other symbolic representations at the same time, and God is the one who "lives forever" (Dan 4:34). In the Greek text of Baruch, God is referred to simply as "the Everlasting" (Bar 4:10 and 7 more times). In the Hebrew expressions just cited, the word occurs with other nouns in the construct state—for example, "king of eternity." The actual term is *'olam,* which refers in spatial terms to the "world," and in temporal terms to an "age." But God is neither of this world nor of this age. God belongs to a different order from those of space and time, in which we live.

This is why, in order to speak of God, the qualities, actions, or sentiments of human persons can be used metaphorically, since the image of God already appears in people as such. The construction of evocative imagery in this way is in keeping with the principle articulated in the Priestly account of the creation: on the seventh day God said, "Let us make humankind in our image, according to our likeness" (Gen 1:26). Here, "image" refers to a manufactured image (*tselem* [Num 33:52]), and the resemblance, "likeness," that exists between God and his human creature is God's *demut.* Because there thus exists a resemblance between humans and their Creator, traits can be borrowed from people and, when pushed to the extreme, be used to evoke God symbolically. Nonetheless, God's absolute transcendence must somehow be clearly indicated. This is how the use of anthropomorphisms in the biblical writings differs radically from their use in the polytheistic mythologies that surrounded the biblical milieu.

Corporeal Symbols Applied to God

Because God is represented in the image of the human person, it should not surprise us to read expressions that speak of God as if God had a body, or as if God carried out deeds or actions that presuppose the use of limbs or organs. This literary convention shows God to be the "Living One," not an abstract metaphysical principle. A person of faith would not think much of having a personal relationship with the "Prime Mover," and a God who designated as the "First Principle" would not be the same kind of God who can see and hear.

The Language of the First Testament

In ancient mythologies God was constantly represented anthropomorphically. In the biblical tradition[3] it is clear that God does not have a body, but anthropomorphisms borrowed from a corporeal conception abound.

Corporeal Representations of God. The Bible speaks frequently of the "face" of God (35x in Psalms). God shows his face to save people, but he hides it to demonstrate his anger. The believer "seeks the face of God" (Ps 27:8), but the sinner who is afraid of God seeks to "flee

---

[3] From this point on, rather than give a complicated bibliography with innumerable references for each word discussed, I invite readers to consult *VTB,* where each of the words I cite is listed with the necessary references. I do not intend here to rewrite an article for each significant word or expression, but rather to give a general idea of the entire question posed by the symbolic language of the two Testaments. [Ed. ET; For English speakers, the words cited will generally be available in *TDOT, TDNT,* or *EDNT.*]

from [God's] presence" (Ps 139:7), since "the face of the LORD is against evildoers" (Ps 34:16). Conversely, God makes "the light of [his] face shine upon" those whom he favors (Ps 4:6; and seven other passages in Psalms). God sees everything from his own invisible residence: "His eyes behold, his gaze examines humankind" (Ps 11:4). His ears hear everything; the psalmist asks God, "Let your ears be attentive to the voice of my supplications!" (Ps 130:2).

At the same time, since the message that comes from God reaches people, it can be said, "The mouth of the LORD has spoken" (e.g., Isa 1:20; 40:5). The intimate dialogue between Moses and God is represented in a metaphorical manner: God says, "With him I speak face to face" (Num 12:8). When God's wrath is furious, it is said that "his lips are full of indignation, and his tongue is like a devouring fire" (Isa 30:27). One psalmist evokes God's anger with these bold images: "Smoke went up from his nostrils, and devouring fire from his mouth" (Ps 18:8). The mouth is the organ that people use to speak, and thus a frequent expression in the prophetic texts is "For the mouth of the LORD has spoken" (e.g., Isa 1:20; 40:5; 58:14; Jer 9:12; Mic 4:4). When God speaks, his voice (*qol*) resounds like a thunderclap (Job 37:2, 5; 40:9; cf. Ps 29:3–9). The multiplication of anthropomorphisms thus permits a forceful evocation of the communication between God and people, whether this takes place in creation, through the prophets as intermediaries, or secretly in one's own conscience.

God's Actions. How can we evoke the actions of an invisible God? The biblical authors are not short of images to speak of God's hand or hands, as is done some 30 times in Psalms. In the Pentateuch it is said repeatedly that God brought the people out of Egypt "with a mighty hand and an outstretched arm" (Deut 4:34; 5:15; cf. Exod 13:3, 9; see also Ps 136:12). As for God's feet, the royal representation of God (to which we will return) depicts him seated on his throne, with the earth as his "footstool" (Isa 66:1).

God is active in the world and in history, because God knows everything: "He who planted the ear, does he not hear? He who formed the eye, does he not see?" (Ps 94:9). The acts of seeing and hearing direct the dynamism that lies behind all of God's interventions. God is intervening all the time; his hands and arms are at work. Thunder is a projectile that God launches at his enemies; bolts of lightning are his arrows (Ps 18:14). The same conventional imagery evokes God's creative activity: God plants a garden in Eden and there places the human that he has formed (Gen. 2:8); God forms from the ground the birds of the air and the beasts of the field (Gen 2:19); God fashions a woman from a rib taken from the man (Gen 2:21–22); God walks in the garden at the time of the evening breeze (Gen 3:8).

It is true that this account is parabolic in form, to evoke both God's creative actions and the human drama that follows them: the temptation and the fall (Gen 3). However, similar images are used to evoke God's presence in the background of historical events and God's providential interventions: God will prune, like a woodcutter, the branches of the trees that symbolize his enemies (Isa 10:33). God will kindle a fire that will devour the useless trees that symbolize the peoples (Ezek 20:47–48). God will stoke the furnace like a foundry worker and cast into it sinners who are compared to impure metals (Ezek 22:18–22). God will tread the winepress like a vineyard worker after tossing in the guilty nations (Isa 63:3–6). We could multiply examples like these of texts in which the activity of God is evoked by means of varied metaphors. What else can we do to make the way that God's active presence is at work in the world accessible to our senses?

God's Feelings. When God is evoked symbolically, his interior dispositions frequently are spoken of as if they were like those of humans, except that the faults that plague human activity are never ascribed to God. God feels sentiments of love (the verb *'ahav*): the love of a father for his son Israel (Hos 11:1); a tragic love for the human community that he made his bride, but that prostituted itself to foreign gods (Ezek 16:15–34 [we will return to this image of betrothal when we take up familial symbols]). In the face of infidelity God experiences anger and jealousy (Deut 6:14–15), but his "jealousy" for his holy name is also accompanied by pity toward the house of Israel (Ezek 39:25). It is by allusion to the sentiments that animate people that God can be defined as "a God merciful and gracious, slow to anger, and abounding in steadfast love and faithfulness" (Exod 34:6). Words such *khesed,* and the verbs *nakham* and *khanan,* which are difficult to render precisely in our language, evoke this merciful love of God. By contrast, God "hates" every kind of evil: the text of Prov 6:16–19 enumerates "six things that the LORD hates, seven that are an abomination to him." Another text specifies that God "hates iniquity" (Jdt 5:17).

Every serious transgression of the law or of cultic practice is presented as an "abomination" in God's eyes, most notably idolatry (5x in Leviticus; 14x in Deuteronomy; 39x in Ezekiel). How could a "jealous God" (Exod 34:14, Deut 4:24 [Hebrew: *'el qanna'*]) put up with Israel when it "made him jealous with strange gods" (Deut 32:16)? This is a description of a loving jealously, like that of a betrayed spouse. But the sense of the verb *qana'* and its derivative noun *qin'ah* varies between "jealousy" and "zeal"—for example, when God is depicted as "jealous for his glory" or for his holy name. The prophets do not hesitate to say that God would "change his mind" about an evil that he had announced as retribution for human sin, if there were repentance, or about a blessing that he had intended to bestow on someone, if that person were to turn away from him (Jer 18:8–10). This clearly is a human interpretation that seeks to understand the meaning of divine benefits and of misfortunes that occur, at a time when it was believed that good and evil would always be repaid here on earth.

On the other hand, God "will rejoice in doing good" to people (Jer 32:41). The psalmist who sings of the glory of God in creation wishes that God may "rejoice in his works" (Ps 104:31b)—that is, that God will receive from them all the honor that he deserves. Our modern sensibilities are hesitant to speak of God's "anger." Nevertheless, the texts of the First Testament, in every group of its books, insist frequently on this aspect of the Holy God, who cannot tolerate it when people impinge upon his honor through their evil conduct. The deserved misfortunes of his people are the effect of his "wrath," of his "anger," of his "jealousy" (terms used frequently in the prophetic texts). God is said simultaneously to be "mighty to forgive" and also the one who "pours out wrath" (Sir 16:11). These things are being viewed, to be sure, from a human perspective, as people deem the varying situations they experience to be the results of contrary divine dispositions. But God's wrath cannot be explained totally as the revenge of an outraged lover. This would not provide an answer to the problem of evil, particularly when the innocent suffer. Job is astonished that God "has kindled his wrath against me, and counts me as his adversary" (Job 19:11; cf. 13:24), since Job is confident (perhaps too confident!) of his own innocence. Thus the problem of evil is posed.

Even as the language of the Bible recognizes in God a holiness that distinguishes him from his creatures, it uses anthropomorphic expressions to evoke his interior dispositions. God is never conceived as an abstract principle, but always as a living being whose image can be recognized in the human body and in human emotions. God is in relationship with the world and with people, and symbolic expressions are able to render the form of this relationship, in its multiple aspects, accessible to our senses, in order to touch the sensibilities of those who receive the message. This biblical imagery is poles apart from those imageries that would debase the "divine" by ascribing human passions to it.

The verb *bara'* is reserved for God alone as a designation of his creative activity: it is used 49 times in the Bible, particularly in Gen 1–6 (11x) and in Isa 40–55 (20x). The human being, created in God's image, therefore allows us to represent God in his absolute uniqueness. Beyond this, two aspects of human society furnish further symbols that the First Testament uses abundantly: the family, in which children are raised, and human society, with its diverse functions. Before examining the symbolism drawn from these two sources, however, let us see whether the New Testament retains the same metaphorical representations when it speaks of God.

The Language of the New Testament

The revelation crystallized in the First Testament constituted, for the living tradition of Israel, a progressive pedagogy that specified the object of faith. It was founded on the experiences granted to those who were spiritual guides—leaders, prophets, sages, seers—and who were charged with transmitting the message of the knowledge of God and of his ways. In the time of Jesus, Judaism had this heritage in a double form: in the books collected into the Hebrew Bible, and in the Greek adaptation of those books made by the Jewish community in Alexandria, a version commonly known as the Septuagint.[4] Several books were added to the Septuagint that are

---

[4] The word "Septuagint" springs from the legend, recounted in the *Letter of Aristeas,* according to which seventy (or seventy-two) scholars were

known only in Greek; either their Semitic originals have been lost or they were written in Greek in the first place.[5] The authors of the New Testament were the heirs of all of these books. It was essentially in them that they found the vocabulary that they needed to speak of the unique God, who had been revealed to Israel, with whom he had first made his covenant. The proclamation of the gospel to Semitic-speaking Jews (Hebrew or Aramaic) and to Greek-speaking Jews required nothing more than an appeal to the language of these Scriptures. However, for those from pagan backgrounds, who belonged to the "nations" (*goyim* in Hebrew, *ethnē* in Greek), could the cults of the day or popular philosophy furnish another language that could speak adequately of the only true God, the living God?

The Affirmation of "One God." Those from the "nations" who had dealings with the Jews, who may even have attended the synagogues from time to time, had some understanding of biblical beliefs and writings. For others, however, it was necessary to find some unambiguous starting points in the common language, and that was a difficult operation. Those who proclaimed the gospel naturally spent a long time offering a critique of idols and idolatry. This can be seen easily by using a New Testament concordance to

---

given the task of translating the Bible into Greek. Their work was done separately, but when it was brought together, it was found to be identical. In reality, it is likely that the five books of the Pentateuch were translated into Greek in the third century B.C.E. upon the orders of the Greek authorities in Egypt, under Ptolemy II, so that an official text would permit them to know the "law" of the Jews who lived in their country. This would enable them to carry out legal proceedings, since this law had been officially recognized for their communities since the decrees of Cyrus and Darius in the sixth century B.C.E. This official version soon was used by the Jews themselves for their prayer services, since the majority of the population that had settled in Egypt no longer understood Hebrew.

[5] The modern discoveries at the Cairo Geniza, and then at Qumran, have enabled us to recover part of the Hebrew original of Sirach as well as the original of Tobit (four copies in Aramaic and one in Hebrew). But still we have no Hebrew original for Judith, 1 Maccabees, and Baruch. Wisdom of Solomon and 2 Maccabees are known to have been written directly in Greek. The Greek additions to Daniel have been translated from Semitic originals, while those to Esther were written in Greek at the time that book was recomposed in that language. The case of Baruch 4:1–5:8 is still debated.

trace the uses of the words *eidōlon* (11x), *eidōlolatria* (4x), *eidōlolatrēs* (7x), and *eidōlothytos* (9x). These uses are found in the book of Acts, in Paul's letters, in Peter's first letter, and in Revelation. Nevertheless, we can see some efforts at apologetics using language directly accessible to Greeks. This is the case with Paul's speech at Lystra, in which he called upon the pagans to "turn from worthless idols" to "the living God, who made the heaven and the earth and the sea and all that is in them," who "has not left himself without a witness in doing good—giving you rains from heaven and fruitful seasons, and filling you with food and your hearts with joy" (Acts 14:15–17). Still, the crowd missed the point!

Paul takes a similar approach in Athens, before the Areopagus. He adds to his general presentation of God as the Creator the idea that God needs nothing (Acts 17:25) and wants people to "search for God and perhaps grope for him and find him" (Acts 17:27), for "(I)n him we live and move and have our being" (Acts 17:28a). Paul even appeals to a quotation from Aratus to explain that "we too are his offspring" (Acts 17:28b). Paul uses this as a point of departure to critique idolatry, but the rest of his speech falls flat when he evokes the Last Judgment, to be presided over by a man whom God has raised from the dead (Acts 17:29–32). Luke apparently is not quoting these speeches verbatim, but rather giving some idea of what, within the Christian apologetics of his own time, could launch a frontal assault against the mentality of pagan communities. Paul himself says, in his letter to the Romans, that pagan peoples had every possibility of coming to know God's "eternal power and divine nature" through his works in creation (Rom 1:20). Thus their idolatry was the error only of their darkened minds (Rom 1:21–23).

It may be that these efforts to enter into dialogue with people who held the common mindset developed in other ways as well. But in general, the language used to speak of God was that which the heritage of the Greek Bible had provided, particularly since many pagans could have had some contact with the Jews. The religiosity of Greek or Hellenized circles made it easy enough to proclaim the "living God" (Acts 14:15; 1 Thess 1:9; 2 Cor 3:3; 6:16; Rom 9:26; 1 Tim 3:15; 4:10; Rev 7:2; 15:7; 4x in Hebrews); the "eternal God" is mentioned less often (Rom 16:26) than his glory (1 Pet 5:10), his kingdom (2 Pet 1:11), or the gifts that are promised to those who believe in him—for example, his life (20x in Acts and the Epistles). But do we find anthropomorphic evocations of God in the New Testament as we do in the books of the First Testament?

The Use of Anthropomorphisms. We do indeed encounter reminiscences of this anthropomorphic biblical language in certain books that occasionally evoke God's "face." This occurs once in the Gospel writings: the angels of the "little ones" "see the face of my Father in heaven" (Matt 18:10). (The picture of the heavenly society here is derived from another analogy that belongs to "mythical" language.) The text of Acts 2:28 is a quotation from Ps 16:11 in the Septuagint, and that of 1 Pet 3:12 is a quotation from Ps 34:15–16. In Heb 9:24 the implication of Christ's entrance in glory into the heavenly sanctuary is that he now appears "in the presence of God on our behalf." But how else could Christ in the "world to come" be evoked? In the same way, to evoke the punishment of the damned in the "world to come," 2 Thess 1:9 explains that they will be driven far from "the presence of the Lord and from the glory of his might." This expression is reminiscent of Isa 2:10, 19, 21, but on a purely verbal level: the Greek phrase *apo prosōpou tou kyriou* ("from the face of the Lord") renders the Hebrew *mippeney,* which has prepositional force. The remaining occurrence is the eschatological description in Rev 22:4, which refers to "God and the Lamb" together in the singular: "they will see his face."

As for the "mouth" of God, the text of Matt 4:4 is only a quotation of Deut 8:3 LXX: "every word that comes from the mouth of God." In the same way, it is a quotation from Ps 33:16 LXX [ET 34:15] that depicts God as having his "eyes on the righteous" and his "ears . . . open to their prayer" in 1 Pet 3:12. Even though it is said more than once that God "spoke" through the prophets, the mention of his "voice" is very rare: Acts 7:31 introduces quotations from Exod 3:5–10 LXX. We should note the voice of the resurrected Christ that speaks to Paul (Acts 9:4, 7; 22:7, 9, 14; 26:14). As for the many voices that transmit messages in Revelation, generally they are those of angels. The voice that addresses the seer at the beginning of the book is that of someone "like the Son of Man"[6]

---

[6] Later in this chapter (p. 62) we will return to this symbol of the "Son of Man," which comes from Dan 7.

(Rev 1:10–16), and the voice that speaks in the final vision is that of God himself (Rev 21:3–4, 6–8). The book's literary genre requires this dramatic convention.

The style of the First Testament sometimes is preserved in the New Testament when it speaks of the "hand" of God. For example, in the Lukan infancy narrative of Jesus it is said of John the Baptist that "the hand of the Lord was with him" (Luke 1:66), and in John's Gospel Jesus himself says, "What my Father has given me is greater than all else, and no one can snatch it out of the Father's hand" (John 10:29). In Acts, when the believers pray for the imprisoned apostles, they tell God that Herod and Pilate have done what God's "hand and plan had predestined to take place" (Acts 4:28), and they ask God to "stretch out your hand to heal . . . through the name of your holy servant Jesus" (Acts 4:30). In Acts 11:21 the preachers of the gospel succeeded because "the hand of the Lord was with them," and in Acts 13:11 Paul announces that "the hand of the Lord is against" Elymas the magician. It is a biblical expression in both cases, but does "the Lord" refer to God or to the resurrected Christ? Among the Epistles, Hebrews is the only one that mentions, following the Greek Bible and its customary vocabulary, the "hands" of God as Creator (Heb 1:10, quoting Ps 101:26 LXX [ET 102:25]). In biblical style, the author also admonishes, "It is a fearful thing to fall into the hands of the living God" (Heb 10:31).

As for God's "feet," once again we are reading a quotation from the Greek Bible when we hear in Acts 7:49 that the earth, as the prophet writes, is God's "footstool" (Acts 7:49 = Isa 66:1 LXX). The quotations in 1 Cor 15:25; Heb 1:13; 10:13, which refer to Ps 109:1 LXX [ET 110:1], as well as those in 1 Cor 15:27; Heb 2:8, which refer to Ps 8:7 LXX [ET 8:6] have in view not God, but rather Christ in glory. In speaking of God's "hands" and "feet," the New Testament is taking up the style of the First Testament.

As for the "eyes" of the Lord in 1 Pet 3:12, once more this is a quotation, from Ps 34:15. Nowhere in the New Testament is God the subject of the verb "see."

God's Emotions. It will not be surprising to see "love" mentioned under this heading, since "God so loved the world that he gave his only Son" (John 3:16). But "wrath"? The metaphor does occur (John 3:36; Rom 1:18; Col 3:6; Eph 5:6; Rev 19:15), and it requires an explanation. It emphasizes God's incompatibility with evil. It is also connected with God's role as the "judge" of humanity (we will return to this idea below). Are "hatred" and "hating" ever attributed to God? We know that the Hebrew of the First Testament freely uses antonyms without qualification, opposing "love" with "hatred." It is in a quotation that God says in Rom 9:13, "I have loved Jacob, but I have hated Esau" (= Mal 1:2–3). But "hatred" by itself is never attributed to God. By contrast, "grace" or "favor" (*charis*) is one of God's essential gifts. In the Lukan infancy narrative Mary "found favor" with God (Luke 1:30), and God's "favor" was upon Jesus (Luke 2:40). In Acts the grace of God, or of the Lord, is mentioned several times by the narrator in the course of the story (Acts 11:23; 13:43; 14:3, 26; 15:40; 20:32). Paul is not outdone by this in his letter to the Romans (Rom 3:24; 4:16; 5:15, 21; 6:1, 14, 15) or in his other letters, although he attributes this disposition and the gift that goes with it equally to Christ. The thought alternates between God, who shows favor to those whom he loves, and the gift that God gives to them, as in the salutations at the beginnings of the letters: "Grace and peace from God, to you . . ."

Related to grace are "pity" and "mercy" toward people: *eleos* with the verb *eleaō* (*eleeō*), and *oiktirmos* with the verb *oiktirō,* which is used in Rom 9:15 in a quotation of Exod 33:19 LXX. The statement describes God's love toward sinners or those who are suffering. But God also shows his "goodness" and "pleasure" toward those whom he has chosen (Matt 11:26; Luke 2:14, 10:21). God's pleasure rests particularly on Christ, whom he addresses as his "beloved Son" because he is the "servant of God" par excellence (Matt 3:17; 12:18; 17:5 and parallels; cf. 2 Pet 1:17). By contrast, Hebrews, quoting the Septuagint, describes those things in which God does not find pleasure: burnt offerings and sin offerings (Heb 10:5–6, 8, quoting Ps 39:7 LXX [ET: 40:6]), and believers who lack faith (Heb 10:38, quoting Hab 2:4).

Thus in the New Testament, as in the First Testament, God is represented as a sensate being, and it is anthropomorphic images that convey this most effectively. They should not be taken literally, of course; God does not have eyes or ears, and God is above human sentiments. However, it is by attributing these things to God that we understand best the disposition and conduct of Divine Providence toward human beings.

Three Essential Metaphors

As for God's deepest nature—and that of Christ, who shares fully in God's existence—certain metaphorical expressions taken from nature or human experience suggest it best.

Light

The First Testament had already connected God strongly with the symbol of light: "Let us walk in the light of the LORD" (Isa 2:5), or even better, "The LORD is my light and my salvation; whom shall I fear?" (Ps 27:1). The New Testament uses the same symbolism, especially in the Gospel of John. The evangelist writes in his first letter, "God is light" (1 John 1:5).

Love

The association of God with love and the verb "love," already present in the First Testament, issues in the astonishing declaration that defines God himself: "God is love" (1 John 4:16) (we will return to this in ch. 5). This analogy from our own experience is worth more than any metaphysical definition. Aristotle spoke of the "Prime Mover" and of the "Perfect Being." This is true on a philosophical level, but it remains abstract. When we hear that "God is light" and that "God is love," however, our sensibilities are immediately touched, even if our philosophical side may remain unsatisfied.

Christ and God

Jesus declares in the Gospel of John, "I am the light of the world" (John 8:12; 9:5; cf. 12:46), alluding to his future glory. In Revelation the author goes even farther, ascribing to Jesus symbolic titles that the First Testament applies to God alone: "I am the Alpha and the Omega, the first and the last, the beginning and the end" (Rev 22:13; cf. 1:8; 21:6). This is a reprise of the title applied to God in Isa 44:6 (cf. 41:4): "I am the first and I am the last; besides me there is no god." In Revelation the allusion to the first and last letters of the Greek alphabet, and to two abstract words that designate the beginning and end of all things, elaborate on the meaning of the double title that the "Message of Consolation" (Isa 40–55) attributes to God. Its words now apply to Christ in glory, underscoring that which the Council of Nicea defined as his "divine nature." The context in Isa 44:6 shows that "the first and the last" is a concrete presentation of the only true God; in Revelation Christ in glory can apply these titles to himself.

SYMBOLS DRAWN FROM FAMILY LIFE

Family life was associated with the divinities of ancient pagan religions in the most literal sense. Natural forces, and the structure of human societies that depended on powers of fertility and fecundity, furnished plenty of "powers" that could be divinized, producing gods who had wives and children! Biblical monotheism steadily detached itself from this general concept of divinity. We have just noted Isa 44:6, where God says, "besides me there is no god." To rephrase this in the style of metaphysical abstraction, "Besides me there is no 'power' that can be considered 'divine' to the extent that it should be worshiped." Must we conclude from this that the family, the building block of society where love and fecundity are found, has no role to play in the biblical representation of God? The answer is slightly different for each of the two Testaments.

Family Symbolism in the First Testament

In the authentic religion centered on the Sinai covenant and, behind it, the covenant with the patriarchs, there is no consort goddess alongside the true God, whatever he is called: "El," "Elohim," or "YHWH." However, archeological discoveries have shown that in the popular religion, among the peasants descended from the ancient Canaanites, the goddess Anat was worshiped alongside YHWH, who had displaced Baal as the patron God of the nation.[7] This type of syncretistic religion demonstrates the profound influence of the ancient Canaanite cult that the prophets fought against,

---

[7] The pairing of Yaho and Anat is attested at Elephantine, where Jews who were enlisted in the Egyptian army, and then in the Persian army, swore "by the temple and by Anat-Yaho." See the text translated in my collection *Documents araméens d'Égypte* (LAPO 5; Paris: Cerf, 1972), 95, no. 10. This was a religion brought from Judah *before* the Deuteronomistic reform.

especially in the northern kingdom. The story of Elijah and the prophets of Baal (1 Kgs 18:20–40) tells of just one episode, along with the preaching of Hosea (e.g., Hos 4:7, 10b–14). But could not the promotion of a pure religion, in which the true God was the object of worship, find adequate expression in the symbols of marriage and family that Canaanite paganism had put to use?

The Symbol of Marriage

Hosea's unhappy experience with his wife provided the occasion for him to use the symbol of marriage in his preaching to depict the state of the covenant relationship[8] that God had established with the people: with regard to YHWH her God, Israel had become an adulteress, like an unfaithful, prostituted wife in regard to her husband (Hos 1). Within such cultures it was the practice of the time to speak of a human community or of a city in feminine terms. We will see in other examples below that the citizens of a country or the residents of a city were considered its "children." But Hosea's language here is original in that it applies the symbol of marriage to the covenant relationship between God and his people. Whatever the date of their editing, the biblical texts that describe the events at Sinai are based on ancient traditions of the covenant that the God of Israel concluded (*karath*) there with his people, or that, in another series of texts, he gave (*nathan*) to them. It is through this original act that Israel became the "people of YHWH," and Hosea describes it as a marriage.

By running after her lovers, who were the false gods of Canaan, Israel, the unfaithful wife, prostituted herself (Hos 2:1–5). This is why misfortunes will suddenly come upon her (Hos 2:6–13), up until the day when God, by his own initiative, will give this love story a new beginning (Hos 2:14–23).

---

[8] "Covenant" (*berit*) is a legal concept that has been transferred to the realm of religion. Covenants are "ratified" (the Hebrew verb is *karat*) after the manner of contracts, between equals or between a suzerain and a vassal. Between YHWH and his people it clearly is an unequal contract. The Priestly texts portray the covenant as something ultimately "given" by God to the people. The symbolism of marriage first introduced by Hosea emphasizes the initiative of God, but it also introduces an affective aspect to the covenant.

In the end, the story that God is rewriting will have a happy ending, but the prophet does not specify when God's design will ultimately be fulfilled. The important thing for us to recognize is the symbolic transformation of the story that began with the exodus from Egypt and the covenant with Israel at Sinai. By means of a daring anthropomorphism God is represented as a loving husband who is betrayed but who ultimately forgives his unfaithful wife. Her children, who symbolize the apostate members of the community, are appropriately the object of a short allusion: "Upon her children also I will have no pity, because they are children of whoredom" (Hos 2:4).

The symbolism first introduced by Hosea, a prophet from the north, is extended in significant ways by Jeremiah, who came from a priestly city in the north[9] (Jer 2:20–23; 3:1–10; 4:1, 29–31). Speaking of the destruction of Jerusalem, Jeremiah says that she has been forgotten by her lovers (Jer 30:14) and "repudiated" by God ("no one cares for her" [Jer 30:17]). But he adds that Israel will be forgiven and taken back as God's "wife" (Jer 31:3–4) and consoled by God for the children she has lost (Jer 31:15–16). Hosea interpreted the covenant with the help of marriage as a symbol; Jeremiah draws out the meaning of the symbol by announcing a new covenant (Jer 31:31–34).

Ezekiel, a prophet of the exile,[10] allegorizes the symbol systematically to depict Jerusalem and her "sisters," Samaria and Sodom (Ezek 16:1–52). He does this to proclaim that at some unspecified time in the future Jerusalem and her "sisters" will be restored (Ezek 16:53–58), thanks to the "eternal covenant" that God has not forgotten (Ezek 16:59–63). A second allegory (Ezek 23), compares the respective fates of Samaria and Jerusalem, which are personified as representatives of Israel and Judah, the kingdoms of which they are the capitals. Samaria is "Oholah," which means "her own tent," while Jerusalem, the city where God's temple is situated, is

---

[9] The sanctuary of Anathoth, situated to the north of Jerusalem, was where the priest Abiathar was exiled (1 Kgs 2:26). Located in the territory of the tribe of Benjamin, it was home to a line of priests different from those in Jerusalem.

[10] Ezekiel, who was exiled after the capture of Jerusalem, was by contrast a member of the local clergy. He was connected with the circles in which the Holiness Code (Lev 17–26) was compiled.

"Oholibah," "my tent is in her." But this time the story of their sins, with allusions to political alliances with foreign nations and the idolatrous worship of their gods, is related without reference to a new covenant coming at the end.

After this, the association of the covenant with marriage becomes a classic literary theme. The Message of Consolation, addressed to the exiles in Babylon, takes up the same imagery to describe the future promised to Jerusalem and her children (Isa 54:1–10). God will bring this drama of love to a close by restoring the Holy City. He will make an "everlasting covenant" with her and with her people (Isa 61:8), and he will restore Jerusalem to her dignity as a wife (Isa 62:3–5). This latter passage (Isa 60–62) comes from after the return from exile and is contemporary with the restoration of the Holy City.[11] Its imagery became the basis of Jewish hopes, and in later Judaism it permitted texts such as Ps 45 and Song of Solomon to be interpreted allegorically.

The Symbolism of Parenthood

In the authentic religion of Israel there was no goddess, and therefore the symbol of parenthood could be applied only to God, and with certain qualifications that we must specify here. The symbol was not used to suggest that people were God's offspring; rather, it was strictly a matter of God's *adoptive* paternity. This concept was found in pagan religions as well. In the various Semitic cultures family terms such as "father," "brother," and "paternal uncle" are used in the composition of proper names, and we see the same thing happening in the Bible. "Abijah" means "YH is my father," "Ahijah" means "YH is my brother," and "Ammiel" means "El (God) is my paternal uncle."

This pious attachment to the God of Israel, analogous to that which we encounter in neighboring religions, is able to accommo-

---

[11] Isaiah 60–62 constitutes a small, independent collection that in a certain sense continues the "message of consolation" (Isa 40–55), but it is clearly distinguished from it by its more sacerdotal emphasis. It may be that the discourse in Isa 61:1–9 was delivered by the high priest, as he received the "anointing" that consecrated him, to the "priests" of YHWH, whom he calls "ministers of our God" and to whom he makes promises about the future.

date more explicit texts in which God himself is brought into the action. Thus Moses receives this mandate from God, in the ancient account of his calling: "Then you shall say to Pharaoh, 'Thus says the LORD: Israel is my firstborn son. I said to you, "Let my son go that he may worship me." But you refused to let him go; now I will kill your firstborn son'" (Exod 4:22–23).

The same filial dignity is accorded to the king of Israel.[12] In a coronation psalm the king declares, "I will tell of the decree of the LORD: He said to me, 'You are my son; today I have begotten you'" (Ps 2:7). This "begetting" clearly is symbolic, but it makes the king, as the adoptive son of God, a sacred person. Psalm 89, which recalls the promises made to David and his dynasty, specifies, "He shall cry to me, 'You are my Father, my God, and the Rock of my salvation!'" (Ps 89:26).

Eventually, by the Greek period, every righteous person came to be considered an adopted child of God. In Wisdom of Solomon the ungodly mockingly use this as an excuse for banditry: "if the righteous man is God's child, he will help him" (Wis 2:18). Just before that statement the ungodly say of the righteous person, "He professes to have knowledge of God, and calls himself a child of the Lord" (Wis 2:13 ["Lord" is the Greek rendering of YHWH]), and later they add, "he calls the last end of the righteous happy, and boasts that God is his father" (Wis 2:16). Thus we can see that symbolic representations of God as father and of God's people as adopted children—first the king, as a type of the future Messiah, and then every righteous person—were current in New Testament times. There is an echo of these representations in Jewish prayers of the period in which believers characteristically address God as "our Father, our King" ('abinu malkenu).[13]

---

[12] Regardless of when the text that describes Nathan's promise to David (2 Sam 7:1–17) was composed, we can recognize in it a divine promise that applies to every descendant of David who would succeed him: "I will be a father to him, and he shall be a son to me" (2 Sam 7:14). If we accept the antiquity of the text, it is source of the theme that the king is the adopted son of the God of Israel.

[13] See the Second Benediction (Ahavah Rabbah), in which God is invoked from the outset as "our Father, our King" ('abinu malkenu). See the translation in A.-C. Avril and D. de la Maisonneuve, Prières juives (CaESup 68; Paris: Cerf, 1989), 24.

As for the maternal role, it is clear that it could not be fulfilled by a goddess, as it was in the surrounding pagan religions. For one thing, the role already had been assigned to the Holy City and to the national community, as the bride of YHWH. But beyond this, certain texts do not hesitate to attribute maternal sentiments directly to God: "Zion said, 'The LORD has forsaken me, my Lord has forgotten me.' Can a woman forget her nursing child, or show no compassion for the child of her womb?" (Isa 49:14–15). In his book on God in Scripture, J. Briend was able to entitle one chapter "The Maternity of God in the Bible."[14] In other words, the God of Israel embraces in his person both paternal authority and maternal compassion. These qualities can be attributed symbolically to the God, whose uniqueness excludes polytheism.

We see, therefore, that the texts of the First Testament and the deuterocanonical writings of Jewish origin make frequent use of symbols drawn from the experience of family life, recast in light of monotheism. Since those who preached the gospel held these texts as sacred, they naturally made use of their symbols, but they transformed them in profound ways in light of the unique position that Jesus Christ holds before God. We will need to take up his title "Christ" and study it in more detail when we come to symbols drawn from experience in society. For now, we turn to the three fundamental symbols of father, mother, and children.

Family Symbolism in the New Testament

The Fatherhood of God

God's symbolic fatherhood, relational but never sexual, is attested in the Jewish Bible and in Jewish prayers. Thus it is not surprising to see it mentioned abundantly in the sayings of Jesus: 5 times in Mark, 45 times in Matthew, and 16 times in Luke, not counting those cases where, in a parable, the figure of a father indirectly symbolizes God, as in Luke 15:11–32 (11x). The 118 references to God as Father in the Gospel of John must be treated separately, since for the most part they have in view Jesus as the Son. In the Syn-

---

[14] See J. Briend, "La maternité de Dieu dans la Bible," *Dieu dans l'Écriture* (LD 150; Paris: Cerf, 1992), 71–90.

optic Gospels, when we examine the texts in Matthew, we discover that Jesus speaks freely to his disciples of "your Father," whether addressing an individual (5x) or the whole group (15x), adding, in the Jewish manner, "who is in heaven" (8x). But he also speaks of "my Father" (13x) and of "my Father who is in heaven" (8x). He even speaks once simply of "the Father" as the one who alone knows "the day and the hour" when the end will arrive (Mark 13:32 = Matt 24:36). The invocation "Father" appears 5 times in Matthew, including once in the prayer that he taught his disciples (Matt 6:9), and the rest in Jesus' own prayers (Matt 11:25, 26; 26:39, 42); and 6 times in Luke, once in the prayer that he taught his disciples (Luke 11:2),[15] and the rest in Jesus' own prayers (Luke 10:21 [2x], with mention of the Son; 22:42; 23:34, 46). In John's Gospel this is Jesus' habitual way of speaking to God, insisting on the specific relationship he has with "the Father," who is for him "my Father."

Certain historians of religion who hold to preconceived theories attribute the initiative to make Jesus a "Son of God" to an influence coming from paganism, whether Greek or otherwise. But this interpretation is untenable. Jesus is using characteristically Jewish language.[16] However, he does so in such a way as to reveal the intimacy of his relationship with "my Father": "no one knows who the Son is except the Father, or who the Father is except the Son and anyone to whom the Son chooses to reveal him" (Luke 10:22 = Matt 11:27). John's Gospel, implicitly making allusion to the revelation of the true God in Exod 3 and Deut 6:4, records the saying of Jesus that "the Father and I are one" (John 10:30).

Later on, when Mohammed was establishing an Islam that he presented as the culmination of the Islam of Ibrahim (Abraham) and of Issa (Jesus), he protested the Christians' claim that Jesus was the

---

[15] There are two versions of the Lord's Prayer in the Gospels. The one in Matthew (6:9–13) adds the Jewish formulation "our Father in heaven." This is a liturgical adaptation. The text in Luke corresponds to the way that Jesus characteristically began his own prayers.

[16] I emphasized this point in my study *Dieu, le Père de Jésus Christ* (Jésus et Jésus-Christ 60; Paris: Desclée, 1994), 60. There I spoke of my interest in a "critical interpretation of symbolic language with an awareness of its different categories" (61 n. 1). This is the work that I have undertaken here.

Son of God: "God is one. Glory to Him! How could He have a son?" (Qur'an 4:171; cf. 9:30–31; 19:34–35). But Mohammed was responding to the way God was represented to him in the oral tradition of marginal Christians in a country where pagan worship was offered to a divine triad: a father-god, a mother-goddess, and a son-god. We can understand why, in this context, Mohammed protested, "Do not say three. . . . God is one. Glory to Him! How could He have a son?" (Qur'an 4:171). The same word "three" in Arabic (*talut*) designates both the "triad" of traditional paganism and the Christian "Trinity"! But faith in Jesus as the Son of God begins with the way in which Jesus addressed God in an existential fashion as "Abba, Father" (Mark 14:36), an expression underlying all of his other prayers[17] (except that from the cross, which quotes Ps 22:1). His word to the apostles in John 20:17 makes no distinction: "my Father and your Father," although he may speak of "my Father" by virtue of the intimacy of his own personal relationship and use "your Father" as an adoptive title already known within Judaism.

In light of these sayings of Jesus, the authors of the New Testament take up the same symbolic terms ("Father" and "Son") and identify God as the "Father of our Lord Jesus Christ" (Rom 15:6; 2 Cor 1:3, Eph 1:3; Col 1:3; 1 Pet 1:3). Revelation does not hesitate to put the Lamb, who is Christ in glory, on the same throne with God (Rev 22:3). But here we have moved beyond the family symbolism found in the First Testament. The symbols "father" and "son" take on a new meaning from the moment Jesus of Nazareth appears as "the Son" in a unique sense. This is a symbolic expression in which the human relationship of father to son takes on a transcendent meaning as a revelation of the intimacy between Jesus and God, thanks to his participation in what the Council of Nicea would call the unique "nature" (*physis*) of God. The New Testament, however, confines itself to a concrete presentation of the

---

[17] See W. Marchel, *Abba, Père! La prière de Jésus et des chrétiens: Étude exégétique sur les origines et la signification de l'invocation à la divinité comme père, avant et dans le Nouveau Testament* (AnBib 19; Rome: Pontifical Biblical Institute, 1963); J. Jeremias, *Abba: Jésus et son père* (Paris: Seuil, 1972), 9–72 ("Parole de Dieu"); idem, *Théologie du Nouveau Testament* (vol. 1; LD 76; Paris: Cerf, 1973), 81–88; Grelot, *Dieu, le Père de Jésus Christ*, 173–87 ("Les prières de Jésus").

relationship between the Son and the Father, which makes them truly one (John 10:30).

Divine Sonship

There is a close connection between the symbolic title "Father," by which God is addressed in order to signify an essential aspect of his person, and the symbol of the sonship that constitutes a concrete realization of that person. In the First Testament the image of a symbolic *adoptive* sonship was used for the chosen people, for their king, and for their righteous ones, as we saw earlier.[18] Jesus, however, represents a new and completely unexpected kind of "sonship." It is not to be understood by a speculative analogy to certain pagan myths, such as the one according to which, at the beginning of our era, the Egyptians expressed their devotion for Harpocrates: "Horus the Child" of divine descent. Christian faith in Jesus as the Son of God begins with the way he addressed God in prayer: "Abba, Father" (Mark 14:36). This was not the typical Jewish formula for addressing God, a formula preserved in Matthew's version of the Lord's Prayer, which assimilates it to Jewish prayers: "Our father in heaven" (Matt 6:9). None of the faithful within Judaism before the Christian era can be shown to have addressed God with the familial affection implicit in the Aramaic term that Jesus used, "Abba." This is the word that a little child would use to address "daddy," and it is even more affectionate than the Aramaic *'abi,* "my father." Yet all of Jesus' prayers, recorded in Greek in the Gospels, begin this way (except for the prayer from the cross, which quotes Ps 22:1).

Throughout the Synoptics and the Gospel of John we encounter the expression *pater* or *ho patēr,* which is a translation of the same Aramaic word (the latter understood in Greek as a vocative address in the nominative case). The expression has nothing to do with the divine genealogies of pagan cults; rather, it translates an internal experience that opens up limitless horizons: "Do you not believe," asks Jesus in John 14:10, "that I am in the Father and the Father is in me?" We will return to this "relational" symbol: the fatherhood of God and the sonship of Jesus are no longer just metaphorical expressions of adoption, analogous to those of Israel, its king, and its righteous ones in the First

---

[18] See above, pp. 42–43.

Testament. The entire New Testament is dominated by the revelation of this mysterious reality that opens up unprecedented and unexpected religious horizons.

Indeed, it gives new significance to the gift of adoptive sonship and daughterhood that God grants to people. Adoption (*huiothesia*) is explicitly mentioned in Paul's writings (Rom 8:15, 23; 9:4; Gal 4:5; Eph 1:5). However, it no longer has the same character that it had for the members of the community of the first covenant: "adoption" then was the privilege of the Jews as a body (Rom 9:4), but now it is those who are "led by the Spirit of God" who have the privilege of being "children of God," in the adoptive sense of the word (Rom 8:14), and the whole creation is straining forward toward the "revealing of the children of God" (Rom 8:19). The words of Hos 1:10 (2:1 LXX), "in the place where it was said to them, 'You are not my people,' it shall be said to them, 'Children of the living God,'" are cited in Greek translation in Rom 9:26, but they are given a new meaning. They are now addressed to Christians: "for in Christ Jesus you are all children of God through faith" (Gal 3:26). Thus it is *in Jesus Christ* that this privilege is now granted to those who believe in him with a living faith, as a result of which "our fellowship is with the Father and with his Son Jesus Christ" (1 John 1:3). We now have much more than a nominal title; we partake in a shared life.

The Son himself is the object of much more than an adoption. Being "the Son" par excellence, he derives his glory directly from the Father, since he is the "only begotten" (*monogenēs* [John 1:14]). This "only begotten" is "close to the Father's heart" (John 1:18). "God so loved the world that he gave his only Son" (John 3:16), and "those who do not believe are condemned already, because they have not believed in the name of the only Son of God" (John 3:18). John returns to this thought in his first letter: "God's love was revealed among us in this way: God sent his only Son into the world so that we might live through him" (1 John 4:9). The use of the word *monogenēs,* which is derived from the verb *gennaō,* "beget," requires some explanation. Because there is not, literally speaking, a feminine principle within the true God, the verb can be used only in a symbolic sense, different from the literal sense that is attached to human sexuality. We must seek to discern the reality here that human language is insufficient to express. The Father plays a role that analogically is both paternal and maternal, in that he begets the Son of his own substance and communicates his own nature to him. This nature is located *above* the sexual differentiation that characterizes human beings.

The Council of Nicea used the word "nature" in order to counter Arian theology, which made Christ the first of the creatures. Hence the council said that the Son was "begotten, not created, of one substance with the Father": *gennēthenta ou poiethenta, homoousios tō patri.*[19] The term "begotten" is the same one used in the New Testament, but here its meaning is specified precisely, to show the difference from how the creatures were produced. It is the *life* of this one who is God's Son "in substance" that is communicated to the adopted sons and daughters by the Holy Spirit, who is given to them, under whose influence they cry out to God, as Jesus did, "Abba, Father" (Rom 8:15; Gal 4:6).

The Motherhood of the Church

In the language of the New Testament the symbol of motherhood is used in the same way as in the Jewish Bible and, more generally, in other Semitic cultures. The community to which an individual man or woman belonged, or the city that presided over this community as its capital or major center, was spontaneously represented with maternal traits. We noted examples earlier of such depictions of the Israelite community itself and of cities such as Jerusalem, Samaria, and Sodom (Ezek 16; 23).[20] The smaller cities that depended on them were their "daughters." The sense of belonging to a community has its psychological background in the relationship that a child, whether son or daughter, establishes with its mother. He or she retains an unconscious awareness of being one with her, having come from her body. By contrast, a father is embraced only through an act of faith, in a relationship that is established with one

---

[19] The word "created" is used here to reflect the meaning of the Greek and Latin versions of the Nicene Creed more precisely. The creed actually uses the word "made," to contrast with the term "begotten." However, because the word "begotten," in its literal sense, presupposes two principles, one masculine and one feminine, it is itself used symbolically, in an analogical sense. It therefore fits the verbal category being studied here.

[20] See above, pp. 40–42.

who is wholly other.[21] If this relationship is not established, it becomes a source of difficulty in the child's psychological development, in different ways for boys and girls.[22] Our sense of social belonging strongly resembles our attachment to our mothers, in that it includes a sense of belonging to a quasi-physical reality of which we are the product. How can we distinguish ourselves, and for that matter, how can we keep from dreaming of reintegration, like a lost child who dreams of returning to the mother's womb?[23]

The distinctive of the Christian community is that it is not intrinsically bound to any city, state, or homeland. With the proclamation of the gospel and the formation of the church, the *ekklēsia* of Israel was opened wide to people of all nations. In Paul's allegory of Abraham's two wives (Gal 4:21–31) the "Jerusalem above," who is "our mother," has for her children all those who are baptized. They constitute the "body of Christ," whether they are "Jews or Greeks, slaves or free" (1 Cor 12:13). The list is expanded in Col 3:11; in the new community, "there is no longer Greek and Jew, circumcised and uncircumcised, barbarian, Scythian, slave and free." Thus in Christ Jesus, the Son of God in the strongest sense of the word, a new fellowship is created. Since the church is his "body" (Rom 12:4–5; 1 Cor 12:12–27; cf. Gal 3:28; Eph 4:4–6; Col 3:11), the unity created among its members by the gift of the Spirit takes precedence over former loyalties to human communities. We are all equally "children of our mother the church" (cf. Gal 4:26). Thus the new humanity, which the book of Revelation represents as a woman crowned with twelve stars (Rev 12:1), appears in the world. Her "firstborn son" has the

---

[21] From this perspective, there is an absolute difference between a child's relationship with its mother, with whom it was entirely united during the time of gestation, and that with its father, with whom it only enters into relationship after its birth, by a mode of relating in which the father takes the initiative. The use of fatherhood to designate God is based on this reality of our experience, by contrast with the "mother goddesses" who are connected in ancient cults with "Earth-Mother."

[22] I will not explore this point, but will leave its investigation to psychologists, drawing on the findings of psychoanalysts.

[23] Significantly, in those religions that worship a mother goddess, the pietism of *bhakti* develops within a mysticism characterized by the doctrine of *advaita* or "nonduality," which is strongly reminiscent of a return to the mother's womb.

biblical characteristics of the Messiah, who will "rule the nations with a rod of iron" (Ps 2:9), but he escapes the clutches of the dragon by being taken up into heaven (Rev 12:5). The dragon then goes off "to make war on the rest of her children" (Rev 12:17). Thus the symbol of the woman is replaced by that of the mother—that is, by the community whose head is the firstborn of the woman.

All of these developments take place within the logic of the maternal symbol, which is the counterpart of the paternal symbol that is used only for the living God. It is true that the symbol of the woman can also be employed with a contrary meaning, as in the case of the "great whore" on whose forehead is written the name "Babylon the great" (Rev 17:1–5). The symbols thereby show the opposition between the new community (the church) and the human empires that oppose it, whatever form they may take. From which of these are we conscious of being descended, or to which have we chosen to belong? The choice is always open to us, no matter what our origins. In any event, it is by the mediation of Jesus, as the "Son" in the strongest sense of the word, that God is revealed as Father. Admittedly, this is in symbolic terms, but the symbol allows us to perceive an essential aspect of the living God. Under the influence of God's Spirit we call out to God as Jesus did, crying, "Abba, Father" (Rom 8:15; Gal 4:6), taking up his words in Mark 14:36.

When feminine symbolism is applied to the church, it can also have another aspect: that of the bride, a symbol tied closely to the covenant between God and his people. As we saw, in the First Testament this symbolic theme was introduced by Hosea in order to denounce Israel's infidelity to her God, which was equated with adultery.[24] The same theme recurs in Jeremiah and Isaiah. The Message of Consolation takes it up in an inverse sense, to declare the renewal of the love between God and his people.[25] In the New Testament a significant passage in the letter to the Ephesians takes up the same theme indirectly to promote conjugal love between Christian spouses: "Husbands, love your wives, just as Christ loved the church and gave himself up for her" (Eph 5:25). Thus the redactor supplies a rationale for a precept already found in the letter to the Colossians (Col 3:19).

---

[24] See above, pp. 40–41.
[25] See above, p. 42.

It is in the book of Revelation that the symbol is used most freely, in an abundance of images. In Rev 19:7–9 a voice from the throne of God announces, "the marriage of the Lamb has come, and his bride has made herself ready." We see the bride "clothed with fine linen, bright and pure," which is the "righteous deeds of the saints." Later on, in a "new heaven and a new earth" (Rev 21:1), the Holy City, the new Jerusalem, descends from heaven, "prepared as a bride adorned for her husband" (Rev. 21:2). Here the author takes up the symbolic representations that we have already encountered in Isa 61:10; 62:4–6. The continuity of the imagery shows that the eschatological hope connected with the glorification of the "Lamb that was slain"—that is, with Christ Jesus crucified and risen—is the complete fulfillment of the Scriptures. It demonstrates that there is continuity between the two Testaments, but when Christ Jesus came into the world, the ancient divine promises were transformed.

SYMBOLS DRAWN FROM SOCIAL LIFE

To speak of the church as "mother" is already to make us of a metaphor that has social content. But we need to return to the First Testament in order to see how several social structures permitted a quasi-technical language to be articulated to describe the "community of salvation." Although salvation, from its origins, was understood as the history of a divine plan to bring about the good of humanity, this salvation, which delivered people from evil in all of its forms, was never presented as the object of an individual quest in which each person is saved by his or her own means.

From this perspective, there is a radical difference between the biblical understanding of evil, from which God sets people free, and the Buddhist cycle of *samsara,* from which each person tries to be liberated by extinguishing desire.[26] Spiritual exercises in both traditions may have some common aspects, but Jews, like Christians later, places themselves in the hands of the living God in order to receive the *grace* of salvation. Thus our task is to see how,

---

[26] See "Samsara," *DR* 2:1815–16 (M. Delahoutre on Hinduism, and P. Massein on Buddhism). The article gives particular attention to the technique of "deliverance" in the various branches of Buddhism.

in the two Testaments, the experience of life in society led to the elaboration of a technical language in which salvation, even though given by the living God to those who trusted in him, reached them by the mediation of a society whose workings constituted a complex mediation of salvation. In the First Testament these workings were connected with functions that had parallels in neighboring societies, but the way they were described ultimately created a symbolic language that the New Testament took up and endowed with a new meaning.

Salvific Functions in the First Testament

The word "salvific" is perhaps a bit too strong, since the salvation that can be obtained through these "functions" depends on certain conditions that are not always fulfilled: everything depends on the disposition of those who perform them. We will be considering the functions of king and judge in the political and social sphere, prophet and priest in the religious sphere, and the wisdom teacher in the cultural sphere. In the preaching of the prophets we also hear about figures who perform salvific functions that do not correspond to precise social roles: the "servant of YHWH" and the "Son of Man," described in the Message of Consolation and the apocalypse of Daniel, respectively. This stream of symbolism in the First Testament creates the language that the New Testament will use to describe the mediator of salvation.

The People

In the First Testament the people are the permanent element in history. In principle, the Hebrew word *'am* could indicate any group of humans, but it applies particularly to Israel as the "people of YHWH." When Israel was joined to God through the covenant, it became "a people of his very own possession" (Deut 4:20). The prophets use the word constantly in this sense (e.g., Isa 1:3; 40:1; 65:10). At the beginning, it was an ethnic designation that could have been used for many other groups of people. However, the nation of Israel, divided after Solomon into two rival kingdoms, was distinguished from its neighbors by a faith that gave its history a particular meaning within the historical realization of the divine plan.

The classic presentation of Israel's history is that the nation was formed of twelve tribes, considered to be descended from the patriarchs. The tribes bear the names of their ancestors, the twelve sons of Jacob, except that the descendants of Joseph form the two tribes of Ephraim and Manasseh.

We do not need to look for historical personages behind the names of the tribes; the essential thing is the assembly of the tribes around a group that experienced the exodus from Egypt, understood as a liberation brought about by God. By the time of the New Testament, the tribe of Judah had given its name to the entire Jewish people ("Jew" = "Judean") throughout its dispersion. In the meantime, the descendants of the twelve ancient tribes, who also assimilated the original inhabitants of the land, had become a political entity whose structure went through several variations over the centuries.

The King

It was not until the ninth century B.C.E. that this tribal league of varying fortunes chose a king for itself as the small nations around it had already done: Edom, Moab, the Ammonites, the Aramaeans of Damascus, and the Phoenician city-states on the Mediterranean coast that had been established for centuries. After the Benjaminite Saul, the throne came to the Judean David, who created a dynasty that received religious legitimization; the idea of a Davidic kingship continued down to New Testament times. Councils of tribal elders gave David his royal authority, first over the various clans of the tribe of Judah (2 Sam 2:2–4), and then over the assembled tribes of Israel (2 Sam 5:1–4). As ruler over the "united kingdom" of Judah and Israel, he conquered and took possession of the city of Jerusalem, which he made the royal capital (2 Sam 5:6–12). There his son Solomon built the temple that housed the ark of the covenant, the ancient symbol of God's presence with the people. Later, in the Deuteronomic reform under King Josiah (622 B.C.E.), this temple became the only place where YHWH, the nation's God, could be worshiped.

Once established, the kingship displaced the traditional functions of the tribal elders. The king retained final authority in judgment and in the conduct of wars. The people expected above all that he would uphold law and justice. However, the monarchy became entangled in the international conflicts between the empires of

Mesopotamia and Egypt, and it met a catastrophic end in 587 B.C.E. with the destruction of Jerusalem. There was a restoration in 538 B.C.E. when Cyrus the Persian conquered Babylon and permitted the Judean elites—the "Jews"—to return to their homeland. Nevertheless, the nation was ever afterwards only a vassal state under successive empires: Persian, Macedonian, then Syrian or Egyptian, and finally Roman. The Jews could only dream of a future king, the supreme "anointed one" or "Messiah" described in their prophetic oracles. Jewish hopes attributed royal qualities to this Messiah: he would uphold law and justice, and create national peace and prosperity, allowing the traditional religious faith to flourish.

The Priests

The covenant inherited from the patriarchs and firmly established at Sinai after the exodus from Egypt made Israel the "people of YHWH," and it required a functioning cult whose regulations were embodied in the law (Hebrew: *torah*). This cult eventually displaced the ancient pagan practices of the land, but only with difficulty, and it was finally entrusted, in the Judean period, to a hierarchical and strictly regulated priesthood. The temple, reconstructed between 520 and 515 B.C.E., was the only place where the sacrifices of the cult could be offered. In the time of Jesus, the twenty-four classes of priests who divided up the temple service over the twelve months of the year were assisted by Levites, who performed practical functions: singers, doorkeepers, and so on. Different kinds of ceremonies were observed: oblations, sin offerings, thanksgivings, burnt offerings—everything being carried out in the temple.

We need to appreciate all of the varied aspects of this cult and its personnel in order to understand the religious language of the New Testament. The temple rituals were still being carried out in the time of Jesus and the apostles. They ceased only with the destruction of the temple by the Romans in 70 C.E., at the end of the Jewish-Roman war described by the historian Flavius Josephus. In the meantime, Christianity was born.

The Prophets

Should not the prophets be grouped together with the members of the priestly hierarchy as people who carried out religious functions? The biblical texts do provide evidence of the existence of cultic prophets connected with sanctuaries (e.g., Jer 23:14–40). Nonetheless, those who truly inspired the faith of Israel, those whom the Bible most significantly calls "prophets," who brought the word of God that has been embodied in the sacred books, were drawn from many different vocations in life. They are the ones to whom the divine revelation is primarily indebted for its preservation and development. These were not "prophets by profession," like the prophets of Baal mentioned in the story of Elijah on Mount Carmel (1 Kgs 18:20–40). A prophetic calling could come to people who were, among other things, priests like Jeremiah and Ezekiel, royal officials like Amos (Amos 7:14–15), king's counselors like Isaiah, and so forth. Their social standing was unimportant; all that mattered was the mission of proclaiming the word of God. John the Baptist belonged to exactly this line of prophets (Matt 11:13–14). But was this the only form that the word of God took?

From the Torah to the Wisdom Tradition

Judaism regarded the Torah supremely as the "word of God." Tradition has attributed all of the Torah to Moses, who can be regarded as the "superprophet." However, the diversity of styles in its books demonstrates that they and the documents from which they have been composed are the product of numerous authors, some of whom have remained anonymous. We can deduce that the authors and editors of texts such as Deuteronomy (itself a complex composition) and the "Holiness Code" of Lev 17–26 worked within priestly circles, in the north for Deuteronomy, and in Jerusalem for the Holiness Code. But where are we to situate the anonymous authors responsible for the materials found in the historical books from Joshua to Kings? What functions did they perform in the society and in the state?

The situation is clearest for the wisdom books. The position of the "wisdom teachers" within the society and state is clearer to us. In a certain way they were, in Israel as in Mesopotamia, the maintainers of the culture. In the case of the wisdom books of the biblical canon, that culture was infused by same religious spirit that animated the genuine legislators and prophets. The "sages" identified the divine wisdom that inspired them as the source of their instruction.

Musicians

The liturgy of Israel has a lyrical quality because it consists of sacred songs originally composed and performed by temple musicians. This was a profession that developed from the time that worship of YHWH first began in Israel. In the ancient East liturgy is unimaginable without singers and musical instruments.

Conclusion

We see, therefore, that members of a number of professions in Israelite and Jewish society were responsible for works that constituted an enormous corpus at the time of Jesus, not even counting the compositions that particular groups cherished that did not become part of the official Scriptures. The discoveries in the caves at Qumran have given us a glimpse into this latter category of literature. In the caves legal, musical, and apocalyptic texts were found alongside commentaries on the prophetic and other Scriptures. The New Testament writers made all of this their heritage, although they left to one side the works that came from sectarian groups. Nevertheless, it is possible that certain of these works have left traces in one or another of the Christian books. The Epistle of Jude, for example, quotes directly from the Greek version of *Enoch,* to which the Qumran community attributed great significance. In addition, the prayers offered in the synagogue had a more or less fixed form, and there is no reason not to believe that the first followers of Jesus and the apostles made use of these prayers when they addressed their own personal needs. However, we must not think that the New Testament writers made unreflecting use of all preceding biblical and extrabiblical literature, because in the meantime, Jesus had come.

This set of functions with the "community of salvation," when limited to Israel, does not constitute a symbolic language; functions that are more or less directly parallel can be identified within the surrounding societies. I list them here only to highlight a particular feature of Israel's religious sociology: it is intimately connected with the first stage in the history of the revelation of the true God. We know of this stage from the literature that it produced. Its custodians were not necessarily aware of the providential role that they were playing, or at least of the role that their society was playing in preparing for the coming of Jesus Christ. But in a retrospective way, the Jews in the time of Jesus already recognized that those who performed the functions that we have been examining were mediators of an authentic revelation that was taking shape over time. Jesus Christ more explicitly revealed the full meaning of these structures, to such an extent that the New Testament could offer a symbolic interpretation of ancient structures that showed them to be "figures" of the new community and of the "world to come," as we will see below.

Two Extraordinary Symbols

We should also note that the prophetic and apocalyptic portions of the First Testament make use of two symbolic titles to designate mediators of salvation: the "Servant of YHWH" and the "Son of Man." Within the literary context in which they appear, these titles do not indicate well-determined functions, nor do they refer to clearly defined individuals, but they do play an essential role in the language of the New Testament.

The "Servant of YHWH"

The general term *'ebed* designates in Hebrew any servant (eventually a bondservant) who is subject to a master. As a result, the expression "servant of God" or "servant of YHWH" is applied in many different cases: to the angels (Job 4:18), to the prophets whom God sent to proclaim his word (e.g., 1 Kgs 14:18; Jer 7:25), and in a special way to Moses (e.g., Exod 14:31). It can also apply to all true worshipers of God (e.g., Isa 65:12–13). But also there are, in the Message of Consolation addressed to the exiles (Isa 40–55), four passages where the expression "servant of YHWH" has a very particular meaning. It is used to designate the one who would bring about salvation for the people in their affliction (Isa 42:1–9; 49:1–9a; 50:4–11; 52:13–53:12).[27] Interpreters have debated the proper identification of this "servant" endlessly. Is it a historical personage from the past, the present, or the future? Is it a fictional character who personifies, for example, the "righteous exiles"? Or is it someone to be expected in

---

[27] I have examined this text and its successive "rereadings" in *Les Poèmes du Serviteur: De la lecture critique à l'herméneutique* (LD 103; Paris: Cerf, 1981).

the future, whose coming the prophet announces in order to stir up the hopes of the Jews in their distress? All the widely varying interpretations have had their supporters. Whatever the servant's identity, we may note that the author of the book of Daniel reminded the righteous who were being persecuted in the time of Antiochus IV, who was trying to force Syrian paganism on the Jews, of the "Suffering Servant" of the fourth poem in the Message of Consolation.[28] The most significant thing for our purposes, however, is to see how the New Testament authors read these texts, giving them a meaning that reflected their faith in Jesus.

The "Son of Man"

The expression "son of man" is a general one that can be used to describe anyone as a human being. In Hebrew, *ben-'adam* has this meaning, as in, for example, Ezek 2:1 (and 87 other times in that book). *Ben-'enosh,* a version of the expression that uses another term for humanity in general, is found in Ps 144:3. In the Aramaic of Dan 7, a passage in which a great number of symbols are intermingled, the term *bar 'enash* refers to the coming of a person[29] who is contrasted with the four "beasts" that appear earlier, which are symbols of four pagan empires that are to hold sway successively in the world. This person, who is said to be "like a son of man" (Dan 7:13), brings salvation with him at the end of the period of tribulation that the people of God are then going through. But whom does this symbol designate? Is it a person to be expected in the future, or a personification that represents the coming of salvation itself? We must, in any event, recognize the importance of the symbol in light of its use in the New Testament.

Sociopolitical Symbols Applied to God

Clearly, there are some sociopolitical symbols that cannot be applied to God, particularly those of people who are in the service of

---

[28] See the discussion of the allusions to Isa 53 in the book of Daniel in ibid., 119–27.

[29] See any of the numerous standard commentaries on the question of the "Son of Man" in Daniel.

God, such as prophets and members of the priesthood, or symbolic personages who are in the service of the divine plan, such as the "Servant of YHWH" and the one who is "like a son of man" in the book of Daniel. Similarly, the symbols of "the people" and "the covenant" cannot be used for God, even though they are directly connected with God, since "the people" are God's partners in "the covenant" that God has made with them. This leaves only the monarchy and the functions directly connected with it: upholding justice by executing judgment, and conducting wars against the enemies of the people. Indeed, we see these two functions used symbolically to depict God in both Testaments, with nuances appropriate to the contexts in which they are employed.

God as Monarch

Royal titles were freely accorded to gods in the religions of the ancient East, as, for example, to Marduk in Babylon. Israel's liturgies frequently made use of such titles as it celebrated the "reign of God." Isaiah was in the temple when he had the vision in which he received his calling to be a prophet of YHWH. In describing this vision, he said, "My eyes have seen the King, the LORD of hosts" (Isa 6:5). In the second part of the book of Isaiah the anonymous prophet describes God as the "King of Jacob" (Isa 41:21) and the "King of Israel" (Isa 44:6). It is especially in Psalms that we find repeated allusions to the divine monarchy, primarily in celebration of it (Ps 5:2; 10:16; 24:7-10; 29:10; 44:4; 47:2, 6–8; 48:2; 68:24; 74:12; 84:3; 89:18; 93:1; 95:3; 96:10; 97:1; 98:6; 99:1; 145:1; 149:2). The liturgy also speaks freely of the reign of God (with the verb "reign": Ps 47:8 [47:9 MT]; 96:10). The Hebrew word *mamlakah,* the Aramaic *malkut,* and the Greek *basileia* can all designate, depending on the context, either the reign, the royalty, or the kingdom of God or of a human monarch.

It is probable that the prayer *'Abinu Malkenu* ("Our Father and Our God") had been introduced to the liturgy of the synagogue by the time of Jesus. Thus royal symbolism was being applied freely to God. It therefore is not surprising to find in the Gospel texts, and particularly in the sayings of Jesus, a proclamation of the coming of the "reign of God" (or the "kingdom of God"), even though the particular details of this proclamation are not explained clearly: is it an eschatological future reality, or something already present?[30] Translators have difficulty rendering the phrase in several places, particularly since the Jews did not make a distinction between "the kingdom of God" and "the kingdom of heaven" (heaven = God), and sometimes spoke simply of "the kingdom" (50x in Matthew, 14x in Mark, 36x in Luke, but only 2x in John). In the apostolic writings the expression occurs in one form or another 7 times in the Acts of the Apostles,[31] and about 15 times in the Epistles and Revelation. We should note the case of 1 Pet 2:9 in particular: the new community is described as *basileion hierateuma,* in an implicit citation of Exod 19:6. But what is this "royal priesthood"?[32] In the New Testament it appears that the phrase is making reference to Jesus Christ as "Messiah-King." The same text in Exodus is paraphrased in Rev 5:10, which says of the martyrs, "you have made them to be a kingdom and priests serving our God" (cf. Rev 1:6). The phrase from Exod 19:6 is no longer being understood in the context of God as king.

But God as king exercises an essential function, that of "judgment," establishing justice among people (expressed by the Hebrew verb *shafat,* "judge"; the derived substantive *mishpat,* "judgment"; and the noun *shofet,* "judge"; and by the Greek *krinein* and its derivatives). It is through this exercise of judgment that God demonstrates his "justice" (*tsedeq*). This justice can be understood in a larger sense as the action by which God proves himself to be the protector of his people and of the righteous, assuring them of his grace (*tsedaqah*). This cluster of words, frequently applied to God in the

---

[30] See the discussion in Grelot, *Dieu, le Père de Jésus Christ,* 71–74; the question of the *basileia* of God is treated at length on pp. 66–90 of that volume. For a discussion at greater length see R. Schnackenburg, *Règne et royaume de Dieu: Essai de Théologie biblique* (Études théologiques 2; Paris: L'Orante, 1965).

[31] Typically, we refer to this book as "*The* Acts of *the* Apostles," inserting definite articles in the title, because we are translating it from the Latin *Actus apostolorum.* However, in the Greek title, *Praxeis apostolōn,* neither word bears an article. Luke is relating "apostles' acts" without any pretense of reporting them all.

[32] For the original meaning of the phrase "a kingdom of priests and a holy nation" see the article by H. Cazelles, originally published in 1976 and reprinted in *Autour de l'Exode: Études* (SB; Paris: Gabalda, 1987), 289–94.

First Testament, shows that God is the supreme judge and that his judgment is at work in the events of the world. The language is taken up in the New Testament with the words *dikē, dikaios, dikaiosynē, dikaiōma,* and the verb *dikaioun.* But we need to be careful about the misleading meanings that modern languages derived from Latin, and even the Greek language, can lead us to find in texts when we read them in translation. In the original Hebrew of the First Testament the roots *shafat* and *tsedeq* differed profoundly in meaning. It is true that "God judges [*shafat*] with justice [*tsedeq*]." But when the Message of Consolation to the exiles speaks of God's "justice" (*tsedaqah*), it draws a synonymous parallel with the "salvation" that God is bringing to the people. Thus in Isa 51:4b–5a we read, "(A) teaching will go out from me, and my justice [or 'judgment'] for a light to the peoples. I will bring near my deliverance [*tsedaqah*] swiftly, my salvation has gone out and my arms will rule the peoples." Justice and salvation go together. It is this "justice" or "righteousness" of God that the apostle Paul presents from the beginning of Romans. The gospel, he says, is "the power of God for salvation to everyone who has faith . . . For in it the righteousness [justice] of God is revealed through faith for faith" (Rom 1:16–17). This "justice of God" is no longer something that judges, but rather something that, through faith, enables people to "become righteous" and thus brings them to salvation by "justifying" them.

Divine justice in this sense is therefore not that of Roman law, which strictly meted out rewards and punishments; that was the concept of the "just judgment" of God in the prophets. Now, rather, it is a matter of "justifying justice": by grace, it "makes righteous" people who are sinners, so long as they put their faith in Christ as the Redeemer. Nevertheless, the New Testament still has a concept of the "day of judgment" (Matt 10:15; 11:22, 24; 12:36; 2 Pet 2:9; 3:7; 1 John 4:17; Jude 6; cf. Matt 12:41, 42; Luke 10:14; 11:31–32; Rom 2:5; 1 Cor 4:5; 2 Pet 2:4; Rev 14:7). But even in the less precise Greek vocabulary, the distinction in Hebrew between *mishpat* and *tsedaqah* can still be felt. The God who "judges with justice" is also the one whose "salvific justice" has appeared on behalf of those who put their faith in Christ Jesus. In this way, God the judge is also the God into whose "justice" (*tsedaqah*) and "salvation" the Message of Consolation gives us a glimpse.

God and War

The king of Israel, like all of the other kings in the ancient East, conducted the wars of his people. Is this symbol applicable to God as king? Let us distinguish here between the two Testaments.

The First Testament. An old collection of Israelite songs was entitled the "Book of the Wars of the LORD" (Num 21:14). We have no direct quotations from this book, unless the "Song of the Well" (Num 21:17–18) and the itinerary in Num 21:10–14 are taken from it. In any case, the very mention of the title suffices to demonstrate an understanding of God as participating in the wars of the nation. The identity of Israel as the "people of YHWH" had this consequence: the realization of the divine plan within the fortunes of the people turned the wars that they needed to conduct for their national survival into "holy wars."

As a result, we should not be astonished to find expressions in the narrative texts that otherwise might surprise us. These texts say, for example, that Israel succeeded in its enterprises because "God fought for the people," both during the exodus from Egypt, as the tradition reports (Exod 14:14, 25), and in the wars that followed (Deut 1:30; 3:22), particularly in the conquest of the promised land (Josh 10:14, 42; 23:3, 10). Even in the later period the idea of a military campaign assisted by the God of the nation did not disappear from people's thinking (2 Chr 20:29, 2 Macc 11:13; cf. 2 Macc 14:34; Sir 4:28). The song in Exod 15 goes so far as to say that "the LORD is a warrior" (Exod 15:3), and the narrative in Exod 17:16 explains that "the LORD will have war with Amalek from generation to generation." The narratives that relate the history of the Israelite kingdom at the time of the wars with the Philistines do not hesitate to say that "the battle is the LORD's" (1 Sam 17:47) and that it was the king's job to "fight the LORD's battles" (1 Sam 18:17; 25:28). Even the Chronicler, writing after the return from exile, has King Jehoshaphat say, "the battle is not yours but God's" (2 Chr 20:15), while an ancient psalm describes the LORD as "mighty in battle" (Ps 24:8).

We must be careful, however, to avoid getting the wrong impression from this imagery, because God was not necessarily entirely identified with the people's *political* struggles. If they were unfaithful to God, they would be threatened militarily once again.

Jeremiah, during his prophetic ministry, interpreted the campaign
of Nebuchadnezzar, king of Babylon, against the kingdom of Judah
as an enterprise that had God's support to chastise the guilty nation:
"Thus says the LORD, the God of Israel: . . . I myself will fight
against you . . . in great wrath" (Jer 21:4–5). The prophet thus interprets international events as decisive acts of divine pedagogy; in this
case, the Babylonian invasion was a just punishment for the infidelity of the people. Every situation in which Israel found itself was
understood in light of the divine plan, which remained unvarying in
the midst of changing circumstances. The people might waver
between religious fidelity and infidelity, but the plan of God was
always the same.

Events, of course, are not symbols. The essential thing is to take
a step back from them and see their meaning. The people wavered
between fidelity to their God and repeated infidelities; how were
they to be made sensitive of this, if not by being exposed to the haz-
ards of history, where they were tossed about by the changing fortunes of international politics? The prophets were there to remind
them of their infidelities and their consequences, and thereby to
educate them in a challenging faith.

The New Testament. It is notable that in the New Testament,
from Jesus forward, wars are never considered "holy wars."[33] If Jesus
speaks of the wars that kings wage against one another (Luke 14:31),
it is only in the perspective of the misfortunes that can come upon

---

[33] For a bibliography on war in the two Testaments see J. Rader-
mackers, "Guerre," *DEB* 546–47. The theological aspect of the theme in
both Testaments is presented by H. Cazelles and P. Grelot in "Guerre,"
VTB 518–24. The question of the Crusades may be raised, but in fact,
whatever the soldiers and the theologians who accompanied them may
have thought, the Crusades were not a religious enterprise, but rather a
political one. They were the result of the opposition between an Islam in
which religion and the state were joined together in the Umayyad and a
Christendom where the "spiritual" and the "political" had been intimately
connected since the decree of Theodosius that made Christianity the official religion of the empire. In such a context the understanding of the Crusades as a holy war was a cultural phenomenon that had only a casual
connection with faith; this understanding was necessary to ensure that the
participants were not engaging in acts that had no foundation in the
church.

people, which are signs of "the end," whose approach will be marked by "wars and rumors of wars" (Mark 13:7; Matt 24:6; cf. Luke 21:9). Jesus himself refused to be made "king" in the temporal sense of the word (John 18:36; cf. 6:15). He forbid even his disciples to defend him at the time of his arrest (John 18:10–12; cf. Mark 14:47–48; Luke 22:49–51; Matt 26:51–54 ["all who take the sword will perish by the sword"]).

Those who believe in Jesus are called to engage in only one combat, that for the triumph of the gospel despite the hostility of those who oppose its proclamation (Phil 1:29–30; 2:25; Col 1:28–2:1). Paul wrote that he had "fought the good fight" all of his life (2 Tim 4:7). This battle is fought by prayer (Eph 6:18–20; Col 4:12; cf. Heb 12:4), with the "weapons of righteousness" (2 Cor 6:7; cf. Rom 6:13), which are both defensive and offensive (cf. Eph 6:11–17). Such is "the good fight of the faith" (1 Tim 6:12; cf. 1:18). This is something entirely different from the political wars of the First Testament; the situation is completely transformed.

However, in the background of the campaigns that are thus conducted for the extension of the gospel in the world and its success in the lives of the faithful, another enemy can be discerned: "Like a roaring lion your adversary the devil prowls around, looking for someone to devour" (1 Pet 5:8). The book of Revelation, through its imagery, reveals the extent of this combat. In the spiritual realm there is the battle between the angel Michael, assisted by his angels, and the dragon (Rev 12:7). But the invisible adversary who engages in this conflict has helpers on this earth, whom the author portrays as a beast with seven heads and ten crowns (Rev 13:1–10), assisted by a false prophet (Rev 13:11–18). On this beast is seated the "great whore" (Rev 17). With her support, the kings who are hostile to the gospel will "make war on the Lamb, and the Lamb will conquer them" (Rev 17:14). This Lamb, seen earlier "as if it had been slaughtered" (Rev 5:6), is none other than Christ in glory. He is also identified as the "rider . . . called Faithful and True," and "in righteousness he judges and makes war" (Rev 19:11). His name is "The Word of God" (Rev 19:13). Behind the symbols we can discern, on the individual level as well as the historical, a *spiritual* combat that ends in a *spiritual* victory.

In the style characteristic of apocalypses, the final battle is described as a gigantic face-off between this "rider," who is Christ, and an evil army composed of the beast, the kings of the earth and their armies, the false prophet, and "those who had received the mark of the beast and those who worshiped its image" (Rev 19:17–21). Their extermination symbolizes the final victory of Christ over evil. This is very different from the wars of the First Testament: the combat now takes place both within human history and within human hearts. And God now has a representative in history who is no longer political: it is Jesus Christ, crucified and risen.[34]

---

[34] In ch. 4 we will consider all of these symbolic representations once again when we examine the "figurative" symbols in the Scriptures.

3

Mythical
Symbols

I do not have in mind here the kind of "mythology" that is woven together of imaginary heroes who embody beliefs connected with pagan conceptions of divinity. What I mean by "myth" is any symbolic construction that evokes, through imagery, certain domains that are inaccessible to observation.[1] A first category of mythical symbols is made up of realities that our spiritual experience conceives of or senses, without having any direct perception of them. On the one hand, there is God and the "world of God" (so to speak),

---

[1] It is quite difficult to define "myth" in general. A good general idea of the concept can be had from J. Vidal, "Mythe," *DR* 2:1392–97. In the end, I favor a definition like that offered by P. Ricoeur: "In no way a false explanation by means of images and fables, but rather a traditional story relating to what happened at the beginnings of history, intended to provide a basis for the ritual activity of people today and, in a general way, to undergird all the forms of action and thought by which people understand themselves in their world" (P. Ricoeur, *The Symbolism of Evil* [Boston: Beacon, 1969], 5). I am looking at categories of symbols from the *literary* point of view, and my focus is on the way the biblical texts understand humanity in its relationship to God. Thus I make a distinction between "myth/mythical sense" and "mythology." I use the latter term in a pejorative way, because of its connection with a polytheistic conception of the "divine," while the terms "myth" and "mythical symbolism," understood from a strictly literary point of view, have a neutral meaning for me: they are imaginary constructions that may be employed in the biblical texts just as easily as in the mythological stories of various paganisms, ancient or modern.

which are removed from our immediate consciousness by an excess of light; on the other hand, there is the whole realm of physical and moral evil, which is inaccessible to our reason because of an excess of obscurity. The second category relates to our experience of time. We have no clear understanding of how time began or of what might have come before it, nor of how time will end and under what circumstances. All we can do in both cases is rely on the construction of imaginary representations. These can be true, to the extent that the things that they suggest offer a perspective that we can consider reasonable, or if divine revelation allows us to identify them as realities.

On many occasions the texts of the two Testaments evoke realities that are situated outside of space and time. It is true that pagan mythologies do the same, but they are connected to polytheistic conceptions that the revelation of the true God excludes absolutely. Nevertheless, this does not mean that their images cannot be appropriated, as long as they are radically purified, by the biblical revelation itself when there is no other means of evoking certain aspects of reality that are inaccessible to our senses. Only a rigorous analysis of the biblical texts can enable us to understand their meaning and significance.

SYMBOLS OF GOD AND SYMBOLS OF EVIL

Neither God nor evil is situated in space and time; rather, they are "presences" coexisting in the same space and time in which we live. We can only represent them by using images created out of whole cloth, unless we content ourselves with abstract ideas developed in an attempt to define them. However, no vigorous mind is content with abstractions, the religious mind least of all. God is for us, by definition, a presence infinitely superior to us. The more we reflect on this infinite presence and try to understand it clearly, the more it eludes our grasp. As for evil in all of its forms, it is even more undefinable, but in these forms it is nevertheless an object of our experience. By contrast, God and what we might call the "world of God" are never the object of direct experience, to such an extent that some have been led to deny their existence. Nevertheless, every religious soul senses this existence and has the certainty that this sense is not deceptive. But this God, who is he? Leaving aside the ways in which various pagan religions have represented God, we will be analyzing only those representations found in the biblical texts, which we receive as true. As for evil, we should acknowledge that it is represented in many different ways, depending on the spheres in which the experience of evil is being examined. In any event, let us examine the diverse "mythical" representations that the biblical revelation employs.

Mythical Representations of the "World of God"

If it were only a question of God himself, the unique God of biblical revelation, we would have no need for the adjective "mythical." When human language considers God directly, it simply makes use of anthropomorphisms, as we saw earlier.[2] However, they are purified anthropomorphisms, if we compare them with those of the ancient paganisms that the biblical revelation was in constant contact with and that it rejects categorically. But even if the biblical revelation is hardly fond of abstractions, it nevertheless poses questions that call for an extensive imagery: Where is God? How does God act in the world? Obviously, certain questions, common in various paganisms, are excluded immediately, such as: For how long has God existed and acted? And until when? For God, there can be no question of dying or of suffering any kind of misfortune; God exists and acts "from eternity to eternity." This is a radical distinction between God and ourselves and the world we live in, this world that is God's creation in the same way that we are. If we want to represent God as "creating" the world or people, we can definitely make use of certain anthropomorphisms; but can we also retain something from the creation imagery of ancient paganism? We will see that the Bible dares to do this, on occasion.[3] However, this is not the essential aspect of its portrayal of God.

Where Is God?

If we want our representation of God to be concrete, we need to do more than just use anthropomorphisms to evoke God's actions

---

[2] See in ch. 2 "Anthropomorphic Representations of God" (pp. 26–27).
[3] See below "Texts of the New Testament" (pp. 75–77).

and feelings; we must also pose an unsettling question related to God's universal presence and action: This living God, where is he? What is God's own dwelling place, as opposed to the place where we live, the earth? Psalm 115 answers this question by contrasting God with idols (Ps 115:4–8). When the pagans, who are attached to their visible idols, ask, "Where is their God?" the believer simply responds, "Our God is in the heavens; he does whatever he pleases" (Ps 115:2–3). But what are "the heavens"? Are they a matter of cosmology or of theology? This question is not meaningful in the realm of symbolic representation. From the metaphysical and religious point of view, God is present where his activity can be discerned. But this activity, and the presence it presupposes, are discernable everywhere. We can grasp the abstract concept of universality in space and time through our unaided reason, but our being cannot be reduced to the "pure reason" of Kant. Our reason needs support from the imagination if our hearts are to be affected.

From this perspective, let us take up once again the question that we posed a moment ago: Where is God? If we were to take this question the way the natural sciences would understand it, we would offer different answers depending on what time and what civilization we lived in. This is because the picture of the world we live in has varied considerably from ancient times up to the present, and the variation has only accelerated since the development of astronomy and nuclear physics. The hypothesis of a "big bang" has given the universe a dimension that the ancients could hardly have imagined.[4] But none of this really matters from the perspective of symbolic language. God is everywhere, but it is impossible to see him or to touch him directly. For us on the earth, God is radically inaccessible. If we wish to situate God's presence, therefore, we must locate it "up above," whatever the picture might be that we have of that

---

[4] All modern astrophysicists speak in terms of a "big bang," when the universe began. For a technical discussion see J. Silk, *The Big Bang* (3rd ed.; New York: Freeman, 2001). Readers should not be intimidated by the technical nature of the presentation or by the mathematics in the appendices. When I read the book, I skipped these technical pages. The hypothesis of an original explosion from which came the universe as we know it today is now generally accepted by astrophysicists. See Hubert Reeves, *La première seconde* (vol. 2 of *Dernières nouvelles du cosmos;* Paris: Seuil, 1995), 2:234.

inaccessible realm. Those in the ancient East pictured several layers of "heavens" that were home to the sun, moon, stars, and so on. The residence of God, however, was *above* those heavens; they were thought to be topped by a sort of platform that certain texts describe cryptically: it is the "firmament" of Gen 1:14, the "pavement of sapphire stones" that the elders of Israel saw God standing on when the covenant was made at Sinai (Exod 24:10).

Ezekiel reports something quite similar in his initial vision: "above the dome over their heads there was something like a throne, in appearance like sapphire; and seated above the likeness of a throne was something that seemed like a human form" (Ezek 1:26; cf. 10:1). In other words, it was an indescribable reality located beyond this world. In the book of Daniel, while the "beasts" that are incarnations of evil rise from the sea—from the abyss!—and while their battles take place on the earth, the prophet sees the "Ancient One" (Dan 7:9),[5] who personifies the divine presence somewhere else, above. However, the book in no way specifies how his location relates to that of the others. But in Deuteronomy we are told that it was "from heaven" that God made the Israelites "hear his voice" (e.g., Deut 4:36), since "heaven and the heaven of heavens" belong to him (Deut 10:14)—in other words, the highest heavens that are to be found above the world. This depiction of a heavenly "dwelling place" for God is found throughout both Testaments. But how can God's presence be portrayed? How has it presented itself to the imagination of seers—or of literary authors?

The description of the elders' vision at Sinai (Exod 24:9–10) says nothing of God's presence. The prophets' descriptions of their visions of God make use of anthropomorphisms. Jeremiah, for example, reports that "the LORD put out his hand and touched my mouth" in order to put his words there (Jer 1:9). Ezekiel uses multiple approximations to portray God. In the book of Kings, Micaiah the son of Imlah provides a few more details in his symbolic depiction of God. But this brings us to a second question: How does God reveal himself, to make known what he is?

---

[5] This is the literal translation of the Aramaic *'attiq yomin.* We are uncomfortable seeing God presented as an old man, even though Christian painters have done this. It needs to be understood that he is an *ageless* old man.

How (in What Form) Does God Reveal Himself?

Visions of God. Let us return to the vision of Micaiah the son of
Imlah, in the ninth century B.C.E.: "I saw the LORD sitting on his
throne, with all the host of heaven standing beside him to the right
and to the left of him" (1 Kgs 22:19). What is this "heavenly host"?
Neighboring paganisms divinized the "powers" that presided over
the functioning of the universe and therefore envisioned an extensive divine court surrounding the supreme deity, whatever name
they gave it: *An* in Sumeria, *Ilu* in Akkadia, or *'El* or *'Ilah* among the
western Semites.

In Israel the supreme God, who had come to be worshiped
under the name "YHWH,"[6] supplanted all other divinities. But he is
described in royal terms ("the King, the LORD of hosts" [Isa 6:5]),
and it is understood that around him he has a court of messengers
(*mal'akim*), the "angels" who carry out his orders.

This is what the "host of heaven" refers to. God does not become
involved directly in the government of the world. In the ancient traditions preserved in the Pentateuch and Judges the "angel of the LORD"
frequently intervenes, substituting for a presence that remains envel-
oped in mystery (e.g., Gen 22:11, 15; 31:11; Exod 3:2; 14:19; Num
22:22–35; Judg 2:1, 4; 5:23). Over time, the terminology changes progressively: instead of the "angel of YHWH" as a manifestation of
God's direct intervention, "angels" come on the scene who are God's
messengers, passing on his orders and acting on his instructions. But
God continues to be surrounded, in the symbolic depiction that progressively gives him more royal traits, by servants, by a "host" of
angels. Thus God is known as "YHWH of hosts." In the book of
Joshua it is the "commander of the army of the LORD" who appears to
Joshua (Josh 5:14–15). A counterpart to this "commander" was known
among the Phoenicians. Thus, during the time of apostasy under
kings of Israel, the people made molten images and "worshiped all the

---

[6]The "revelation" of this divine name is described in Exod 3:1–6.
However, it is actually the development of an older terminology: *Yo,* or *Ya,*
or *Yaho/Yahu,* explained by reference to the Hebrew verb *hawah,* which
means "being-there," as opposed to the Greek *einai,* which indicates existence. See in ch. 1 "The Name of God" (pp. 12–15). The NRSV translates
this LORD.

host of heaven" (2 Kgs 17:16). For their part, the Judeans did the same under King Manasseh (2 Kgs 21:3, 5). During the reform under Josiah all of the cultic objects were burned that had been made "for Baal, for Asherah, and for all the host of heaven" (2 Kgs 23:4). In 2 Kgs 23:5 this "host of the heavens" is associated with astral cults.

But let us return to the titles of God, who is the sole object of worship in the biblical revelation. The texts frequently call God *YHWH tseba'ot,* "YHWH of hosts," referring to the "host" or "army" of celestial "messengers" who carry out the missions on which God sends them into the world. No longer are there divine powers in heaven apart from God, but there are celestial "powers" who carry out God's orders: God is the head of these "heavenly hosts" (1 Kgs 19:10, 14; 2 Kgs 19:31; Hos 12:5; 9x in Amos; Isa 1:9 and more than 50 other times; similarly in Jeremiah, but never in Ezekiel; Ps 24:10 and in a dozen other psalms). Thus the worship of the true God is confident enough to make use of this "mythical" expression whose origin is to be found in neighboring paganisms.

Messengers of God. With time, the portrayal of the "messengers" who carry out YHWH's orders was transformed. Already in Ezekiel, the "living creatures" who support the divine throne are personified by means of an image borrowed from the Babylonians: the *karibu.*[7] Later, in the Persian period, the concept of angels is developed more extensively (already in Zech 1:11 and 22 other times; Dan 3:28; 6:22; 7x in the Greek; 19x in Tobit). Persian religion came to have an increasingly greater influence on the way surrounding cultures developed their imagery;[8] we see this particularly in the apocryphal

---

[7] This image is found in several places in the First Testament, notably in Ezekiel (Ezek 9:3; 10:4–22), but also in the temple furnishings (1 Kgs 6:25–28; 8:6–7; Exod 25:18–22; 37:7–9). Psalm 18:10 (18:11 MT) makes the "cherub" the mount on which God rides in a theophany. The Akkadian prototype (*karibu*) was a winged bull. See J. Trinquet, "Kerub-Kerubim," *DBSup* 5:161–86, an article that examines the origins of the image and documents the uses of the word in both Testaments.

[8] It was within the context of Persian influence that the book of *Enoch* developed its extensive angelology, which was tied to a parallel demonology. The canonical texts of the Bible are more restrained. But we should note that in the book of Tobit, the demon Asmodeus takes his name from an evil spirit in Iranian religion.

book of *Enoch*, whose oldest portions may go back to the third century B.C.E.[9] This is where the conventional names of the four throne angels come from, which actually are descriptions of their functions: Michael, Gabriel, Raphael, and Uriel[10] (who is not mentioned in the Bible). In short, theological ideas were in place that generated symbolic representations; the doctrine gave rise to what are obviously literary elaborations. In this way, God's "heaven" was populated. But it is important to understand what the symbols mean, so as not to confuse the theological ideas themselves with these imaginary constructions. Imagination has an appropriate place in the work of the inspired authors, but we need to interpret it prudently.

The development of the doctrine of angels left the true God in his supreme position. It is in the apocalypse of Daniel that the portrayal of God is the most "mythical," but even so, God loses none of his sovereign majesty. The text of Dan 7:9–10 appears to depend on a more detailed depiction in the book of *Enoch* (*1 En.* 14:8–23, especially vv. 14–23). The scene in the book of Daniel is much more restrained, but it uses many of the same clichés.[11] For the moment, we will leave aside the royal character of the "Ancient of Days," who

---

[9] See A. Dupont-Sommer et al., eds., *La Bible: Écrits intertestamentaires* (trans. A. Caquot; Bibliothèque de la Pléiade 337; Paris: Gallimard, 1987), lxi–lxx. The primitive Aramaic text was discovered among the incomplete manuscripts in Cave 4 at Qumran. The astronomical and meteorological treatise (chs. 72–82) is abridged in the translated versions; it may be older and could go back to the fifth century B.C.E. It may have been based on Babylonian treatises.

[10] In *1 En.* 20 seven archangels are named, and their functions are indicated. They are also mentioned, without their names, in Tob 12:15. But *1 En.* 9:1 mentions only four archangels, and the name of the fourth varies between "Uriel" and "Sariel." "Sariel" is attested in the Aramaic and Greek versions of *1 En.* 20:6, but the name is "Uriel" in the three Ethiopian manuscripts and in 2 Esd 4:1. In *Tg. Neof.* 1 on Gen 32:35 the name of Sariel is mentioned. The names given to the archangels are in keeping with the functions that are attributed to them: in the book of Tobit, when Tobit is old, he is healed by Raphael ("God heals").

[11] See P. Grelot, "Daniel 7:9–10 et le livre d'Hénoch," *Sem* 28 (1978): 59–83. For the dependence of Dan 7:9–10 on *1 En.* 14:18–22 see p. 68 of that article, where *1 En.* 18–19 is retranslated from the Greek, the Ethiopian, and the Aramaic fragments. It is quoted again in *Transeu* 15 (1998): 146 n. 22.

is enthroned amidst a group of judges.[12] Let us simply note how many servants are at his disposal: "A thousand thousands served him, and ten thousand times ten thousand stood attending him" (Dan 7:10b). The same image is found in *1 En.* 14:22b. The heavenly scene itself is particularly characterized by fire: "his throne was fiery flames, and its wheels were burning fire" (Dan 7:9d). We should stress once again that these are not actual wheels; the scene here is borrowing a characteristic element of Mesopotamian art, in which divinities went about on a *melammu,* a platform whose degree of brightness reflected their place in the hierarchy.[13] This is a significant instance of literary borrowing, in that the image also appears in the scene in *1 En.* 14:18, in which we also see a "stream of fire" flowing beneath the throne (Dan 7:10a; cf. *1 En.* 14:19).

Thus the entire scene is designed to exalt the image of God. His thousands and tens of thousands of servants are pointedly described, but angels are not mentioned explicitly. Nevertheless, the author of the Aramaic portion of the book (Dan 2–7) is familiar with angels: one of them delivers the young men who are thrown in the furnace (Dan 3:25). As for the Hebrew conclusion to the book, it refers explicitly to the angel Michael (*Mikael*) as well as to Gabriel (Dan 8:16; cf. 9:21). We will have to return later to the theme of the divine court, which is intimately tied to a royal depiction of God. For the moment, let us simply note the "mythical" form of the imagery that evokes the glory of God here.

The Texts of the New Testament

In order to speak of God, the New Testament takes up the language of the biblical texts at the stage it had reached in the time of Jesus and the apostolic community. As a result, heaven (or the heavens), without losing the physical meaning known within Hellenistic culture, still indicated the symbolic place where God resided. God is "your Father in heaven" (Mark 11:25–26). The story of Jesus'

---

[12] The "thrones" that are set up in Dan 7:9 are for those who assist the supreme Judge. In Dan 7:10 we are told, "The court sat in judgment, and the books were opened."

[13] See my commentary in the article cited on p. 145 in *Transeu* 15 (1998). This image would be the source of the future iconography of Christ in glory.

baptism shows the heavens being "torn apart" (Mark) or "opening" (Matthew and Luke); the Spirit descends from them, and the voice of God is heard from there. It is not only God who dwells in heaven, but also the "assembly of the firstborn" (Heb 12:23). It was to heaven that Jesus, after his resurrection, "ascended" (Luke 24:51, Acts 1:11), and it is from there that he will "descend"[14] on the day of the general resurrection (1 Thess 4:16). Through its literary conventions, the book of Revelation[15] describes several scenes that take place in heaven. But in order to depict the new Jerusalem descending from heaven (Rev 3:12; 21:2), it explains that in the new world "the first heaven and the first earth had passed away" (Rev 21:1). Thus a clear distinction is drawn between the physical heavens and the "mythic" portrayal of them as the abode of God.

Similarly, the New Testament books take up the depiction of angels at the point it had reached within late Judaism, particularly within its apocalypses.[16] The text of Luke 2:13 even shows a familiarity with the "heavenly host," which appears with "an angel of the Lord" there in a scene right out of an apocalypse. Luke 1:19, 26 portray the angel Gabriel as a divine messenger, and Michael enters the action with his angels in Rev 12:7. The "angel of God" (or the "angel of the Lord") appears once again, with the indeterminate sense that the expression has in the First Testament, 5 times in Matthew, 5 times in Luke, once in John, and 5 times in Acts. And angels in general are mentioned many times, particularly in Revelation. In all of these cases, the language of the New Testament takes up the termi-

---

[14] It is obvious that this "ascent" and "descent" are not to be understood in the physical sense, but rather in keeping with the symbolism of "heaven." In the scene of Jesus' ascension the apostles and the other participants "see" Jesus in a way that is characteristic of manifestations of the risen Christ: the symbolic elements of the vision are intermixed with the reality of his presence and of their living relationship with him, and as a result they can give an authentic testimony to his resurrection.

[15] I will not go into detail here about the visions in Revelation. In the next chapter we will see that in Revelation "mythical" symbols frequently are intermixed with figurative ones.

[16] I have already discussed the book of *Enoch,* alongside which we should put the other apocryphal apocalypses, including the fragments recovered from the caves at Qumran. A list of these works may be found in the "Index thématique" in Dupont-Sommer et al., *La Bible,* 1811–12.

nology bequeathed to it by the Scriptures. This does not mean that angels are simply mythological images devoid of reality. But how else would it be possible to speak of the communications between an invisible God and the people to whom he reveals himself and who experience his interventions in their lives?

Mythical Representations of the "World of Evil"

The experience of evil is common to all people, in all times and in all cultures. How are its causes and its agents to be defined? We search with good reason for the causes of certain evils, whether they be bodily,[17] physical,[18] or psychological,[19] and we find it difficult to penetrate even into the human psyche. But even if we could explain the cause of these evils, we would not have explained the "mystery of evil." It is a "mystery"[20] not because it is surrounded by too much light, as in the case of God and what we might call the "supernatural," but because it is too darkly obscured. This is why, in order to

---

[17] Our search for relief from bodily ills dates back to the work done in antiquity within the framework of Greek medicine. Sirach praises physicians (Sir 38:1–15) among those of other noble occupations. He does not posit supernatural causes for illness such as the work of evil spirits, and so he does not prescribe exorcisms as a remedy. People went to doctors in the time of Jesus: the woman who had an issue of blood "had endured much under many physicians and had spent all that she had; and she was no better, but rather grew worse" (Mark 5:25–26)! In the parallel passage in his Gospel, Luke the physician leaves out these details that reflect poorly on his profession.

[18] Popular beliefs, which we find reflected in the book of *Enoch,* attributed storms, earthquakes, and the like to the work of evil spirits. The names given to the twenty chiefs of the evil angels in *1 En.* 6:7–8 are connected with their malevolent functions, which are detailed in *1 En.* 8.

[19] The classic case is that of the Gerasene (or Gadarene) "demoniac" described in Mark 5:2–7. The nature of his insanity can be diagnosed from the details of the story. An exegetical reading of the passage also involves a critical interpretation of the "legion" of demons that possessed him, and of the herd of swine that rushed into the Sea of Galilee after the exorcism performed by Jesus.

[20] I am not using the word "mystery" in the apostle Paul's sense, but in a more neutral, modern sense in which any preternatural or supernatural causes of evil that may exist are not taken into consideration. In other words, "mystery" refers to realities that are inaccessible to our reason.

speak of evil, we need to develop "mythical" representations that suggest the direction from which come the evils that we experience.

The "Location" of the Causes of Evil

Ancient mythologies spontaneously located the causes of good "above": they came from heaven as the "abode of God" and from the agents that God sent to bring us good things. Conversely, everything that belonged to evil was seen as "below," "underneath," in a place that is as inaccessible as the realm of good, but for the opposite reasons.[21]

To a living person, death appears to be more or less the worst evil. The ancients[22] situated death in the Mesopotamian *Arallu,* the Israelite *Sheol,* the Greek *Hades,* and the Latin *Inferi.* But what is death? Is it an accident that happens to a living person that cuts off the life that the person is leading, or is it a mysterious "power" that stalks and attacks us? This power was personified as one or more divinities within ancient paganisms; we may leave such mythology aside. We should note, however, that in certain biblical texts death is personified as a malevolent power (Ps 49:15; Isa 28:15; Jer 9:21; Hos 13:14) and is paralleled with hell (= Sheol: 2 Sam 22:6; Ps 6:5; 18:5; 49:14; 55:15; 89:48; 116:3; Prov 5:5; 7:27; Isa 28:15; 38:18; Hos 13:14; Hab 2:5). A person's death is understood as the result of an attack by this infernal power.

However, death, thus personified, is not assimilated with a divinity, as in the paganisms of the Middle East. Among the Akka-

---

[21] Hell is no more a proper matter for cosmology than heaven is for astrophysics. These are symbolic constructions arising from the psychological impressions that people have of realms that are inaccessible to them. The causes of evil are no more accessible to our reason than is the existence of the Creator, even though the experience of evil in its various forms is universal. It is a matter of suggesting a "place" for its causes by recourse to imaginative constructions.

[22] In *DBSup* there is no article on "Hell" or "Hades" or "Sheol," but simply an article "Descent into Hell," which barely touches on the depiction of this place in Eastern or Greek antiquity. One may consult the article "Enfers et Enfer," *VTB* 352–56, which mentions "basic representations" (col. 353). The article by M. Carrez, "Séjour des morts," *DEB* 1184–85, deals with *Arallu, Sheol* in First Testament, and *Hades* in the Septuagint and the New Testament.

dians[23] the "land of no return," dusty and obscure, had for its queen the goddess Ereshkigal, who was assisted by her husband, Nergal. The Egyptians' concept was more complicated. Isis, an ancient fertility goddess, became the goddess and ruler of the dead in the grain fields of the underworld. It was possible to escape from the forced labor of this place of punishment and to participate in the eternal life of the stars in Am Douat after one had passed through the judgment that all of the dead were subject to.[24] The solar cult of Horus developed in such a way that participation in the eternal life of this god, a privilege originally reserved for the pharaohs, eventually was extended to anyone who was properly mummified after death. Such persons, it was felt, could expect to share in the happiness of the "field of reeds." It was this hope, passed on from the Egyptians, that the Greeks expressed with their myth of the "Elysian Fields."

None of these beliefs, however, were accepted in Israel, and this provided an excellent defense against the various paganisms that were all around. The Israelites believed instead that the dead who descended to Sheol lived a diminished life there: they are those whom God remembers "no more" and who are "cut off from your hand" (Ps 88:5 [the whole psalm is a cry of distress for deliverance from death]).

The "Agents" of Evil

There are other evils on earth besides death. The Israelites sensed that behind them lay "evil spirits," and that they were led by someone called, in "mythical" language, "Belial"[25] (Hebrew *beliya'al,* meaning "worthless"). The number of evil spirits that were thought to exist multiplied over time, particularly in the Persian and Greek periods. Speculation about the fallen angels mentioned in

---

[23] See H. Limet, "Enfers (Religions akkadienne et sumérienne)," *DR* 1:619. The names of the divinities (Nergal, Ereshkigal) are of Sumerian origin.

[24] The section on "Religions" by P. du Bourguet in the article "Égypte (Religion)," *DR* 1:602–4, touches briefly on this theme. The judgment of the dead often is depicted as a "weighing of souls," a theme that was bequeathed to Christian art.

[25] In the Septuagint, the Jewish apocalypses, and the New Testament (2 Cor 6:15) the word is transcribed as *Beliar.*

Gen 6:1–4 contributed to this multiplication: in the book of *Enoch* (third century B.C.E.) the imagery that is developed around this theme organizes the evil spirits into phalanxes, whose leaders are named (*1 En.* 6) and whose punishments are described in detail (*1 En.* 10–11). This is where the idea of hell began in Judaism.[26] The Gospel parable of the Rich Man and Lazarus (Luke 16:19–31) gives us some concept of this idea. We can say more definitely that by the time of the Gospels it was the common belief that the righteous would be rewarded in the afterlife (we will return to this below).

These evil spirits had a leader, who was given the name of the Phoenician god Beelzebul (Matt 10:25; 12:24, 27; Mark 3:22; Luke 11:15, 18, 19), which literally means "Prince Baal," but which should be understood as "the prince of demons."[27] However, the name "Satan" (meaning "the accuser"), known since Zechariah (Zech 3:1–2; 1 Chr 21:1) and used in the book of Job (Job 1–2), had become the common name for the chief of demons by the time of the New Testament. These demons, the Hebrew *shedim* who became *daimonia* in the Greek Bible (e.g., Deut 32:17), eventually received individual names—for example, "Asmodeus" in the book of Tobit (the name appears 2 times and is a transliteration of the Old Persian *Aeshma-Daeva,*[28] the "demon of anger"), and "Legion" in Mark 5:9. However, this was on the level of popular beliefs, in keeping with

---

[26] In his visionary journeys (*1 En.* 17–22) Enoch sees the abyss, where the wandering stars and the fallen angels are locked up (*1 En.* 18:12–16), then the hell for stars and the prison for angels (*1 En.* 21), then four caverns where the spirits of the dead await the great judgment (*1 En.* 22). One of them is reserved for the righteous, who will "testify against the murders that have been committed against them" (*1 En.* 22:12); this is a sort of purgatory since, if they suffer, "they will not be punished on the day of judgment" (*1 En.* 22:13 [this phrase is attested in an Aramaic fragment]). The Epistle of Jude (14–15) quotes the text in *1 En.* 1:9 that announces the great judgment. There probably is an allusion to Jewish beliefs in 1 Pet 3:19, where it is said that Christ, after his death (and descent into hell!), went and "made a proclamation to the spirits in prison."

[27] The mythology of Ugarit knew of a *Zbl B'l,* "Prince Baal." But the pagan gods were reduced to demons by the Jews, who gave *Baal Zebul* an ironic change of name to *Baal Zebub,* "Lord of the Flies."

[28] Unfortunately, the name of Asmodeus (Tob 3:8, 17) is absent from the four Aramaic fragments and the one Hebrew fragment from Qumran, but it is definitely an allusion to Persian mythology.

which Jesus' adversaries accused him of casting out demons by "Beelzebul . . . the ruler of the demons" (Mark 3:22 and parallels). The New Testament writers equated the gods of the pagans with "demons" (1 Cor 10:20–23; cf. Rev 9:20; 16:14; 18:2).

We should not regard these abundant representations as definite dogmas; the language involved is borrowed from that of the surrounding cultures to evoke what we may call the "world of evil,"[29] of which Satan came to be seen as the ruler. This is why the Gospels present a duel between Jesus and Satan, briefly in Mark 1:13 but developed in three scenes in Matt 4:1–11 and Luke 4:1–13.[30] The duel, in which Jesus confronts the "world of evil," is fought through biblical quotations: Jesus cites Deuteronomy three times (chapters 6 and 8). In Revelation this same world of evil is deployed around the dragon and the beasts that personify its earthly supporters. Here again, the language is clearly mythical. Nevertheless, the use of conventional imagery takes nothing away from the reality of Jesus' temptations. Not during his time in the wilderness only, but throughout his entire life, he shared in this aspect of humanity's common experience:[31] the temptations of fleshly desires (Matt 4:3 [the bread]), of an attention-seeking showmanship that provokes only human admiration (Matt 4:5–6 [with a quotation from Ps 91:11–12]), and of a vainglory that would detract from the worship of the true God (Matt 4:8–9). Jesus' vocation as the "Son of God" ruled out these diabolical mirages, but it did not spare the human Jesus from constant testing: he was "in every respect . . . tested as we are, yet without sin" (Heb 4:15).

In the Judaism of the time the hidden cause of every illness was believed to be a demon or an evil spirit. This was the case for the dumb (Matt 9:32–33), the insane (Mark 5:1–9 and parallels), epileptics (Mark 9:17–22 and parallels), and those with paralysis or other

---

[29] See my study "Jésus devant le 'Monde du mal,'" in *Foi et culture à la lumière de la Bible: Actes de la session plénière 1979 de la Commission Biblique Pontificale* (Turin: Elle di Ci, 1981), 131–201. The article concludes with a "Réflexion sur le 'mystère' du Mal" (pp. 191–201).

[30] For an exegetical and theological study of the three passages that relate the temptations of Jesus see P. Grelot, "Les tentations de Jésus," *NRTh* 117 (1995): 501–16.

[31] Ibid., 503–6: "Les tentations *historiques* de Jésus."

kinds of infirmities (Luke 13:10–11). Jesus never discussed this interpretation of human sickness, which was far removed from the
understanding of Greek medicine. He contented himself with using
his power to heal the sick. But he did explain the meaning of these
healings: with the coming of the reign of God,[32] human sicknesses
were being healed in keeping with the promises of the Scriptures
(Matt 11:5 = Luke 7:22). His opponents, even though they carried
out exorcisms of their own (cf. Matt 12:27), found another explanation:[33] "It is only by Beelzebul, the ruler of the demons, that this
fellow casts out demons" (Matt 12:24). Jesus answered them deci-
sively with the parable of the kingdom divided against itself (Matt
12:25–26).

Should we conclude that Jesus "believed" in the devil and in
demons? The answer depends on how we understand the verb
"believe." The object of faith, of gospel "belief," is God and his
reign. But alongside faith there are "beliefs" whose content may
vary: they seek to give meaning to those human experiences in which
one senses the insidious presence of the "mystery of evil." The purpose of the gospel of the reign of God is not to offer a clear explanation of the "mystery of evil"; rather, its object is to make known who
God is and what God is doing to set us free from the grip of evil in
all of its forms. Evil itself is, for us, an *object of experience* and, as a
result of the experience that we have of it, an *object of beliefs* of various kinds. The essential thing is that the reign of God, by its coming
on earth, triumphs over evil and delivers us from it, at least where
we have been its prisoners and victims, and to the extent that it has
separated us from God. Jesus has given us this promise of salvation
as the object of our faith and hope.

A passage in the Gospel of Luke is significant in this regard.
Jesus has sent out seventy-two disciples (Luke 10:1–12). They were to
preach simply that "the kingdom (or 'reign') of God has come near"
(Luke 10:11b). They "return with joy," exclaiming, "Lord, in your
name even the demons submit to us!" Jesus replies, "I watched Satan
fall from heaven like a flash of lightning. See, I have given you

---

[32] See the study of Jesus' response to the messengers from John the
Baptist in P. Grelot, *Jésus de Nazareth, Christ et Seigneur: Une lecture de
l'Évangile* (2 vols.; LD 167, 170; Paris: Cerf, 1997), 1:273–77.

[33] Ibid., 286–89.

authority to tread on snakes and scorpions, and over all the power of the enemy;[34] and nothing will hurt you" (Luke 10:18–19). It is the reign of God that triumphs supremely over the power of the enemy, whose activity in the world is an object of experience. Thus it is imperative that God's victory over this power also become an object of experience. As for the details of the enemy camp, these seem to be unimportant. Jesus never gave his disciples a course in demonology; it was enough for them to see that "in his name" the "demons" were subject to those who proclaimed the good news of the reign of God. For now Satan has "fallen from heaven like lightning." There is an allusion to Isa 14:12 in the image, which is itself taken up in the book of Revelation (Rev 12:9). It is not Satan and his world that are the object of gospel faith, but rather the triumph of the reign of God over this mysterious empire of evil, by the invocation of the "name of Jesus" (Luke 10:17). Even though the "world of evil" in all of its forms can only be described through the reveries of the human imagination, God's victory over evil is a decided fact.

We should remember that the "agents" of evil can also be identified with human beings. The conflict between good and evil, between light and darkness, runs all the way through the Gospel of John. "(T)his is the judgment"—in other words, this is the principle that operates automatically to sort people into one or another of the two realms—"that the light has come into the world, and people loved darkness rather than light because their deeds were evil" (John 3:19). The narrative of this Gospel traces the development of this conflict. At the point where the last act of the drama is about to begin, the evangelist notes the disposition of Judas: he tells us that after Jesus has given Judas the piece of bread (which may represent a final attempt to keep him from slipping into evil), "Satan entered into him" (John 13:27). And when Judas leaves the room, we hear, "after receiving the piece of bread, he immediately went out. And it was night" (John 13:30). After Judas enters into the darkness, Jesus begins his last discourse, which is followed immediately by the story of his passion. Thus the passion is Jesus' final combat with the forces of evil.

---

[34] On this text see P. Grelot, "Étude critique de Luc 10, 19," *RSR* 69 (1981): 87–100, as well as the commentaries on Luke.

To describe the symbolic "place" where evil carries out its actions, John uses a word that seems banal, but one that, in many of its occurrences, has satanic overtones: the "world" (*kosmos*).[35] Or rather, we should say, the "world" presents itself in an ambiguous fashion. On the one hand, "God so loved the world that he gave his only Son" (John 3:16), and "God did not send the Son into the world to condemn the world, but in order that the world might be saved through him" (John 3:17; cf. 12:47). But when the hour of Jesus' passion comes, it is the time of "the judgment of this world" (John 12:31a), when "the ruler of this world will be driven out" (John 12:31b). Jesus returns to this essential idea in his final discourse: his death will constitute the judgment of "the ruler of this world" (John 16:11). This is why Jesus' discourse can end on a note of hope: "take courage; I have conquered the world!" (John 16:33b). Jesus is not using the term "world" in a mythical sense. However, the phrase "ruler of this world" certainly is mythical, and the ending of the discourse gives the term "world" itself a similar resonance.

Evil within the Human Person

The agents of evil that we have examined so far have all been, in a sense, exterior to the human person. But some people seem to suffer the most from the agents of evil that they contain within themselves. The study of these agents ordinarily would be limited to the confines of experiential psychology, unless we wished to speak of them in "mythical" terms. And in several passages in Paul's writings the evil forces that we sense to be at work within ourselves are *personified,* to such an extent that they can be included in the category of myth. This personification happens in the cases of Sin, the Flesh, and Death.

The development of Paul's argument in Rom 5:12–21 provides a clear example of this. From the beginning, the interior agents of the drama that plays out in the conscience are openly personified: "Therefore, just as sin came into the world through one man,[36] and

---

[35] See, briefly, the following articles in *VTB,* which I coauthored: "Jugement," "Monde," "Satan."

[36] See my study of this text in *Péché originel et rédemption, examinés à partir de l'épître aux Romains: Essai théologique* (Paris: Desclée, 1973), 115–26. The emphasis in the passage is not on the uniqueness of Adam, who is eponymous with humanity; the references to "one man" are made

death came through sin, and so death spread to all because all have sinned—" (Rom 5:12). Sin and Death are no longer just interior experiences here, as sin becomes in the final phrase ("because all have sinned"). They are actors in the history of humanity, presented in the form of a drama. Thus Paul can go on to say, "death exercised dominion from Adam to Moses, even over those whose sins were not like the transgression of Adam" (Rom 5:14). The word "sin" (*hamartia*) oscillates between two meanings, that of a psychological experience that everyone recognizes, and that of a shadowy power that reigns over humanity just as death does.

Paul introduces a third figure into the drama who, theoretically, is on God's side, but who proves incapable of overcoming Sin: the Law (Rom 5:20). Paul says earlier, "sin [in the psychological sense] was indeed in the world before the law" (Rom 5:13). "But law came in, with the result that the trespass [in the psychological sense] multiplied" (Rom 5:20). As a result, until the coming of Christ, "sin exercised dominion in death" (Rom 5:21). Thus we are "slaves to sin" (Rom 6:17; cf. 5:20) from birth, and the final outcome is "death" (Rom 6:21). Paul's thought thus oscillates between a psychological presentation of the interior conflict that every person experiences and the "mythical" background against which it plays out. This drama can never be brought to a conclusion until Christ intervenes with his liberating grace.

Another conflict is intermingled with this first one; it is entirely interior. Paul speaks of it in its psychological aspect in Rom 7:14–25, but elsewhere (Gal 5:15–18) he personifies the interior force that constitutes one of its two combatants: the "flesh," which only the "Spirit" can triumph over. The "Spirit" must be understood in the sense of the Spirit of God, who intervenes in our lives to bring about our deliverance. However, the psychological aspect of this conflict must be kept in mind: "For what the flesh desires is opposed to the Spirit, and what the Spirit desires is opposed to the flesh; for these are opposed to each other" (Gal 5:17). In other words, "I am of the flesh, sold into slavery under sin" (Rom 7:14). Paul's thought thus

---

only in comparisons that refer to Gen 3. Paul's essential point is the parallel between the entrance of sin into the world and the grace that comes through Jesus Christ alone. Here we are paying primary attention to the personification of Sin and Death in this text from Paul.

oscillates between two perspectives that give the same words different shades of meaning. The spirit is that good tendency within me that inclines toward following God's law; but behind that good tendency, which is a matter of psychology, it is also the Spirit of God that "bears witness with our spirit that we are the children of God" (Rom 8:16). The Flesh is the evil tendency that shows that we are under the control of Sin as an evil power. Here we are on the border between psychological language and "mythical" language: abstractions—or, we should say, the psychological aspects of interior experience—are being personified so that the force of the drama can be felt. This use of personified abstractions is found both in Paul's writings and in the Gospel of John: Death, Sin, the World, and the Flesh are forces at work in the service of evil.

Reversal of Death's Meaning

For every living person, death is the supreme evil. To all appearances, it deprives us of that which we hold most dear: life. But the coming of Jesus Christ to our world brings about a radical transformation in this situation. The supreme paradox in the plan of God is that the Son of God, the Lord of Life, manifest in human form in the person of Jesus, should carry the logic of his incarnation to the extreme by identifying with humanity in its experience of death. Death personified, that evil power which entered the world after Sin (Rom 5:12), seemed to overcome Jesus, the one righteous human, but was instead overcome by him. His resurrection from the dead demonstrated his victory over Death.

This experience of victory over death now belongs not just to Jesus as "Christ in glory," but also to everyone who identifies with him by faith. Paul explains this in his same letter to the Romans. Baptism, the sacramental act that marks the entrance into the Christian life, unites believers with Christ in his death so that they can also be united with him in his resurrection from the dead. "(W)e have been buried with him by baptism into death" with a very specific end in mind: "so that, just as Christ was raised from the dead by the glory of the Father, so we too might walk in newness of life" (Rom 6:4). Being plunged into the waters of baptism becomes a symbol of being plunged into death, and not just any death (such as by drowning!), but the death of Christ, by virtue of the sacramental symbolism that, understood properly, is efficacious by virtue of what it signifies. "(I)f we have died with Christ, we believe that we will also live with him" (Rom 6:8). The sacrament, which is a sacred sign, brings about that which it signifies for those who are internally disposed to receive the grace that it is bringing.

Here the symbolism is not just significant; it is operational. The efficaciousness of the symbolic sign derives from the historical reality of Jesus' death, which was the prelude to his resurrection, his decisive victory over death, not just for himself, but also for everyone who ultimately will be resurrected in him. "Then the saying that is written will be fulfilled: 'Death has been swallowed up in victory' [Isa 25:8]. 'Where, O death, is your victory? Where, O death, is your sting?' [Hos 13:14]" (1 Cor 15:54–55). The symbolic language of the Scriptures makes Death an evil power, the enemy of humanity, but the historical death of Jesus, the prelude to his resurrection in the glory of God, has tied death to Death in all of its forms.

After all, for the human person, sin is another kind of death. But, Paul explains to the Colossians, "you were dead in trespasses" (Col 2:13), but "when you were buried with him in baptism, you were also raised with him through faith in the power of God, who raised him from the dead" (Col 2:12). Thus the symbolic death of baptism brings to an end the state of death (and was it just a spiritual death?) into which they were plunged by the domination of the power of Sin. Human life is thus a drama in which opposing powers face off. Through the death and resurrection of Christ, however, it is God who has the final word.

It is thus through symbolic language, which we may describe here as "mythical," that the Christian reflection in the New Testament depicts certain essential aspects of the life of faith that are intimately connected with the most dramatic aspects of human experience. A purely objective account of these matters would be unmoving, but because this language offers a "poetic" account instead, it enables the gospel to reach not just our spirits, but our hearts as well.

THE APPROPRIATION OF EXTRABIBLICAL MYTHS

The authors of the two Testaments did not live in a vacuum, with no contact with the surrounding cultures. Those cultures constructed abundant mythologies; that was how they expressed their polytheism and set down their religious thought. Let us consider several examples of images in the Bible behind which we can sense an appropriation of mythological characters or events that have been adapted to biblical monotheism.

Texts in the First Testament

Echoes of Creation Myths

Genesis does not really begin with two creation accounts (Gen 1:1–2:3a and 2:3b–3:24).[37] These are not, strictly speaking, myths. The first passage is a hymn of liturgical character from which all mythic language has been excluded:[38] the presentation of God as Creator is determinedly demythologized. The second passage is a parable whose narrative has two phases. There is first a parable of creation, in which God plays his unique role and brings forth all of the creatures, finishing with the man and the woman. At the end comes the man's enthusiastic exclamation; "This at last is bone of my bones and flesh of my flesh; this one shall be called Woman, for out of Man this one was taken" (Gen 2:23). (The Hebrew contains a play on words, juxtaposing the masculine *'ish*, "man," with the feminine *'ishah*, "woman."[39]) We may understand the terms as referring

---

[37] I will be omitting critical suggestions that the two passages discussed here make reference to myths found in the pagan cults of the ancient East; these views may be found in the commentaries on the two biblical texts.

[38] In this biblical text there is a verb that is applied only to God: *bara'*, "create." However, its use, which is without parallel or etymology in neighboring Semitic languages, is not limited to the original "creation." A full list of its uses in the Bible is provided by F. Zorell in *Lexicon Hebraicum Veteris Testamenti* (Rome: Pontifical Biblical Institute, 1984), 126b. The Arabic word *bara'a*, borrowed from Hebrew through Aramaic, retains its biblical sense. The Akkadian *banû* indicates creation in the sense of "construction"; a cognate is found in Hebrew (*banah*).

[39] It is, in fact, a faulty play on words, since it is based on the juxtaposition of two words that actually have separate origins and etymologies. The word *'ish* begins with a long vowel, while *'ishah* begins with a short one. Etymologically, when this stands before the consonant *sh*, doubled (but left single in the English transliteration here), it indicates that the con-

to "husband" and "wife," given the conclusion of the story: "Therefore a man leaves his father and his mother and clings to his wife, and they become one flesh" (Gen 2:24).[40]

As for Gen 3, it is a parable with four characters. The continuing drama of temptation and sin is carried all the way back to our origins. We experience this drama every day, but here it is projected onto the beginnings of human history to explain its constant character. This is very far from the creation myths developed within polytheistic cults! Nevertheless, we may ask: Does the Bible ever appropriate images from those myths?

Daring Poetic Images

Why not appropriate mythological images, for example, to depict God's creative act of bringing order where chaos once had reigned? In Babylonian mythology the goddess Tiamat, a monster who personified the sea, was vanquished by Marduk, who cut her in pieces and used these pieces to make the world. The Bible takes up this mythical image in several places where it speaks of God's creative acts. But the Akkadian feminine *tiamat* is actually derived from the Hebrew masculine *tehom,* which means simply "the abyss" in Gen 1:2.

The poets, for example, describe the creation as God's victory over the monsters that personify chaos, as we can see in briefly looking at some texts from Isaiah, Job, the psalmists, and prophetic oracles.

In Isa 51:9–10 the poet addresses the "arm" of God, which is a symbol of his power. God demonstrated this power in the beginning by vanquishing the disorder of the original chaos: "Was it not you

---

sonant is replacing a *th* and that a preceding *nun* has been assimilated. Thus the original word for "woman" would have been *'inthah* (compare the Aramaic *'intah*).

[40] Jesus later would interpret this text as providing the religious basis for lifelong, monogamous marriage. However, the text actually alludes only to the union between one man and one woman that occurs in the sexual act itself, considered in its "animal" aspect. Nevertheless, the passage also makes an allusion to the fact that a man "leaves his father and his mother" to "cling" to his wife; this verb is very strong from the psychological perspective.

who cut Rahab [the "Furious One"] in pieces, who pierced the dragon [*Tannin*]? Was it not you who dried up the sea, the waters of the great deep [*tehom*]?" (Isa 51:9c–10a). Given this, why should God not deliver the people who have been deported to Babylon?[41]

The poet of the book of Job similarly describes the action of the Creator, who separated light from darkness (cf. Gen 1:4): "By his power he stilled the Sea; by his understanding he struck down Rahab. By his wind the heavens were made fair; his hand pierced the fleeing serpent" (Job 26:12–13). The mythology of Ugarit provides the background here. One of its poets says to the divinity he is praising, "You will crush Leviathan,[42] the fleeing serpent; you will smash the twisting serpent, the tyrant with seven heads." The poet in Job makes other allusions as well to this mythical image of the sea monster (Job 3:8; 7:12).

The psalmists take up this theme in the same way in order to praise God: "You divided the sea by your might; you broke the heads of the dragons in the waters. You crushed the heads of Leviathan; you gave him as food for the creatures of the wilderness" (Ps 74:13–14). Rahab and Leviathan are no more than literary reminiscences (cf. Ps 89:10): the true God has shown his omnipotence by establishing order in the world, which thereby escapes from chaos. This is just like the way the Latin poets of the Renaissance made allusions to Roman mythology, even though it was foreign to their religious faith.

The prophetic oracles can also use the image to stir up hope, by projecting the same victory of God into the future, obviously without specifying the date: "On that day the LORD with his cruel and great and strong sword will punish Leviathan the fleeing serpent, Leviathan the twisting serpent, and he will kill the dragon that is in the sea" (Isa 27:1). The allusion to the mythology of Ugarit is almost

---

[41] The reason for this allusion to the "myth" of origins, which is perfectly demythologized here, is understandable: the return from exile will be a kind of new creation of the people of God. In any event, it would be the origin of Judaism.

[42] In the text from Ugarit the monster's name is spelled *lwtn,* which usually is written as *Lôtân.* However, the *w* can retain the consonantal value that it has in the Hebrew *liweyathan,* which is written as *lwytn* in the manuscript tradition.

word for word, but it is being used only as a poetic image that explains the antecedent context: "For the LORD comes out from his place to punish the inhabitants of the earth for their iniquity; the earth will disclose the blood shed on it, and will no longer cover its slain" (Isa 26:21). Behind the mythical monster it is the "city of chaos" (*qiryath-tohu*) that is clearly in view (Isa 24:10): because it has attacked the people of God, it will be paid back in kind when God delivers them.

Thus we see from the "Message of Consolation" addressed to the exiles, as well as from the psalmists, the book of Job, and the little apocalypse included in the book of Isaiah, that the biblical poets were free to take their images from wherever they liked, even from pagan mythologies.

There are similar allusions to foreign myths in the various biblical poems that offer ironic elegies over the fall of kings such as those of Babylon (Isa 14:3–23) or Tyre (Ezek 28:12–19). In the former poem the author exclaims, "How you are fallen from heaven, O Day Star, son of Dawn!" (Isa 14:12). The metaphor that describes the pagan king here has been borrowed from a Phoenecian myth: *heylel ben-shakhar* corresponds exactly to the title "Phaeton son of Eos,"[43] found in a Greek myth derived from the Phoenicians. "Phaeton" is related to the verb *phainō,* "shine," and "Eos" is the word for "dawn." This artifice recalls that of the painter who decorated the chamber of Louis XIV at Versailles with mythological images borrowed from solar cults in order to flatter the "Sun King." This does not mean that at Versailles there was a residual community of sun worshipers.

In the same way, Ezekiel uses multiple mythological images to describe the king of Tyre as the "signet of perfection" in the elegy in which he laments his fall (Ezek 28:12b–19).[44] Some of these images are also used in the description of Eden, the "garden of God," in

---

[43] I demonstrated this in an early article, "Isaïe 14, 12–15 et son arrière-plan mythologique," *RHR* 149 (1956): 18–48.

[44] In this case, the mythological background is harder to identify, even though the multiplication of extrabiblical images leaves no doubt that it is there. The prophet has perfectly assimilated the imagery that he is using, but nevertheless it belongs solidly in the category of "mythical" symbols.

Gen 2. Ezekiel 28 is the story of a fall: the "glittering cherub" who was "on the holy mountain of God" and who walked "among the stones of fire" (= live coals) was ultimately "cast from the mountain of God" (Ezek 28:13, 16). Here we can once again presume that a Phoenician myth is being appropriated, one that spoke of the "garden of God," and *kiroubi* (cherubim) are being borrowed from Babylonian mythology.

Nevertheless, Ezekiel has skillfully incorporated these images into a lament (*qinah*) whose realistic allusions to the commerce of Tyre indicate that it is a free composition, closely tied to the oracle against the king of Tyre (Ezek 28:1–10). In both texts the reproof of a king who considers himself a god (Ezek 28:2b) and who prides himself on his wisdom (Ezek 28:3; cf. 28:17) has affinities[45] with the parabolic account of the fall of humanity (Gen 3). Thus we see in both Genesis and Ezekiel the skillful use of images drawn from elsewhere. Eden, the "garden of God" (Ezek 28:13), is a close parallel to the "planting" of Gen 3:8. But the word "Eden" comes from the Akkadian *edinu,* which is itself derived from the Sumerian *edin,* "a fertile irrigated field."[46] Therefore this probably is the original source of the mythical imagery here. The same image is used in Isa 51:3, where it is found in a promise, but the primitive myth is now quite distant, and the allusion to its theme is just a metaphorical expression.

Mythical Images of God in Poetry

Poetic language is symbolic by its very nature. Religious literature in the Hebrew language was born in a milieu in which this form of expression had been known for a long time. Even if Phoenician mythology and its associated cults are known only secondhand, the discoveries of Ugarit have uncovered mythological texts and poetic works belonging to a religious literature that is several centuries older than the "classic" biblical texts. From these discoveries we have learned of the myths that were associated with Baal, the "lord"

---

[45] "(W)hen you eat of it your eyes will be opened, and you will be like God, knowing good and evil" (Gen 3:5). The "knowledge of good and evil" is one of the fruits of wisdom, as the woman of Tekoa asserts in her speech to David (2 Sam 14:17).

[46] See F. Zorell, *Lexicon hebraicum Veteris Testamenti,* 575a. Zorell draws on a previous study by Deimel.

(*ba'al*) of storms and of fecundity. We thus can appreciate what a battle the prophets of Israel had to fight against the Canaanite Baal, to whom the Israelite peasantry would have been spontaneously attracted. In order to glorify YHWH, the true God, creator of all of nature and master of cosmic forces, the poets of Israel brazenly appropriated the imagery that originally was used for Baal.

Psalm 29, a storm psalm in which thunder plays the role of the "voice of God" (Ps 29:3–8), probably is derived from an ancient Canaanite hymn in honor of Baal, but its opening (Ps 29:1–2) and its conclusion (Ps 29:9c–11) celebrate the grandeur of YHWH, the eternal king. The same imagery is found in other psalms, as if it were a well-known literary cliché (Ps 18:14–16; 77:18–19; cf. 104:7). In other places we see that the poets of Israel had mastered their art to such an extent that they were able to transform completely this appeal to images from nature. Thus Ps 104 musters all of creation to sing the greatness of its Creator, even if it has to transpose certain exceptional phenomena to show what happens when God "hides [your] face" and then "send[s] forth [your] spirit" (Ps 104:29–30). Poetic language has the freedom to do this kind of thing! Thus Ps 107 sketches out four scenarios to show how God rescues people who are in peril (Ps 107:4–30), and Song of Solomon pulls together a group of love songs in which YHWH is only named in one conventional expression (Song 8:6). It required a great deal of ingenuity for Jewish interpreters, and then Christian ones, to make these songs an allegory of the love between God and his people. But we are getting away from our consideration of the mythical aspect of language.

The Construction of Original Myths

If we consider "mythical" any story or any imaginative construction that is not inspired by actual experience, but which instead uses the imagination to create images or even entire scenes, why should we deny the biblical authors the possibility of using their imaginations in this way to convey their message, particularly when they were speaking of the future, which is necessarily removed from our experience? We will consider two specific cases: the imagery used for the resurrection, and the depiction of the "world to come" as a new creation.

The Resurrection. We will not be examining here the technical vocabulary used to indicate the resurrection of the dead: "wake up" (*'ur*), "arise" (*qum*). We are concerned instead with how scenes are constructed in which this "awakening" or "arising" is depicted in detail. The artist already has to know what death is, but the depiction is of what comes after death. The great promise proclaimed in Ezek 37:1–14 provides a model of this, in the form of a parable. The death of the "house of Israel" clearly is understood metaphorically: it is the disappearance of the nation after the destruction of Jerusalem and the exile of the Judeans. Thus the "arising" and the return to "life" promised by the prophet also are to be understood symbolically, even though the scene is of the resurrection of the dead.[47] All the details are there: the bones that come together, the flesh and nerves that grow back on top of them, the skin that covers everything. The conclusion is, "I [will] open your graves, and bring you up from your graves, O my people!" (Ezek 37:13). But the realism of the scene is only conventional, since it is a metaphor for the future restoration.

These images are taken up in an abbreviated way in the promise of the resurrection from the dead that is found in one of the passages of the apocalypse of Isaiah. In Isa 26:14 there is a scene of death, understood metaphorically, to which Isa 26:19 is the response. It is a scene of resurrection, set in the future with a fictitious realism: "Your dead shall live, their corpses shall rise. O dwellers in the dust, awake and sing for joy! For your dew is a radiant dew, and the earth will give birth to those long dead" (Isa 26:19). The scene is not based on any experience; it imitates the imagery of Ezekiel but enlivens it with the image of the "birth of the shades [*refa'im*]." Therefore we may recognize this as an example of the construction of "mythical" imagery, in the sense in which we have defined that term. The same mythical imagery, which is a distinctively biblical construction without any analogues elsewhere, is used to describe the righteous in Dan 12, which depicts the "awakening" of those who are called to eternal life (Dan 12:1–2). Thus this imagery is an original creation of the Bible.

The New Creation. A second example is provided by passages where promises about the future, which are indeterminate as to time

---

[47] The promise that Judah will be "raised from the dead" can be interpreted literally, in a way that can be described as "mythical," since all of the elements in this extended metaphor cannot be allegorized: it is a story whose apparent content suggests another kind of realism.

but nevertheless definite because they describe what God intends to do, are expressed in terms of "creation" (the verb *bara'*). These include Isa 4:5–6; 41:18–20, which present a scene of nature transformed; Isa 45:8, which speaks of salvation; and Isa 65:17–18, whose depicts the creation of a new heavens and a new earth, as well as creation of "Jerusalem as a joy." These depictions, which are "mythical" in the sense that we are using the term here, enable the reality of these promises to take shape literarily. Eschatological oracles generally make use of a style in which "mythical" symbols abound, unless the authors are actually projecting an idealized memory of the people's past experiences ahead to "the last days." In that case, they are making use of "figurative" symbols, which is a third category that we will take up later.[48]

Texts in the New Testament

There is less to say about the appropriation of extrabiblical myths when we come to the New Testament, since in its language it typically makes allusion to texts in the First Testament. However, the "symbolism of evil" does have a prominent place in its pages, from the sayings of Jesus, in which we hear of "evil spirits" and of Satan, to the text of the apostle Paul that mentions Beliar (2 Cor 6:15 [the Greek *Beliar* is the equivalent of the Hebrew *Belial*]). But it is particularly in Revelation that this symbolism abounds. The imagination of its author, who is heir not only to Ezekiel and Daniel, but also to the apocalyptic tradition that developed within intertestamental Judaism, literally crams mythical images into his text. He stops using them only when he is employing "figurative" symbols instead. The Epistle of Jude shows a familiarity with the imagery of the book of *Enoch* regarding fallen angels (Jude 6), and also with a curious discussion between the devil and the angel Michael concerning the body of Moses (Jude 9).

We should also note the mythical images in the New Testament of "the end," the day and hour of whose coming the Son of Man himself does not know (Mark 13:32). The scene of wars (Mark 13:7–8a), earthquakes and famines (Mark 13:8b), the "abomination of desolation"

---

[48] See in ch. 4 " 'Figures' in the History of Israel" (pp. 112–16).

spoken of in the book of Daniel (Mark 13:14), and the eclipse that follows the stars falling from heaven (Mark 13:24–25) is woven from images that have many scriptural antecedents, but in their combination here they take on a mythical aspect. The parallel passages in Matthew and Luke do not give these conventional expressions any greater precision. In Revelation we find sometimes decipherable historical allusions mixed together with conventional images (which often are taken from the First Testament but given a new significance), and both are then combined with "figurative" allusions that are not, properly speaking, "mythical." Nor is the use of numerical symbolism[49] mythical; rather, it is a cultural convention of the time in which the author lived. In any event, the announcement of "the end" creates an atmosphere that is itself mythical. The attempt to decipher these accumulated symbols poses numerous problems, particularly when they have no scriptural antecedents.

Among the mythical symbols in the book of Revelation we must note the dragon of Rev 12:3–4, who is said to be "that ancient serpent, who is called the Devil and Satan," who is defeated from the beginning by Michael and his angels (Rev 12:7–9). It also includes his minions, the monstrous beasts who arise from the sea and the land (Rev 13:1–8). There is also the "great whore," who is "Babylon the great" (Rev 17:1–8). The dragon of Rev 12 is identified by the author himself. But his minions, the beasts, are images that represent the Roman Empire (symbolized by Babylon) and of the paganism that was tied to it. Thus the manifestation of evil powers within earthly realities is given a symbolic face that the wise reader is to

---

[49] This convention was common to a number of ancient civilizations. In the Gospel of John the number of 153 large fish (John 21:11) is the triangular number based on 17, but its significance is unclear. In Revelation the number of the 144,000 elect—12,000 multiplied by 12 (Rev 7:4)—represents a perfect totality: 12, the perfect number of the tribes of Israel and of the months of the year, multiplied by 1,000. Later in the book the number of the beast, 666, represents, on the one hand, the repetition of the bad-luck number 6, and on the other hand, the triangular number 36, which itself equals 6 times 6. Moreover, by gematria, 666 corresponds to the transcription of the name of the persecuting emperor, Nero Caesar, into Hebrew letters: QSR NRN, *Qesar Nerōn*. But these plays on numbers are not, strictly speaking, symbols; they are nothing more than riddles, undecipherable to those who do not have the key.

decipher: we are in the time of the persecutions that the Roman Empire unleashed against Christians.

But what about the theme of the "resurrection," which will take place when Christ inaugurates the "world to come" and gives it a concrete content that necessarily escapes our present sensory experience? We can only take the symbolic language as the texts present it and seek to make sense of it the best we can.

THE COSMIC FRAMEWORK OF HUMAN EXISTENCE

Can the physical world in which we live provide symbols eloquent enough to be integrated into the revelation of God and of his plan? Even as we discussed texts that borrowed elements from various Eastern mythologies or that contained scenes that were original creations of the biblical authors, we were already considering images that the cosmic framework of human existence underlay. But we can go farther than this, and note appeals to symbols drawn specifically from the cosmic framework within which human existence unfolds. Two kinds of images come to mind immediately in this regard. The first are images that depict the great day of judgment that will bring human history to a close. The others, by no means less significant, have to do with the reality of God himself.

The Outlines of the Day of Judgment

Just as the beginnings of cosmic history can only be depicted mythically, since a realistic description of them is impossible, so the end of cosmic history can only be envisioned by the imagination, as we carry some aspects of our present experience in the world to an extreme. The scenes of the end that the biblical authors present are necessarily tied to their conception of sacred history, which God sovereignly oversees. Thus they envision this world ending in a way reminiscent of its beginning, in keeping with the general principle that guides the plan of God.

In the biblical portrayal the end of the world has two different aspects, corresponding to how people have lived: depending on whether they have done good or evil, God will either shower his blessings upon them or bring them under his judgment. Thus the "last day," the "Day of YHWH," can be depicted in two opposite ways.

The Day of Judgment

The first depiction, which is the more frightening because it portrays the judgments by which God will punish a sinful world, relies on the symbolic accumulation of cosmic catastrophes: this is the most common portrayal of the "Day of YHWH,"[50] a day that will be "darkness, and not light" (Amos 5:18). All the prophets describe this day in order to bring about the conversion of their unfaithful contemporaries. Let us consider some examples. In the book of Joel a great plague of locusts has come upon the country like an invading army (Joel 2:2–9). As these locusts rush against the guilty city, "(t)he earth quakes before them, the heavens tremble, the sun and the moon are darkened, and the stars withdraw their shining" (Joel 2:10). These images will reappear in the book of Revelation (Rev 9:3–11) as signs of the final judgment. But even before that they will show up in abbreviated form in the apocalypse that is preserved in the Synoptic Gospels (Mark 13:24–25; Matt 24:29; Luke 21:25). In Matthew's depiction of the death of Jesus the same cosmic signs show that the judgment of God has already been pronounced against the enemies of his plan (Matt 27:51–52). In another passage, Joel depicts a judgment with a similarly cosmic framework: he describes a final harvest and vintage in the Valley of the Judgment of God (Joel 3:12–13). Revelation makes use of the same images (Rev 14:14–20). Among the texts that depict the "Day of YHWH" along similar lines, we may mention the one in Zephaniah, which piles on frightening details as it describes that day (Zeph 1:14–18). Parallel texts may be found throughout the prophetic corpus.

The Day of Salvation

This day of wrath and terror has a beneficent counterpart. God does not forget his promises; he punishes sinners, but he saves the righteous. Thus all of the forces of nature are also associated with the final fulfillment of God's plan to bless those who are righteous and

---

[50] *DBSup* has no article on the "Day of Yahweh" (or the "Day of the Lord"); rather, it refers readers to its article "Judgment of God." One may consult the article "Jour de Yahvé" in *DEB* 688–90, and the article "Jour du Seigneur" in *VTB* 618–23, which covers both Testaments and presents both aspects of the "Day" in the New Testament.

faithful. In Joel's own prophecy the locust plague gives way to a vision of agricultural abundance (Joel 2:21–26); the land where God's people live will come to know an Edenic prosperity (Joel 3:18). The book of Amos ends with a similar depiction of fantastic agricultural prosperity (Amos 9:13–15). We can find the same thing in the second part of the book of Isaiah, where the author describes the "new heavens and the new earth" (Isa 66:17–22). He is making an allusion to the portrayal of a restored paradise in an oracle from the prophet Isaiah himself, which has been placed right after a description of the future ideal king (Isa 11:6–9). A "new heaven and a new earth" reappear at the end of Revelation (Rev 21:1), but they immediately give way there to a symbolic depiction of the New Jerusalem (Rev 21:2–22:15).

From the Wind to the Spirit of God

In the First Testament

A single word (Hebrew *ruakh* [fem.], Greek *pneuma* [neut.]) designates several different realities, among which we can distinguish a natural phenomenon, the "wind"; a psychological characteristic of human beings, their "spirit" (referring to an interior disposition rather than to the intellectual faculty); and a divine power that manifests itself in various ways.[51] So in which sense should we understand Gen 1:2, where it says that "a wind from God swept over the face of the waters" or "the Spirit of God brooded over the waters"? This simple example shows the difficulties attached to

---

[51] In DBSup the article "Saint Esprit" ("Holy Spirit") has several coauthors for the First Testament and Qumran (H. Cazelles, R. Kuntzmann, M. Gilbert, E. Cothenet, J.-É. Ménard). A. Vanhoye offers an excellent presentation on the New Testament (cols. 172–334). There are briefer articles on "Esprit" and "Esprit de Dieu" by P. van Imschoot and J. Goldmann in *DEB* 433–39. The two articles "Esprit" and "Esprit de Dieu" in *VTB* 388–401 are written by J. Guillet. For a more technical presentation see S. Tengström and H. J. Fabry, "רוּחַ *Rûaḥ*," *TDOT* 13:365–402 (with an extensive bibliography), and J. Kremer, "πνεῦμα *pneuma*," *EDNT* 3:117–22, which has a bibliography that is very complete up to 1982, and which refers the reader to F. Baumgärtel, "πνεῦμα," *TDNT* 6:359–67 for even more details.

the word *ruakh* in the First Testament, which is translated by the Greek *pneuma.*

Nevertheless, there are places where this "breath" of God has the well-attested meaning of "wind" (e.g., 1 Kgs 19:11; Ezek 13:13; 27:26). In the same way, *ruakh* is also used unambiguously to mean an interior human disposition: the spirit of justice (Isa 28:6), of uncleanness (Zech 13:2), of distrust (Judg 9:23), and so on. In the New Testament the apostle Paul speaks of the body, soul, and spirit (1 Thess 5:23) that make up a human being. But is it by analogy to this characteristic of people, or rather to the natural force, that the First Testament speaks of the "Spirit" of God? The Spirit appears first as the "power" of God: in this capacity the Spirit takes hold of people to enable them to do extraordinary things: the judges (e.g., Judg 11:29), the kings (e.g., 1 Sam 11:6), and ultimately the messianic ruler (Isa 11:2). In the same way, the Spirit takes hold of the prophets and makes them bearers of the word of God (e.g., Num 11:25–26, Ezek 3:14). It is the Spirit who consecrates the "Servant of YHWH" (Isa 42:1). One of the most important promises of the prophets was that the Spirit would be poured out upon the people as a whole (Ezek 36:26; 39:29). When the Spirit came into an individual heart, that assured its complete fidelity (Ps 51:10, 17). These references move us from the natural force of the wind that renews "the face of the ground" (Ps 104:30) to a divine reality that transforms people from within.

In the New Testament

The New Testament picks up from the First Testament at this point as it speaks of the Spirit of God. Jesus was conceived by the power of the Spirit (Matt 1:20; Luke 1:35). The vision that Jesus received at the time of his baptism was of the Spirit (Mark 1:10 and parallels); thus John the Baptist could say of him that he would "baptize with the Holy Spirit" (Matt 3:11). It was in the Spirit that Jesus faced Satan (Matt 4:1) and "brought good news to the poor," in the words of Isa 61:1–2, which he applied to himself (Luke 4:18–21). The Spirit is mentioned on numerous occasions through-out his ministry, particularly in the Gospel of John, which records his promise that those who believed in him would be given the gift of the Spirit (John 7:39; 14:17; 15:26; 16:13).

From the way this promise is made, it becomes clear that the Spirit is not simply a force that comes from God, since the Spirit is described as a person (although not said specifically to be a person in the text). The multiple uses of the word in the book of Acts and in Paul's letters to designate God's sanctifying activity within the lives of those who receive the Spirit (e.g., Rom 8:9–16) show that the Greek word, even with its Hebrew background, has lost its meaning as a reference to a natural force and is now descriptive of one of the most intimate mysteries of God. The Spirit is not simply a "force," as in the First Testament, but a "person" just like the Son, a person whom the Father will send in the Son's name and at his request (John 14:26). The sending of the Spirit accounts for the events of Pentecost, when the church was launched into history (Acts 2:1–20). Paul specifies the results of this sending: the Spirit will now sanctify believers and grant them the status of adopted sons and daughters, by which they will address God the way children address their fathers (Rom 8:15–17). We see how this word, which originally designated a natural force, came, through its symbolic use, to indicate a divine reality. This reality was already secretly active in the world, but now its presence has been unveiled.

4

Figurative
Symbols

The biblical texts include a third type of symbol, which is found nowhere else. This point requires a special explanation because it is not generally recognized by historians of religion,[1] who, although they do discuss symbols in general, typically give insufficient attention to this particular variety. Figurative symbols depend essentially on the close relationship, which is exclusively biblical, between the revelation that has been put into writing in the scriptural texts and the historical experience of the community within which these texts were written. First I will explain this relationship, and then I will examine the use that is made of it in the Hebrew and Greek versions of the First Testament, and then its use in the texts of the New Testament. We will see that the person of Jesus provides an essential framework within which the biblical authors describe the passage from one "covenant" to another.

REVELATION AND HISTORY IN THE BIBLE

There are many different ways to describe the course of history as it is being related. First we must establish in what sense we are

---

[1]Nevertheless, the integration of history into religious symbolism is noted by M. Eliade, *Le mythe de l'éternel retour: Archétypes et répétition* (Paris: Gallimard, 1949), 152–66, and it is also developed in the works of P. Ricoeur.

using the word "history": history *lived* or history *related?*[2] All of them are shaped by culture. The records of Sargon's campaigns are historical documents written from the political and religious perspective of seventh-century B.C.E. Assyria. The story of the Peloponnesian War, composed by Thucydides, is an example of a different kind of narrative art, whose standards of precision are not the same as those of today's historians. Titus-Livy wrote his history of Rome beginning with the founding of that city, but in order to do so he needed to incorporate traditional legends about Romulus and other early kings. Without these legends, his history would have been judged incomplete, since his contemporaries were raised on them. And who would claim that all of the information that Herodotus collected on his voyages is as accurate as we would expect it to be today? History is a narrative art; it carries readers back to a more-or-less distant past, but since this past can be described in a thousand different ways, the narrator can be seeing and speaking truth even if the details of the story do not meet the standards of exactitude to which we hold professional historians today.[3] Moreover, the historian is not content simply to relate bare facts, but rather seeks to understand what has happened in a certain place, to a certain people or to a certain person, in the period of time under consideration. Thus, in telling the story, the historian necessarily also interprets.

An Interpreted History

History in the Bible, whether it is directly in view, as in the narrative books, or whether it is contained in books with a different aim, such as those of the prophets, is always seen from the perspective of its religious significance, through faith in the God uniquely revealed to Israel. The fabric of this history is composed, on its surface, of the events that take place, the people who experience them

---

[2] I discuss this relationship in *La Bible, parole de Dieu: Introduction théologique à l'étude de l'Écriture sainte* (Bibliothèque de théologie 1, Théologie dogmatique 5; Paris: Desclée, 1965), 238–50.

[3] I made this point in *Évangiles et histoire* (Introduction à la Bible 3, Le Nouveau Testament 6; Paris: Desclée, 1985), 101–16: "L'histoire: Évocation et interprétation." What is true of the history in the Gospels is equally true for the history in the First Testament.

or make them happen, and the varying fortunes of the nation. However, all of these things are depicted from a particular angle, because the story is truly woven together from the unfolding of God's plan, which is what really underlies the events, characters, and successes and failures of the tiny nation that is looking back at its past. It follows from this that not everything recorded in the Bible will have equal value for us as "history" in the modern sense. As the biblical narrators undertook to relate the origins of their nation, even though they lived within a literary culture, the only sources available to them had come down through the oral tradition. Moreover, their goal was not to satisfy the curiosity of their contemporaries, but rather to train them in the faith by composing—please excuse the modern terminology—a "catechism" in the form of narratives. As they did this, they would at times include things such as legal codes, practical wisdom teachings, conversations about how God works in the world, and details of the arrangements for the worship of this God, who had been uniquely revealed through the patriarchs and the prophets, through whom the history of Israel was to be traced.

This is what distinguishes the religion of Israel from that of its neighbors. In the period for which we have the best understanding of this religion from its texts, it does not appear to be something that has flowed on undisturbed from time immemorial. The religion of Egypt was a successful synthesis of the various cults that had developed in the different great sanctuaries of that country (not counting the revolutionary monolatry that Amenophis IV Akhenaton[4] attempted to introduce, which lasted only a short time). In Israel, by contrast, the religion that the prophets of the nation's God sought to maintain at all costs, advancing and deepening it by their very struggles, always strikes readers of the Bible as a militant

---

[4] The name "Amenophis" is a Greek transcription of "Amenhotep." An excellent study of the religious revolution that he attempted, a study that includes primary texts both in hieroglyphics and in transcription, is P. Grandet, *Hymnes de la religion d'Aton: Hymnes du XIVe siècle avant J.-C.* (Sagesses 97; Paris: Seuil, 1995). This was not a "monotheism" in the biblical sense, but rather a "monolatry" centered on the worship of one natural element, the solar disk. It would be absurd to see this religion as the precursor of Mosaic religion and Israelite monotheism, in which the sun and the other stars are simply created objects; the sun is a lamp to give light on the earth during the day (Gen 1:14–17).

religion.[5] This religion had to be maintained and finally imposed
against the continual revival of the ancient fertility cults of the land
in which the "people of God" had settled, the land of Canaan. In
every century of the nation's history the battle against these cults is
patently the driving force of the historical experience. There are ups
and downs; there are times when religious compromise takes hold,
and other times of sharp conflict between leaders who are loyal to
the true God and the common people or their representatives who
keep falling back into the rut of a paganism that must unfortunately
be called traditional. If we recognize it as the continuation, among
agricultural and pastoral populations, of an ancient pagan tradition
that was tied to the soil, we will acknowledge it as the religion that
was always practiced by the "people of the land." But this puts us precisely in a position to see that the essential aspect of Israel's history as
the "people of God" is the maintenance and progressive development
of a new religion, whose traditions record its own origins.

   The tradition about the "Hebrew patriarchs" is not historical in
the modern sense of the word; rather, it preserves the memory of distant ancestors under names that are organized genealogically: Abraham, Isaac, and Jacob. There is no need here to establish exactly how
the Israelites were related to these ancestors; this is a very complicated question whose answer depends on the individual histories of
the tribes into which the people of Israel were finally divided.[6] The
essential thing, from the religious perspective, is the reference to the
God of the patriarchs, who is not to be defined by metaphysical
speculations, but rather worshiped loyally as the "God of our
fathers."[7] It is highly significant that the Genesis traditions fre-

---

[5] I will not offer here a detailed bibliography on history and religion
in the First Testament. The essentials may be found in H. Cazelles, ed.,
Introduction critique à l'Ancien Testament (rev. ed.; Introduction à la Bible
2; Paris: Desclée, 1973).

[6] In recent years the question of the formation of the Pentateuch has
once again been the subject of much discussion. See P. Haudebert, ed., *Le
Pentateuque: Débats et recherches* (LD 151; Paris: Cerf, 1992). There is much
useful information in H. Cazelles, *Études d'histoire religieuse et de philologie
biblique* (SB; Paris: Gabalda, 1996); see especially pp. 195–217, "Peut-on
conscrire un événement 'Exode'?"

[7] See H. Cazelles, "Patriarches," *DBSup* 7:81–155; for the "religion of
the patriarchs," see cols. 141–55.

quently employ, in texts that present the "words of God," the expression "I am the God of your father" or "the God of your fathers," citing the names of Abraham, Isaac, and Jacob. The expression recurs in Exodus and Deuteronomy. It figures prominently in the text in which God reveals his liturgical name: "I am the God of your father, the God of Abraham, the God of Isaac, and the God of Jacob" (Exod 3:6). Moses is instructed to say to the Israelites, "The God of your ancestors has sent me to you" (Exod 3:13). This is where the liturgical name of God is introduced in the text, in the (developed) form of the tetragram "YHWH."[8]

The stories of the patriarchs have a very clear religious goal: to establish and illustrate by example the faith to which the Israelites must hold. By introducing their hearers to the traditional shrines and by acquainting them with the rites that have been practiced since the time of the patriarchs, these stories instill in them a loyalty to the worship of the "God of the ancestors." In the process, they also inculcate a practical monotheism that begins with a glimpse of the religious experience that the believer can have in relationship with this God. This is the starting point for the biblical revelation, and it was the shared inheritance of the tribes that continued the line of the patriarchs in the land in which they had lived. One group of tribes, probably the "house of Joseph" and perhaps also Benjamin, migrated at one point into Egyptian-controlled territory and returned to the land of the ancestors only after a difficult exodus and a time of wandering in the desert south of Canaan. The leader of this exodus had an Egyptian name, "Moses."[9] He gave Israel two fundamental components of its national and religious tradition: the law, which naturally developed over the centuries, and the covenant with God. This covenant made the Israelites the "people of YHWH," a

---

[8] See in ch. 1 "The Name of God" (pp. 12–15); also Cazelles, *Études d'histoire religieuse et de philologie biblique*, 36–47.

[9] On Moses see Cazelles, *Introduction critique à l'Ancien Testament*, 37ff.; idem, *À la recherche de Moïse* (Études annexes de la Bible de Jérusalem; Paris: Cerf, 1979). For an article written from a critical point of view see "Moïse," *DBSup* 5:1308–37. The name "Moses" is found in several Egyptian compounds, including "Thutmose" ("son of the god Thot") and "Ramses" ("son of the god Ra"). The Hebrew *Mosheh* retains only the Egyptian suffix *–mw*, "son of."

people who had YHWH for their own God and who were aware
that he had chosen them from among all the nations of the world.

These people already had the promises of God, and now they
belonged to the covenant as well. The promises were an inheritance
from the patriarchs and included the blessings of posterity and the
possession of the land of Canaan. The texts that describe these
promises being made were naturally written after the fact; clearly
they have been shaped by the intervening history. In the same way,
the texts that describe the "exodus from Egypt"[10] and the migration
through the desert of Sinai are "retellings" that describe the past in
their own way; they tell the story of these wanderings from the perspective of the time when the people had already settled in the
"promised land." The important thing is for the people to discover a
meaning in this history, as an expression of God's plan for them.
The history of Israel is thus finalized, and these foundational epi-
sodes take on a meaning within the religious memory. The group
that had come from Egypt became the unifying core of all the
groups that had settled in the land of Canaan, and they acquired a
stable national self-consciousness: they were the "people of the covenant." The nation reached its greatest heights with the institution of
the monarchy, the advent of David and his dynasty, the conquest of
Jerusalem and the establishment of the capital there, and the construction of the temple as the religious center. But toward what end
was all of this history leading?

The Changing Fortunes of the People

Since the Israelites understood themselves as the "people of
God" and believed that the events of their national life had meaning

---

[10] These texts are a compilation in which three different sources can be
identified: the Yahwist and Elohist (northern Israelite) traditions, and the
Priestly history that was written during the Babylonian exile. The separate
contributions of these three sources are discernable in, for example, the
account of the Red Sea crossing (Exod 14:1–31). I illustrated this some time
ago in a collection written for secondary school students, *Pages bibliques* (2d
ed.; Paris: Belin, 1965), 42–44 (Yahwist tradition), and 180ff. (Priestly history). The song of deliverance in Exod 15:1–16 is a liturgical composition that
carries the story right up to the establishment of the temple in Jerusalem.

for their faith, they naturally saw their political and cultural ascendancy as the realization of a providential design. To be sure, the surrounding peoples also attributed their successes to their national divinities,[11] but in Israel the situation was different: within the framework of the covenant, national successes and fulfillments of the divine promises were subject to conditions specified by the law. The law, understood as God's most basic expectations of the people, consisted of religious and social requirements summarized in the Decalogue.[12] Unfortunately, after the golden age of Israel during the reign of Solomon (972–932 B.C.E.), these requirements were not met. In the religious sphere, the worship of "strange gods" (primarily the Canaanite fertility god Baal) continued to flourish, rivaling the worship of the nation's God in the temple that Solomon had built in Jerusalem and in the traditional sanctuaries that were scattered throughout the country. In the social sphere, the royal administration's exactions put an increasingly heavy burden on the common people.[13]

The result was the nation's first crisis. The Israelite tribes in the northern part of the country, gathered around the group that preserved the tradition of the exodus (Ephraim and Manasseh, plus Benjamin), separated from the southern tribe of Judah, within whose territory the royal capital of Jerusalem was located.[14] This political schism had religious consequences: the northern kingdom established rival royal sanctuaries at the sites of two ancient shrines,

---

[11] In Babylon, for example, it was believed that it was Marduk who had subjugated the other gods. See the prayer to Marduk in A. Barucq et al., *Prières de l'ancien Orient* (CaESup 27; Paris: Cerf, 1979), 16–17; also the "Prayer of Nebuchadnezzar to Shamash," in which the king insists that his reign has been righteous and asks for protection for his armies (p. 37); the prayer of Nabonidus to Sin, whom the king has chosen to worship even at the risk of alienating the priests of Babylon (p. 38).

[12] See H. Cazelles, "Dix paroles: Les origines du Décalogue," in *Autour de l'exode: Études* (SB; Paris: Gabalda, 1987), 113–23.

[13] See J. Briend, "Solomon. I. Dans les livres des Rois," *DBSup* 11:431–50 (especially col. 449 on the social crisis).

[14] Jerusalem and the surrounding territory were conquered by David and remained in the possession of his family; they did not belong to any of the tribes (2 Sam 5:6–10). Their inhabitants enjoyed special privileges, including exemption from certain taxes.

Dan and Bethel.[15] There YHWH was represented by means of a forbidden image: the "golden calf," symbol of the Canaanite fertility
god. Thus there was a political schism and a religious schism, and
what the faith of Israel regarded as the plan of God seemed to have
suffered a first defeat.

This defeat issued in the slow decline of the two kingdoms[16]
that emerged from the modest empire of David and Solomon. Each
kingdom experienced high and low points in its national life, and
although the two sometimes were allied, often there were periods of
tension between them. It was a time of steady religious decline in
Israel, during which the Canaanite cult of the fertility god Baal
returned in force, but it was also the time when the prophets conducted a vigorous campaign against social and religious decadence:
Elijah and Elisha in the ninth century B.C.E. in Israel, and then, in
the seventh century B.C.E., Amos and Hosea in Israel and Micah and
Isaiah in Judah and Jerusalem. The northern kingdom ultimately
experienced a catastrophe: Samaria fell in 722–21 B.C.E., the country's
elites were deported to Assyria, the people from five Mesopotamian
cities were brought in to replace them, and the country was annexed
to the Assyrian Empire.

The tiny kingdom of Judah survived. Its religious decadence
reached its lowest point during the reign of Manasseh, in the seventh
century B.C.E., with the recrudescence of the Canaanite cult of Baal
and his consort Astarte. During the reign of Josiah (640–609 B.C.E.)
there was a radical reform based on the Deuteronomic legislation
(622 B.C.E.). But Judah was also caught in the wash of international
politics, where Babylon had replaced Assyria. In 609 B.C.E. Josiah
was killed in combat against the Egyptians, and his successors were

---

[15] See 1 Kgs 12:26–33. The bull was the sacred animal of the Canaanite
cult of Baal; the Decalogue had forbidden the making of such images
(Exod 20:4, commented on by Deut 4:15–20). The first of the northern
kings, Jereboam, thereby opened the door to the idolatry that proliferated
in his kingdom.

[16] It is not useful for our present purposes to survey the history of the
two kingdoms in detail. A broad outline suffices to explain the decadence
that led to the annexation of Israel by Assyria in 722 B.C.E. and of Judah by
Babylon in 587 B.C.E. It was during the two-kingdom period that the great
prophets brought their message.

never able to recover either politically or religiously, despite the intervention of several prophets: Zephaniah, Habakkuk, and especially Jeremiah. Jeremiah was originally from one of the sanctuaries in the north—he belonged to the school of priests in Anathoth, in the territory of Benjamin—but he came to Jerusalem to preach the word of God, which put him on bad terms with both the temple priests and the civil authorities. His long career began during the reform under Josiah (626 B.C.E.) and continued until sometime after 587 B.C.E. As he cried out against the social and religious abuses of his day, he alienated all of his hearers, since he proclaimed that Jerusalem and the temple would be destroyed.

This happened as Jeremiah predicted, but in stages. Babylon finally defeated Assyria and took over its empire in 609 B.C.E., and then it began a westward advance. It first besieged Jerusalem in 597 B.C.E. and deposed the king; Jehoiachin (or Jechoniah) was deported and replaced by his uncle Zedekiah, a son of Josiah, who became a vassal of Babylon. But Judah could not stay out of political intrigues, and it joined a coalition of small kingdoms that Egypt instigated. In response, Nebuchadnezzar mounted a second campaign against Jerusalem. This time the city was captured and destroyed, the temple was burned to the ground, and a second group of Judeans was carried off into exile to join those whom the Babylonian king had deported after the first siege. Ezekiel, a Jerusalem priest who had been among those in the first group, carried out a prophetic ministry among the exiles. Like Jeremiah, he had predicted that the city would be destroyed if his compatriots did not genuinely repent. In Jerusalem, the Judeans who were left behind hatched yet another conspiracy against Babylon, and they finally had to flee to Egypt for safety. They took the prophet Jeremiah with them.

This should rightfully have been the end of the nation's hopes, but as these hopes had taken shape, starting with the patriarchs and Moses and continuing in the time of the conquest and of the nation's greatest heights under King David's, they had always been founded on promises that the faith of the most devoted Israelites recognized to be the word of God himself. And so these hopes persisted, despite everything. To understand how, we must return to the preaching of the prophets, who taught that the nation's fortunes were an outworking of the principles of the covenant that God had made with the people. Their success and prosperity were granted freely by God, but to maintain them, they needed to remain faithful to God's religious requirements and to his law. Otherwise, they could only expect to experience the judgment of God. The misfortunes that they had suffered at the hands of Assyria and Babylon were tangible expressions of this. There was now only one thing for the people of YHWH to do: repent, in order to see the plan of God resume its course. But if they did, how was their future then to be envisioned?

THE FIGURATIVE VALUE OF THE PAST

From this perspective, let us once again consider the prophetic texts that, from the eighth to the sixth centuries B.C.E., envisioned the future of God's plan. The signs of God's judgment were evident in the nation's misfortunes and, ultimately, in the destruction of Jerusalem and of the temple, which symbolized God's presence among the people.[17] However, the prophets also taught that in the future, even if the precise circumstances could not be specified, God's plans to bless the people would still be realized. As the prophetic texts openly envision this future, how do they present it?

"Figures" in the History of Israel

It is here that we encounter for the first time the figurative reinterpretation of past historical experience.[18] The approach is slightly different for each of the prophets in whose oracles this reinterpretation occurs: Amos (assuming that Amos 9:11–15 comes from the prophet himself), Hosea, Micah, Isaiah, Zephaniah (Zeph 3:9–20), Ezekiel, and the author of the "Message of Consolation" spoken toward the end of the Babylonian exile (Isa 40–55). Nevertheless, we can offer a common description of their method and of the themes

---

[17] See the theological summary in *VTB* 625–31, which provides the essential biblical references.

[18] I have already discussed this figurative interpretation in *Sens chrétien de l'Ancien Testament: Esquisse d'un traité dogmatique* (Bibliothèque de théologie 1, Théologie dogmatique 3; Tournai: Desclée, 1962), 209–46, 286–326.

they treat by saying that they offer a "figurative rereading" of the past, in order to show how, under the veil of figures, it has disclosed the durable intentions of God that will be realized in the future. Not all of the prophets, however, make equal use of all of the events in the history of the people of God. Depending on whether they prophesied in Judah or in Israel, they tend to speak more either of the time when the covenant was made at Sinai or of the time when the people enjoyed the height of their national fortunes in the promised land.

The Time of the Patriarchs

This was the time when the first promises were made.[19] Abraham is mentioned only once in Micah (Mic 7:20, which could be an addition of the inspired editor), once in Isaiah (Isa 29:22), once in Jeremiah (Jer 33:26, possibly an editorial addition), twice in the Message of Consolation (Isa 41:8; 51:2), once in Ezekiel (Ezek 33:24), and once in later texts (Isa 63:16). Isaac is mentioned in Amos 7:9, 16 and Jer 33:26 as one of the three patriarchs. Jacob is named as a representative figure for his "house," the kingdom of Israel, 6 times in Amos, 3 times in Hosea, 11 times in Micah, 4 times in Isaiah, once in Nahum, and 3 times in Obadiah. However, this is never in connection with the divine promises; the emphasis is placed on descent and the inheritance that it assures.

The Covenant

Several prophets recall the covenant in order to warn the people that they have broken it: Hosea, who speaks of it under the symbol of marriage, Jeremiah (Jer 3:16; 11:2–10; 22:9), and Ezekiel (Ezek

---

[19] Certain contemporary critics tend to consider the traditions of the patriarchs to have been fixed only late in Israel's history, around the time of the Babylonian exile or perhaps even later. But the references we will be discussing here seem rather to be *allusions* to known texts: those in the "Yahwist" tradition, likely written around the tenth century B.C.E., and those in the "Elohist" tradition, written probably a little later in Israel. We should note that the double name "Jacob/Israel" represents two ways of referring to the tribes that were believed to have been descended from this eponymous ancestor. Two of those tribes, the half-tribes of Ephraim and Manasseh, considered themselves descended from someone who bears an individual name in the tradition, Joseph.

16:8, 59; 44:7). But these prophets also promise that in the future God will make a new covenant with the people. Hosea says that God will "speak to her [Israel's] heart [*'al-libah*]" (Hos 2:14 [2:16 MT]) and enable them to maintain a new fidelity (Hos 2:15b–23). Jeremiah speaks of a new covenant that will be written on their hearts (Jer 31:31–33) and will be irrevocable and perpetual (Jer 32:40), while Ezekiel says that it will be unbreakable (Ezek 16:60–62). The Message of Consolation says that the "servant of YHWH" will be the mediator of this covenant (Isa 42:6; 49:8). It will be a "covenant of peace" (Isa 54:10) that nothing will be able to shake (Isa 55:3). This is because God is "ever mindful of his covenant," as Ps 111:5 says, despite the people's infidelities.

King David

In other prophetic texts, particularly those of Isaiah and Micah, it is the memory of King David that is projected into the future. Micah depicts a future king, a descendant of David, coming forth from Bethlehem to "feed his flock in the strength of the LORD" (Mic 5:2–4). Isaiah speaks of the "sign" of a young woman[20] who will "bear a son" and give him a name that means "God with us" (Isa 7:14–15). Later, this child is given a series of ceremonial names[21] that express the expectation that he, even more than his ancestor David, will establish the kingdom in justice and peace (Isa 9:1–6). This heir to the throne will be filled with the Spirit of God, and as king he will uphold justice in a land where Edenic harmony[22] prevails (Isa

---

[20] In Hebrew *ha'almah* designates an unmarried young woman, who ordinarily would be a virgin (*betulah*). The Septuagint translated this expression as *hē parthenos,* "the virgin." Isaiah here seems to be offering an oracle about the birth of a royal heir in the time of Ahaz, but the Septuagint projects the oracle into the future.

[21] As Isaiah celebrates the birth of the royal heir, he gives him names that express the benefits that he expects him to bring: "Wonderful Counselor, Mighty God, Everlasting Father, Prince of Peace" (Isa 9:6). All of the various gifts expected from God are contained in this formula. The text remained even after the dynasty had ended. As it was reread over the ages, and particularly in later Judaism, the collection of names became an expression of hopes in the future Messiah.

[22] According to Dilmoun, the end of the text (Isa 11:5–9) presents a picture of paradise that is earlier attested in Sumerian mythology.

11:1–9). The vision here is for a royal program of government in which the rule of justice will make the people the beneficiaries of the best gifts God has for them (Isa 32:1–4).

The same theme appears in the book of Jeremiah. The prophet makes a play on the name of the king, Zedekiah ("YHWH is *my* righteousness"), in order to predict the coming of a "righteous branch" from the line of David whose name will be "the LORD is *our* righteousness" (Jer 23:5–6). In this prediction of a perfect king to come in the future there is an implied criticism of the current king, who is mistreating the people. Even if Pss 2; 72; 110 represent ancient liturgies of coronation or enthronement,[23] they nevertheless express the same line of thinking, going so far as to underscore the adoptive sonship that God has granted to the king (Ps 2:7; an idea repeated in Ps 89:27) and insisting on the righteousness of his reign (Ps 72:1–2, 7–8). This future king will not only be a David *redivivus;* he will dominate the world (Ps 2:8–9). From this perspective, the reign of David was just the imperfect prefiguration of this king, whom God will send to his people and ultimately to the whole world.

The Experience of the People of Israel

There is, finally, in the experience of the people of Israel collectively an aspiration that the prophets do not hesitate to project figuratively into an indefinite future. It is that of a land[24] whose amazing fecundity and perfect harmony recapitulate the mythic traits of paradise.

Isaiah briefly sketches out a picture of this (Isa 11:6–9). The Message of Consolation depicts it symbolically in a text (Isa 41:17–20)

---

[23] R. Tournay, writing in the *Bible de Jérusalem,* argues that these are instead compositions of late Judaism that are directly messianic. I believe, however, that they were anthems connected with the royal anointing or coronation, and that later they were reinterpreted from a messianic perspective, to which the New Testament appealed in order to apply them to Jesus Christ. See my *Le mystère du Christ dans les Psaumes* (Jesus et Jesus-Christ 74; Paris: Desclée, 1998), in which I go beyond a literal reading to discuss the reinterpretations that were offered after the exile, to set the stage for the rereading of these psalms in the New Testament and by several of the church fathers. A few of the examples in the study could be developed still further.

[24] See Grelot, *Sens chrétien de l'Ancien Testament,* 373.

that is characterized by the use of the verb "create"[25] (cf. Isa 44:2–5): the image is intermingled with that of the exiles' return to the promised land (Isa 49:10–26). Alongside are put scenes of Jerusalem, the Holy City, which reawakens (Isa 51:17–23): it is the time of the new Jerusalem (Isa 54). We must give poetry its due, but we also must recognize what this rhapsody is saying to us through its symbols. Here the allusion to a primeval paradise suggests a world that has been perfected by being returned to its "original" state, which is necessarily mythical.[26] Nevertheless, the myth is undeniably meaningful when it speaks to human desires that are currently unsatisfied. All of these images are combined because this is the only way to depict the indescribable end toward which the plan of God is moving; they are superimposed to show that all of the events in which the eye of faith can discern God at work have a hidden meaning that points to the same mysterious reality: the ultimate salvation of humanity gathered into the people of God. The partial, temporary realizations of this salvation that occurred in the past were evocative but incomplete figures of it.

Analogical Symbols and Figurative Symbols

In the Later Prophets

The experiences and institutions that God granted to the people were thus given a figurative meaning. They were turned into symbols that expressed the same kind of beliefs as the "analogical" and "mythical" symbols that are also found in the biblical texts, which we examined earlier. The various kinds of symbols were then used together, but in very different ways by different writers. The book of Ezekiel contains a sort of blueprint that describes in advance what the Holy Land, Jerusalem, the temple, the priesthood, and the worship of God will look like in the future (Ezek 40–48). In the

---

[25] The verb "create" (*bara'*) refers exclusively to God's creative acts (see above, p. 88, n. 38).

[26] See my comments above on the use of the word "mythical" (p. 67, n. 1). Any conception of the paradisaic state is by definition "mythical," in the literal sense of the word.

apocalypse of Isaiah (Isa 24–27)[27] a series of scenes depicts not just the return of Israel to the land, but the renewal of the whole world: death will be suppressed, and the righteous dead will be raised to life. In the second part of Zechariah (Zech 9–14), which is a later composition (fourth century B.C.E.), we are told that the world will be transformed, that God will be victorious over all the enemies of his people, and that all the families of the earth will go up to Jerusalem to celebrate the Feast of Tabernacles (Zech 14). We need not look for any logic behind these pictures; the accumulation of symbols aims to inspire true faith by speaking to the imagination. The essential thing to note is the use that is being made of a thousand and one memories drawn from the historical experience of the past—memories of the great architects of the work of God, of the great events in which God demonstrated his intentions toward the people, and of the great institutions that God progressively provided for them. All of these are transferred into a future when God's secret designs will be fully realized.

The Idea of Eschatology

As the centuries passed and all of these texts were continually reread,[28] their symbolic details were arranged into a general scenario that gave the Jews a picture of what their hope and faith could lead them to expect. In the apocalypse of Isaiah (Isa 24–27), the second part of Zechariah (Zech 9–14), and the visions of the book of Daniel (Dan 7–12), this synthesis of earlier Scriptures is already taking

---

[27] The word "apocalypse" is the conventional designation that critics have adopted for Isa 24–27, but it is, in fact, a collection of separate oracles that have the final crisis and its marvelous outcome in view.

[28] When we read the biblical texts today, we seek to determine what they meant within the historical and literary context in which they were written. However, such was not the approach of the faithful people who reread them after the exile. For them, the sacred texts still had a meaning and contained a message as the "words of God," but the context of faith and hope had changed, so that faith instinctively applied them to an indefinite time in the future. Later, the apocalyptic thought that dominated literary conception and composition after the third and second centuries B.C.E. would apply them to the "last times," from a strictly eschatological perspective that can be recognized in, for example, the book of Daniel.

place", in keeping with the literary style of each author.[29] Later, during the centuries that led up to the appearance of the gospel in the world, this same kind of literary endeavor was carried on incessantly. We can recognize it in the writings of each of the separate streams into which Judaism divided in the second century B.C.E.: that of the Pharisees, which was closest to the reading and study of the Scriptures in the synagogues; that of the Essenes, who isolated themselves and therefore were cut off from the temple and the official leadership, but who produced a literature in which images of the future played an incontestable role; and that of the Hellenists, who, in the Judaism of Alexandria and the Egyptian countryside, had adopted the Greek language.

In the context in which Jesus lived and taught he would not have had direct contact with Hellenistic Judaism. Through his participation in worship in the synagogue and at the temple, however, he would have encountered the teaching of the Pharisees and also picked up echoes of the hope that inspired those living in the Galilean countryside.[30] How, then, did Jesus himself read the Scriptures that had been written over the course of the preceding ten centuries?

JESUS' READING OF THE SCRIPTURES

A Highly Personal Reading

Jesus waited until he was thirty years old (Luke 3:23) to leave his family occupation of carpenter (Mark 6:3; Matt 13:55) and begin a preaching ministry. When he did, he astonished and irritated his immediate family (Mark 3:20–21; 3:31 and parallels). Leaving Nazareth,

---

[29] A good example is provided by the rereading of Jeremiah's oracle that after "seventy years" the exile would end and Jerusalem would be restored (Jer 25:11–12; 29:10). This text is taken up in the book of Daniel and reinterpreted, by means of numerical symbolism, as "seventy weeks of years" (70 x 7 = 490 years).

[30] In *L'Espérance juive à l'heure de Jésus* (11th ed.; Jésus et Jésus-Christ 6; Paris: Desclée, 1994) I have assembled Jewish texts from around the time when the Christian era began. The Sadducees are not represented in the collection, but there are texts from the Pharisees, the Essenes (Qumran), and Hellenistic Judaism.

a small town in the Galilean countryside, he took up residence in
Capernaum (Matt 4:13), but his ministry took him throughout Galilee, with occasional trips to Jerusalem for festivals. There is no text
that indicates that he was the student of any Jewish rabbi; when it
came to studying and teaching the Scriptures, he was self-taught.
Certainly, he was able to read[31] them in the original Hebrew (Luke
4:16), but the people were astonished at the things he taught as
he explained these Scriptures, without any formal studies (Matt
13:53–57). "Where did this man get this wisdom?" (Matt 13:54b).

Luke records the tradition that when Jesus was twelve years old,
he sat with the teachers in the temple court, "listening to them and
asking them questions" (Luke 2:46–47). His memory and his reflections enabled him not only to remember the texts that he had heard
in worship on the Sabbath or during festivals, but also to understand
their meaning and their implications, and to develop a method of
teaching different from that of the scribes: as he taught from these
texts, he communicated his own understanding with a singular
authority that astonished his hearers (Mark 1:22; Matt 7:28).

But was his teaching traditional? The answer depends on what
is meant by "traditional." Unlike the scribes of his day, he never
appealed to the authority of recognized teachers. Although he did
take up the halakah,[32] which established rules of conduct, he left
juridical discussions aside and concerned himself only with moral
wisdom, in keeping with the Scriptures, to which he eventually

---

[31] Of all the ancient peoples, the Jews were unquestionably those
among whom the teaching of reading was most developed, given the need
to read the Scriptures in the synagogue. Small schools were maintained
next door to synagogues in which students were taught to read the Scriptures. We can compare this to the Koranic schools that operate today in
Islamic parts of Africa. Jesus could have learned to read as a child in the
small school that likely existed next to the synagogue in his village of Nazareth. For the details of this elementary education see H. L. Strack and G.
Stemberger, *Introduction au Talmud et au Midrash* (trans. M.-R. Hayoun;
Paris: Cerf, 1986), 30–31.

[32] The halakah (from the verb *halak,* "walk, conduct oneself") fixed
rules of conduct that were considered obligatory and that were, in principle, derived from Scripture by means of certain rules of interpretation.
These rules were first established by Hillel (see Strack and Stemberger,
Introduction au Talmud et au Midrash, 38–43).

always referred. But he never hesitated to go beyond the "letter of the law": "You have heard that it was said . . . but I say to you . . ." (five times in Matt 5:21–47). He said this not to abolish the Torah, but rather out of a concern to fulfill it (Matt 5:17), down to the last detail (Matt 5:18–19). His goal was to understand the implications of each of these details, but not in a juridical sense. The essence of his teaching was faith in the coming reign of God: it had drawn near (*engiken*), it summoned people to conversion, it was the "good news" in which they needed to believe (Mark 1:15). Jesus' personal method of teaching was characterized by the frequent use of parables, which are a symbolic genre par excellence. The scribes of his day used parables as well, but they did so to illustrate the teachings they derived from the *letter* of the texts, in keeping with the oral tradition maintained in their schools. Jesus' parables were his own original creations, designed to make his hearers think[33] in the hopes that they would progressively discover "the mystery of the kingdom of God" (Mark 4:11). But they could discover it if only their hearts were ready, if they were open to the good news.

Jesus' Method

When Jesus discussed the Scriptures, did he cite them in their original, literary sense, or did he appeal to their symbolic meaning(s)? The answer to that question depends on the particular case.

Two Examples of Interpretive Reading

Two examples of interpretive reading can help us appreciate Jesus' method, which was characterized by great freedom in its use of texts. When he spoke to the crowds about the mission of John the Baptist, Jesus told them that they should understand John to have been "more than a prophet." To explain this, he appealed to a text from the book of Malachi, but he adapted it to the circumstances.

---

[33] See J. Dupont, *Pourquoi des paraboles? La méthode parabolique de Jésus* (Lire la Bible 46; Paris: Cerf, 1977). See also the discussion of Jesus' parables, along with many other topics, in Dupont's *Études sur les évangiles synoptiques* (2 vols.; BETL 70; Leuven: Leuven University Press, 1985), 1:213–331.

The quotations of this text, Mal 3:1, in Matt 11:10 and Luke 7:27 are not literal translations of the Hebrew, nor are they taken from the Septuagint. Instead, Jesus first quotes Exod 23:20a exactly, "See, I am sending my messenger ahead of you," and then cites the second part of Mal 3:1, "who will prepare [*kataskeuasei* = Hebrew *pinnah*] your way before you." But the text from Malachi has been modified. It actually reads, "See, I am sending my messenger to prepare the way *before me*." Do we have the actual words of Jesus here, or have they been adapted by the source that Matthew and Luke are using? The question could be discussed endlessly, but in any event, this is what the Gospel tradition has preserved, to show how Jesus understood John the Baptist's mission.

The original text in Exodus, we should note, has to do with Israel's journey to the promised land: the angel of God will travel in front of them to prepare the way. The text in Malachi has to do with the final manifestation of God himself on the "day of judgment." The Gospel text has augmented the statement in Malachi by inserting the material from Exodus at the beginning. Nevertheless, Malachi's meaning remains: the statement is the announcement of God's coming in person on the day of his eschatological manifestation. Thus Jesus was defining John the Baptist's mission as the precursor of that day. It follows that Jesus himself, by preaching the good news of the reign of God, was introducing this day that the Jews anticipated and expected. After Jesus' death and resurrection, Christian faith came to understand that he was, in his own person, the longed-for presence of the reign of God itself. He was, in Origen's term, an *autobasileia*.[34] Thus John the Baptist, who was the precursor of the appearance of the reign of God, was actually the precursor of Jesus himself. What Jesus said to the crowds about John therefore had an ambivalent meaning. It was to be understood first in reference to the reign of God, for which John had indeed prepared the way, but when reread from the perspective of the Gospel as a whole, it shows that John was the precursor of Jesus.

---

[34] Origen, *Commentaire sur Matthieu* (trans. R. Girod; Paris: Éditions du Cerf, 1970–), 24.4. The term and reference are found in G. W. H. Lampe, *A Patristic Greek Lexicon* (Oxford: Clarendon Press, 1961), 268.

What Jesus said therefore had a direct relation to the question that he was asked by the messengers from John ("Are you the one who is to come, or are we to wait for another?" [Matt 11:3 = Luke 7:20]) and to the answer that he gave them. Jesus limited himself to reminding them of the signs that were accompanying his mission (Matt 11:4–5 and parallels). Everything that he listed, with the exception of cleansing lepers, was also mentioned in the promises made by the prophets about the great day of salvation, promises that Jesus' contemporaries transferred to the last day as they reread the prophets (e.g., Isa 26:19; 29:18–19; 35:5–6; 61:1). All of these were signs that pointed to the coming reign of God.[35] But how would it come? The miracles of Jesus were signs of it; thus the reign of God was present in his person. But this fact could be understood only at the end of his mission, after his death and resurrection from the dead. Then it could be recognized that Jesus himself was what the good news was all about.

How Jesus Revealed Himself

The two sayings of Jesus that we have just considered demonstrate his amazing finesse. He never revealed all of his personal secrets. He made them accessible only to those whose hearts were open to the revelation of the mystery of God, a mystery that he bore within himself. When the situation called for it, he knew how to argue in the rabbinic manner, as when the Sadducees challenged him with a question about the resurrection of the dead (Mark 12:18–27 and parallels).[36] The deduction that he makes from God's reference to the three patriarchs in Exod 3:6 depends on the premise, shared with the Pharisees, that they were then alive. And how could they have been, unless they had entered into eternal life so that they could participate in the "great feast of God," which Jesus describes in his own parable of Lazarus and the Rich Man (Luke 16:19–26) and which is announced in the text of Isa 25:6–8? Jesus therefore takes this symbolic promise literally.

---

[35] P. Grelot, *Jésus de Nazareth, Christ et Seigneur: Une lecture de l'Évangile* (2 vols.; LD 167, 170; Paris: Cerf, 1997–1998), 1:274–77.

[36] Ibid., 2:145–47, based on more detailed studies by F. Dreyfus and E. Main in *Revue biblique*.

In Jesus' great discourse on "the end" (Mark 13:9–37; Matt 24:1–42; Luke 21:5–36),[37] allusions to stock images from the prophetic writings are easily discernable. In Mark, where a concern over the destruction of Jerusalem dominates the composition, there are three allusions to the book of Daniel: Dan 9:27 (cf. Dan 11:31; 12:11) for the "abomination of desolation," Dan 12:1 for the great tribulation, and Dan 7:13–14 for the appearance of the Son of Man. But Jesus does not explain the meaning of the scriptural symbols that he uses; he simply applies them to a future whose date is undetermined: "But about that day or hour no one knows, neither the angels in heaven, nor the Son, but only the Father" (Mark 13:32). Thus Jesus offers an eschatological reading of the prophetic oracles, even if he adds to the scene—in the manner of the ancient prophets!—a threat against the unfaithful city that has rejected the good news. While he also brings in the perspective of "the end," he does not explain who the Son of Man is (Mark 13:26), so that the relationship between the symbolic figure from the book of Daniel and the expression that he characteristically used to designate himself remains unexplained. When his words were reread after his resurrection, however, the transcendent meaning derived from the book of Daniel was attached to them.

In Mark 14:62 there is already an association between Jesus and the "Son of Man" who "comes with the clouds of heaven." But did Jesus identify himself definitively with the person whom the allusion in Dan 7:13–14 associates with the Davidic Messiah of Ps 110, who is "seated at the right hand of God"? The precise wording of this saying varies in the different Gospels: "*You will see* the Son of Man *seated*"in Mark 14:62 and Matt 26:64, but "*from now on* the Son of Man *will be seated* at the right hand of the power of God" in Luke 22:69. The accusation of blasphemy that follows assumes that Jesus has identified himself with the symbolic personage in Daniel. This is why, in Luke's account, the members of the Sanhedrin cry out, "Are you, then, the Son of God?" (Luke 22:70a). But Jesus replies, "You say that I am." Is he agreeing with the interpretation that they consider blasphemous, or is he simply holding them responsible for what they have said? Either way, the texts of Dan 7 and Ps 110 are being read in the way that the Jewish interpretation of the time understood them.

---

[37] Ibid., 2:167–87, with reference to J. Dupont, *Les trois apocalypses synoptiques: Marc 13; Matthieu 24-25; Luc 21* (LD 121; Paris: Cerf, 1985).

Psalm 110 appropriately occasioned a discussion with the scribes in which Jesus had the initiative (Mark 12:35–37 and parallels). In the Gospel narratives this discussion is based on the Greek text of the psalm.[38] The psalm is understood to have been composed by David, and so this question arises: How could he have referred to the Messiah, who was his son, as "Lord," using a divine title? The question would have been just as pertinent if it had been posed of the Hebrew text of the psalm, since in liturgical reading the word "YHWH" that designated God was replaced by *'Adonay,* "the Lord." But in posing the question, Jesus is careful not to identify himself directly with the Messiah: he appeals only to the current reading (*ne'um 'Adonay la'adoni,* "the word of the Lord to my lord"). In short, Jesus limited himself here to quoting the Scriptures according to the ordinary interpretation, without betraying the secret of his identity.

We get a glimpse into this identity only through other things instead: the way in which he spoke to the Father, and especially the way in which he addressed him in prayer, saying "Abba!" in his Galilean Aramaic;[39] and the way in which he spoke of himself as "the Son" (Mark 13:32; Matt 24:36). In this regard, the numerous texts in John's Gospel in which this expression is found pose a particular problem; John may have used it more generally, in keeping with his own theological understanding. Jesus himself concentrated his teaching on the reign of God and the practical consequences of its coming, without putting himself forward and revealing the secret of his identity. He let his teaching and his actions speak for him, and they could indeed speak for him to those of his contemporaries whose hearts were open to believing in him. But at the same time, through his life, which ended in death on a cross, and then through his appearances to his disciples after his resurrection from the dead, he introduced into history the key to interpreting the ancient Scriptures.

BIBLICAL FIGURES IN THE NEW TESTAMENT

In the prophetic writings the future of the people of God is depicted symbolically through a figurative interpretation of the

---

[38] Ibid., 2:148–49.

[39] See P. Grelot, *Dieu, le Père de Jésus Christ* (Jésus et Jésus-Christ 60; Paris: Desclée, 1994), 183, 185 (with bibliographic references).

major events and essential institutions of their history.[40] These writings do not offer an interpretation of *the texts* that describe this history, but rather refer to *the facts* of this history itself, in the belief that they reveal the plan of God for his people. However, the figurative interpretation of these facts, of these events and institutions, necessarily involves a rereading of the texts that describe them, in such a way that their essential details take on a symbolic significance that makes them prefigurations of the "end of history"—that is, the goal that God has been pursuing in history as his plan has unfolded. But because the goal of God's plan in history has now been accomplished by the life, death, and resurrection of Jesus, the Messiah of Israel and the Son of God, it follows that all of the prophetic Scriptures that speak of this "end" in one way or another have also been "accomplished." As a result, it is only natural that all of these Scriptures should be reread in such a way that they are seen to point to the Christian faith. Let us see how this general principle is worked out in the development of the theological language of the New Testament.

The Language of Christology

In its reflections on the identity of Jesus the New Testament is able to make use of a technical language that essentially is borrowed from earlier biblical texts, following the principle of reinterpretation just described. This language does not apply essentially to the material aspects of Jesus' life, although those who tell the story of his life are often ingenious enough to incorporate certain details that are in keeping with their presentation (I will discuss some examples of this). The events and institutions of Israel's history already have a literal meaning in the Scriptures that record them; this meaning is extended when they are used as figurative symbols in the prophetic texts, and it is extended even further by the reinterpretive principle that enables the New Testament writers to see, scattered throughout them, glimpses into the mystery of Jesus' identity. Let us consider some significant examples of this.

---

[40] See above, " 'Figures' in the History of Israel" and "Analogical Symbols and Figurative Symbols" (pp. 112–18).

The Titles of Jesus

Jesus of Nazareth came from a human family that was well known to his contemporaries. Legally, he was the son of "Joseph the carpenter" (Matt 13:55; Mark 6:3). This was how his compatriots knew him. But this Joseph, from whom was he descended?

Son of David. The Jews who lived in the time of Jesus had not completely lost the record of their tribal lineages or of their "great ancestors." Saul of Tarsus knew that he came "from the tribe of Benjamin" (Phil 3:5). Hillel the Elder, who lived roughly in the time of Jesus, was regarded by a later tradition as a descendant of David.[41] Thus it should not be surprising that the family of Jesus could be traced back to that same stock. This may explain why Jesus was addressed with the title "Son of David" (e.g., Matt 9:27), and why the two differing genealogies in Matthew and Luke do agree that Jesus was descended from David. The secret of his divine conception was a family matter that the general public knew nothing about (John 7:42).[42] However, it is revealed in the christological texts of the New Testament (Matt 1:20; Luke 1:27, 32; 2:4, 11; Acts 13:34; Rom 1:3; 2 Tim 2:8; Rev 3:7; 5:5; 22:16), since it is crucial to his identification as the Messiah, the son of David.

Messiah of Israel. Jesus, in his preaching, never claimed the title "Messiah" for himself. This was because the title had, at the time, an essentially political resonance: it was believed that the Davidic Messiah would be a national liberator. His coming was even more eagerly anticipated at this time, when the Jewish nation was under Roman domination.[43] When Peter confessed his faith that Jesus was

---

[41] See Strack and Stemberger, *Introduction au Talmud et au Midrash,* 94. Hillel is known to have come originally from Babylon and to have lived in Trachonitis, on the other side of the Jordan.

[42] Thus it is not surprising that the general public and even his family (the "brothers and sisters" of Mark 3:32, and the "family" of Mark 3:21) considered Jesus to be the son of Joseph; that was his legal identity.

[43] Bar Kosiba, some of whose letters have been recovered from a grotto at Murabba'at, led a Jewish revolt against Roman occupation from 132 to 135 B.C.E. His coins are dated in the "era of Israel's liberation." Rabbi Aqiba ben Yoseph declared him to be the Messiah of Israel but paid with his life for this political adventurism (see Strack and Stemberger,

the Messiah (Mark 8:29; Matt 16:16; Luke 9:20), Jesus ordered his twelve disciples to keep silent about his identity and used the occasion to speak to them about what the future held for him: he would be rejected, mistreated, and finally executed (Mark 8:30–31). Jesus rebuked Peter very severely when the latter contradicted him.[44] The fallacious theory of a "messianic secret" has been built on this episode.[45] We can leave that theory aside. It was only when the disciples had seen Jesus after he rose from the dead and entered into the "world to come" that they recognized him as the Messiah, in a completely different sense from that suggested by political hopes. Luke records this recognition in the book of Acts, beginning with Peter's speech on the day of Pentecost (Acts 2:36). From then on, the title "Christ"—a Greek translation of the Hebrew *Mashiakh* (*Meshikha* in Aramaic, transliterated as *Messias* in John 1:41; 4:25)—is used regularly in the New Testament, to such an extent that the people of Antioch give the name "Christians"[46] to the followers of Jesus (Acts 11:26; cf. 26:28; 1 Pet 4:16).

Son of God. This title also comes from prophetic promises that have been interpreted from an eschatological perspective (2 Sam 7:14; Ps 2:7; 89:26). The title originally refers to an adoptive sonship

---

Introduction au Talmud et au Midrash, 100). Bar Kosiba became known as Bar Kokeba, "Son of the Star," in light of his messianic pretensions (see E. Nodet and J. Taylor, *Essai sur les origines du christianisme: Une secte éclatée* [Initiations bibliques; Paris: Cerf, 1998], 179–82).

[44] The language is even more severe in Matt 16:22–23 than in Mark 8:32–33.

[45] The theory is based on the way that Jesus, in the Synoptics, responds to Peter's confession of faith by imposing silence on the apostles. The theory essentially holds that since Jesus knew himself to be the Messiah, and since from the earliest days of the church he was presented as such to Jewish audiences, the Gospel tradition must have artificially introduced this demand for silence into the texts. However, the actual situation is quite different: Jesus was not, and did not want to be, the Messiah of Israel in the sense that the Jews of his time expected, in light of their hopes for political liberation.

[46] This name is Latin in form (the Greek is *Christianoi*), and it was given to Jesus' followers in Antioch with satirical intent (Acts 11:26): they were "partisans of *Christos*." In 1 Pet 4:16, however, it is taken up as a badge of honor.

granted by God to the king. In the New Testament Jesus never says directly, "I am the Son of God," but the theophany at the time of his baptism identified him as such (Mark 1:11 and parallels). This was something that Jesus experienced personally, but when it was repeated at the time of his transfiguration, the three apostles who witnessed it were let in on the secret as well (Mark 9:7 and parallels). Were they able to understand it at the time? Whether or not they were, it is paradoxical that this initial revelation was followed by Jesus' arrest, trial, and execution. Nevertheless, it was right after Jesus' death that, according to Mark and Matthew, the Roman centurion declared, "Truly this man was God's Son!" (Mark 15:39; Matt 27:54).

What did Jesus himself think? All of his prayers, except for the one from the cross in Mark and Matthew, show that his relationship with God was one of astonishing intimacy. He always called God "Father," and the record of his prayer in Gethsemane preserves the literal form of this address in Aramaic, "Abba" (Mark 14:36)[47]. This is the strongest indication we have of his divine sonship. This is why every book of the New Testament gives him the title "Son of God." The Gospel of John shows that Jesus' entire career was defined by the question of his relationship to God, his Father (a point that we examined earlier).

Lord. The Greek title *Kyrios* was used officially for the Roman emperor, but in the biblical tradition it is reserved for God. It was used in the Septuagint to translate the Hebrew tetragram "YHWH."[48] The word *kyrios* does have the everyday meaning "sir," but in Christian writings it takes on a much more solemn sense, as in the expression "the Lord Jesus Christ." This expression is found in all of the books of the New Testament. The book of Revelation characteristically refers to "the Lord God" (*Kyrios ho Theos*), but it closes with the appeal "Come, Lord Jesus!"

---

[47] See above, p. 46, n. 17.

[48] In the manuscripts from Qumran this tetragram is rarely written out. Often it is replaced by four dots. In ancient Greek manuscripts of Jewish origin the word *Kyrios* is itself replaced more than once by the four Greek letters that most closely resemble the Hebrew tetragram, so that it will not be pronounced. In the manuscripts of the Greek Bible preserved by Christians, however, the word *Kyrios* takes the place of the divine name.

Lamb of God. This image is liturgical in origin: it refers to the Passover lamb (Exod 12). It is found in the first letter of Peter (1 Pet 1:19), in the Gospel of John (John 1:29, 36), and especially in the book of Revelation ("a lamb as if it had been slain"[49] [29x]). This is a figurative interpretation of the Passover lamb, which is assimilated symbolically to Christ on the cross (cf. 1 Cor 5:7).

Suffering Servant. This image is an application of the prophecy in Isa 52:13–53:12 to Jesus and his death on the cross. The application is made directly in Acts 8:32–35, and it underlies the passages in which Jesus describes his death as a redemptive sacrifice (Mark 10:45; Matt 20:28), or in which he says that his blood will be "poured out for many" (Mark 14:24 and parallels). But is this a figurative interpretation of Scripture? That depends on what we consider to be the literal meaning of the text in Isaiah: does it refer to a single historical individual, or to a group?[50] Whatever the case, Jesus incarnates in his person the Suffering Servant described in this text.

Son of Man. Jesus used the periphrasis "son of man"[51] to identify himself in an ordinary sense (meaning "the human being that I am"), but in his response to the high priest (Mark 14:62), he used it to express his vision of the future by allusion to Dan 7:13–14, which predicts the future glorification of the Davidic Messiah (Ps 110:1). Although his words may have been understood ambiguously at the time of his trial, the Gospel tradition saw in them a prediction of his resurrection, since he was identified with the Son of Man in glory. From there the Gospel texts applied the title to him personally wherever it appeared. Although he was the Messiah and the Son of Man, he appeared to be only an ordinary human being during his public ministry. However, his death led to a resurrection that made him the Son of Man in glory. The same title is used in Acts 7:56; Rev 1:13; 14:14.

---

[49] As a symbol of Christ in glory, the Lamb cannot be seen as "slain," but in light of the cross, he is shown "as if he had been slain": he still bears in glory the traces of his sacrificial death.

[50] See in ch. 2 "The Servant of YHWH" and "The 'Son of Man'" (pp. 58–59).

[51] See in ch. 2 "The 'Son of Man'" (p. 59).

Christ as High Priest. The theme of Christ Jesus' priesthood is presented only in the letter to the Hebrews.[52] Its Alexandrian author is not content merely to show by an appeal to the text of Ps 110:4 that Melchizedek (Gen 14:17–20) was a prefiguration of Christ (Heb 7:17). He develops at length a presentation of Jesus as the "high priest of the good things that have come" (Heb 9:11), thanks to his entry into the heavenly sanctuary that the temple prefigured (Heb 9:11–28). The entire argument depends on a figurative interpretation of the ritual of the Sinai covenant (Heb 9:19–21, cf. Exod 24:6–8) and of the ritual of the Day of Atonement (Heb 9:7–9a), with appeal to Isa 53:12. Jesus is both priest and sacrifice at the same time. Thus his death is interpreted as a sacrifice, or, more accurately, as an oblation of his body, which began with his entry into the world and which was completed by his physical death (Heb 10:5–10).

Christ as the Word of God. Is this a figurative title? We use the English term "word" to render a term that, in Hebrew and Aramaic as well as in Greek, designates the spoken word of God, which is active and revelatory. This term is never used in the First Testament to indicate God's messengers. But in Isa 55:10–11 the word of God is presented as an active power that, in creation and in history, never returns to God "without accomplishing the object of its mission."

But is this a revelatory mission, or is it a mission of carrying out the divine government of the world? It is both at once. In the hymn to the Word at the beginning of the Gospel of John (John 1:1–5, 9–18), the Word is not just personified by a literary fiction; it is hypostasized as a real person who participates in the being and the actions of God.

The symbolic idea of the Word of God is thereby elevated to a plane on which an essential aspect of the mystery of Jesus Christ is revealed. This revelation actually occurred only after his glorification as the risen Lord, but John projects it back upon his human condition, beginning with his conception and birth, when "the Word became flesh and lived among us" (John 1:14). Thus the figurative interpretation of the biblical notion of the "word of God" is

---

[52] For a detailed discussion of the texts see the commentaries on this epistle. I take up the question in *Corps et sang du Christ en gloire: Enquête dogmatique* (LD 182; Paris: Cerf, 1999), ch. 8.

pushed to the limits of possibility. We should not think that some speculation about the divine Logos, after the manner of Alexandrian philosophy,[53] lies behind this image; no one would propose such an interpretation for the first text in which Christ Jesus is represented as the Word of God (Rev 19:13).

The Functions of Christ in Glory

The Book of Revelation. Revelation attributes to the "Lamb as if it had been slain" other symbolic titles that most often presuppose a figurative interpretation of various biblical texts. The "Word of God" of Rev 19 is also "the One who judges in righteousness." This was a title of the future king who was announced in Isa 11:4 (cf. Rev 19:11). The statement that this king will "rule the nations with a rod of iron" (Rev 19:15) is appropriate in light of the royal imagery of Ps 2:9. But the royal image of a king who "judges in righteousness" is also applied to God in Ps 98:9; in the same way, the title "King of kings and Lord of lords" (Rev 19:16; cf. 17:14) takes up an expression that is applied specifically to God in Deut 10:17; Dan 2:47. Thus the imagery oscillates between a figurative application of messianic royalty and an indication of participation in the divine dignity itself. We can say the same thing about the title "Faithful and True": it may refer to human qualities attributed to the royal Messiah, who "judges and makes war" (Rev 19:11), but it may also indicate participation in divine prerogatives that are frequently mentioned in Psalms (Rev 19:11; cf. 1:5; 3:7, 14). Christ's identity as a warrior (Rev 19:11, 15) is similarly ambivalent. The "sharp sword that comes out of his mouth" is a figurative interpretation of the image of the royal Messiah in Isa 11:4, but the allusion to the "wine press of the fury of

---

[53] The "prologue" to John (John 1:1–5, 9–18) appears to be a hymn to the Word of God. I am not convinced that this was an Alexandrian hymn to the Logos that has been taken up and amplified by the evangelist (as suggested by G. Rochais in P. Grelot et al., *La liturgie dans le Nouveau Testament* [Introduction à la Bible 9; Paris: Desclée, 1991], 272–87). As I see it, *ho logos* is an exact translation of the Hebrew *haddabar* or the Aramaic expression that occurs frequently in *Targum Yerushalmi: memra*. It is a personification of the Word of God, which is active in creation. But the prologue moves beyond personification to what Greek theology called the "hypostasis" of the Word (in one of the possible meanings of *hypostasis*).

the wrath of God" goes back to Isa 63:3, where God himself is the one who executes vengeance. The cooperation of the glorified Lamb with God is confirmed by their close association in Rev 21–22: together they constitute the temple of the new Jerusalem (Rev 21:22); they give light to the city (Rev 21:23); and they share a single throne (Rev 22:1). The Lamb declares, "I am the Alpha and the Omega, the first and the last, the beginning and the end" (Rev 22:13); thus he has the same name as God (Rev 1:8; cf. Isa 44:6). Here the titles of Christ in glory are a mixture of messianic titles from the First Testament, interpreted figuratively, and of divine titles. This is the summit of Christology.

The Gospel of Matthew. In his regular preaching Jesus did not push himself forward and claim to have transcendent attributes.[54] However, the Gospels were written at a time when faith in Jesus instinctively projected onto his words the full meaning that his resurrection had given to them. As a result, they present "rereadings" that show how those who proclaimed the gospel understood his definitive role in bringing about salvation. Let us consider several examples, starting with the Gospel of Matthew.

The chapters that describe Jesus' early years (Matt 1–3) repeatedly quote the prophecies of the First Testament in order to show that Jesus came to the world to "fulfill" them. However, the original meaning of the texts is generally forced, sometimes even modified, in order to express a christological reflection by means of the Scriptures. Even if we leave aside plays on words such as the explanation of the name "Jesus" (which is the Greek form of "Joshua," meaning "the LORD saves" [Matt 1:21]), we still can recognize that the oracle of Isa 7:14 has been used independently of its original meaning when applied to the virginal conception by which Jesus the Messiah was born in order to portray him as "God with us" from his birth (Matt 1:23). Later, the tradition that Jesus was born in Bethlehem—a tradition that Matthew and Luke both record but that they obtained through separate sources—is justified by the oracle in Mic 5:2. However, the words of the text are modified

---

[54] This is true except for his discussions with the "teachers of the law" in Jerusalem, as they are reported in the Gospel of John. See Grelot, *Jésus de Nazareth, Christ et Seigneur,* 1:319–27, 2:58–72, 98–105.

from the Septuagint[55] in order to show how the fact conforms to the Scriptures. The flight into Egypt is illustrated by a quotation from Hos 11:1, which refers to the people of Israel as the "firstborn son" of God; as such, the people prefigured Jesus, who is the Son of God in the most significant sense. The oracle in Jer 31:15 (38:15 LXX) is adapted in a secondary sense to the massacre of the infants of Bethlehem because of the similarity of the situations. Finally, an oracle of "the prophets," which is otherwise unidentified, is used to justify somehow the fact that Jesus grew up in Nazareth;[56] this is a literary adaptation rather than a figurative prediction.

The same applies to the quotation of Isa 9:1–2 (8:23–9:1 MT) in Matt 4:15–16, although the image of a "great light" is appropriate to the evangelical proclamation that is about to begin. However, the portrayal of the healings that Jesus performed in terms reminiscent of Isa 53:4 is more difficult to appreciate, as it depends on a figurative interpretation of the Suffering Servant, who is in view in the original text. On the other hand, the quotation of Isa 42:1–4 in Matt 12:18–21 identifies Jesus clearly with the Servant who is spoken of in the Message of Consolation: Jesus is doing exactly what was predicted of him.[57] Isaiah 6:9–10 is quoted in Matt 13:14–15 and in the parallel texts in Mark and Luke, but also in John 12:40 and at the end of the book of Acts (Acts 28:26–27). The original text is adapted so that what the Christian authors want to say can be expressed through it. The proclamation of the gospel, like the preaching of Isaiah, is blocked by its hearers' hardness of heart. In this respect, the Jews living in the time of the apostles are just like the Judeans in the time of Isaiah. This is not a prefiguration, but rather a reflection of the persistence of the same disposition

---

[55] Mic 5:2 reads, in Hebrew as well as in Greek, "You are the least of the clans of Judah." By contrast, Matthew writes, "You are by no means least among the rulers of Judah."

[56] In what First Testament text do we read, as we do in Matt 2:23, "He will be called a Nazarene" (*Nazōraios*)? Even if the Greek *zeta* corresponds to the Hebrew *tsade,* there is still no such text to be found. There is a Hebrew term *natsor,* derived from the verb *natsar,* "observe." Does the quotation refer to an "observer" of the law, by means of a play on words with the name "Nazareth"? It is difficult to know what to think.

[57] See the discussion in P. Grelot, *Les Poèmes du Serviteur: De la lecture critique à l'herménéutique* (LD 103; Paris: Cerf, 1981), 166–69.

of heart. Paul observes the same thing about the Jews of his time (Rom 11:8).

We may make a similar observation about the quotation of Isa 29:13 in Matt 15:7–9. This time it is Jesus himself who gives a critique of the superficial worship that his contemporaries are offering, but now the quotation is word for word. Let us consider once more the phrase in Matt 3:17b, which is repeated, but in the third person, in Matt 17:5b. The voice of God that identifies Jesus as his Son, as we saw earlier, makes allusion to Ps 2:7, which is now being fulfilled in a new way. But why is Jesus called God's *"beloved* Son"? The only explanation for this qualifier seems to be that it is a reference to the Greek version of Gen 22:2, 16,[58] and this enables us to understand why it has been added: Jesus is in the same position relative to God that Isaac was in relative to Abraham. This gives us a further insight into his divine sonship. In Matt 22:2 the evangelist transforms the parable of the banquet recorded in Luke 14:16–24.[59] In Matthew it is "a king" who gives a "wedding banquet for his son." The change is significant. It makes the parable an allusion to Isa 25:6, which concerns the eschatological banquet, and to Hos 2:21–22, which has to do with an eschatological wedding. But since "the king" can only represent God, who can "his son" be except for Jesus? Matthew thus introduces a christological theme into the parable.

Let us also consider the way in which Matthew presents the final judgment (Matt 25:31–46).[60] In Matt 25:31 the judge is the "Son of Man" in glory; the "throne of his glory" is appropriate for one who is later presented as "the king," through a figurative interpretation of the prophetic texts that predicted the coming of an eschatological king to Israel. But "the king" calls the elect "you that are blessed by *my Father"* (Matt 25:34). Thus a Christian rereading of the text has indicated the divine sonship of "the king" in a sense that is unknown to the prophetic texts and that the words of Jesus alone could have revealed. Here I conclude the specific analysis of Matthew and turn to the four Gospels together to consider scriptural allusions in the narratives of Jesus' passion.

---

[58] See Grelot, *Jésus de Nazareth, Christ et Seigneur,* 1:116–17; *Dieu, le Père de Jésus Christ,* 163.

[59] See Grelot, *Jésus de Nazareth, Christ et Seigneur,* 2:154–56.

[60] Ibid., 2:187–89.

The Passion Narratives. All of the texts in the First Testament that speak of the future king, whom the Jews of Jesus' day understood in eschatological terms, depict this king as a glorious victor. The idea of a suffering Messiah is nowhere attested. The texts that describe the Suffering Servant (Isa 52:13–53:12) are applied in the book of Daniel to all of the righteous who suffer and die for their faith.[61] Jesus did not apply this text of Isaiah to himself when he told his disciples that he would suffer and be put to death, and that he would then rise from the dead "on the third day," using an expression that was commonly applied to the day of judgment[62] and that appears in the texts of each of the three Synoptic Gospels (Mark 8:31–32; 9:31; 10:32–34 and parallels). His only apparent reference to himself in connection with the Suffering Servant passages is in the saying found in Mark 10:45 (with a parallel in Matt 20:28), "The Son of Man came not to be served but to serve, and to give his life a ransom for many." This is likely an allusion to Isa 53:10–12. There is an echo of this in what Jesus says about the cup at the Last Supper (Mark 14:24 = Matt 26:28). Luke is less specific about this, but he does cite Isa 53:12 explicitly a short while afterwards (Luke 22:37).

It is actually on another basis that the Gospel narratives show that the passion took place "according to the Scriptures." This claim can hardly be grounded on the quotation from Zech 11:12–13 that Matthew includes in the account of Judas's payment for his betrayal (Matt 27:9–10). Leaving aside the fact that Matthew attributes the quotation to Jeremiah, it is only a secondary application of the text, based on the mention of the thirty pieces of silver that later will be used to buy the "Field of Blood" (Matt 27:8). The parallel text in Acts about the death of Judas tells such a different story that it may well reflect a later and much less reliable tradition.[63]

When we consider John's narrative together with those of the Synoptics, we recognize a significant number of references, sometimes explicit, to "psalms of supplication" in the background of the

---

[61] See in ch. 2 "The 'Servant of YHWH' " (p. 58).

[62] See Grelot, *L'Espérance juive à l'heure de Jésus,* 187; P. de Surgy et al., *La résurrection du Christ et l'exégese moderne* (LD 50; Paris: Cerf, 1969), 28, 38–39.

[63] See Grelot, *Jésus de Nazareth, Christ et Seigneur,* 2:288–90.

narratives.[64] In John 13:18 Jesus himself quotes Ps 41:9 (41:10 MT) to describe his betrayal by Judas. Similarly, in Mark 14:34 Jesus expresses his sadness through a formula that appears to have been borrowed from Ps 42:6, 11 (42:7, 12 MT; 41:6, 12 LXX). To express his feeling of abandonment by God (Mark 15:34 = Matt 27:46), Jesus quotes Ps 22:1 (22:2 MT) in Aramaic, while in Luke's Gospel (Luke 23:46) he commends his spirit into the Father's hands in words reminiscent of Ps 31:5 (30:6 LXX). His cry "I thirst!" has parallels in Ps 22:15; 69:21. Indeed, the vinegary drink that he is offered as he is dying (Mark 15:36; Matt 27:48; Luke 23:36) is a detail preserved precisely because of its appearance in Ps 69:21; John emphasizes it as a "fulfillment of scripture" (John 19:28–29). In the same way, the fact that the soldiers divided up Jesus' clothes, as they customarily did at executions, is described because of the reference to this in Ps 22:18. John 19:23–24 calls attention to this explicitly, and it is implicit in Mark 15:24; Matt 27:35; Luke 23:34. John (John 19:36–37) even connects the fact that Jesus' executioners, after examining him on the cross, "did not break his legs" and "pierced his side with a spear" with the fulfillment of two texts of Scripture: one is a combination of Exod 12:46 and Ps 34:20,[65] while the other, regarding the examination, is from Zech 12:10 (cf. Rev 1:7).

None of these texts had to do originally with the future Messiah, but as they are adapted to Jesus' situation, their literal sense is generally respected. Should we say that the faithful Jews whose prayers are preserved in the psalms were "prefigurations of Christ"? The expression is not quite appropriate. We should rather say that Jesus, as a Jew, prayed these psalms himself, and that their words marvelously expressed his inner feelings as he underwent his passion.[66] By taking on the human sufferings to which these psalms refer, Jesus

---

[64] See Grelot, *Le mystère du Christ dans les Psaumes,* 94–98, 106–9, 114–16, 135–36, 141–45, 176–81. For each of the psalms that it discusses, this commentary cites patristic texts that follow the interpretation of the New Testament.

[65] See the detailed discussion in T. M. Dabek and T. Jelonek, eds., *Agnus et Sponsa: Essays in Honor of A. Jankowski* (Krakow: Wydawn. Benedyktynów, 1993), 109–22.

[66] See Grelot, *Le mystère du Christ dans les Psaumes,* 11, 40–41, 179–80, 253–54.

gave them a deeper meaning within the mystery of salvation. Those who believe in Jesus Christ as the Savior of the world will necessarily associate the suffering that so many innocent people experience with the cross of Christ. For example, how could they not think in this connection of the Holocaust, in which so many innocent Jews, who prayed these same psalms, lost their lives? We are not talking here about "post-Holocaust Christian theology," but rather about how to reflect in a Christian way on the mystery of evil that was perpetrated against this people, whose prayers are the psalms, and to whom Jesus belonged. If they experienced suffering like that of Jesus, how could they not also have found *with him* a salvation like his, from the true God in whom they, *like him*, believed?

The Infancy Narratives in Luke. Space does not permit us to examine the entire Gospel of Luke in detail here.[67] Nevertheless, we may consider the chapters devoted to Jesus' infancy and childhood (Luke 1–2), which are particularly dense in scriptural references. Some of the allusions are purely literary. The angel Gabriel, who brings messages to Zechariah and to Mary (Luke 1:11–20, 26–38), is mentioned in the book of *Enoch*. And it is a scene right out of an apocalypse when, at the birth of Jesus, heaven and earth join together to sing God's praises and promise peace to people everywhere (Luke 2:13–14). However, other references are more figurative. In Luke 1:17 the impending birth of John the Baptist is described as a fulfillment of the promise in Mal 4:5–6. The salutation to Mary in Luke 1:30, "Do not be afraid," is the same one addressed to the "daughter of Zion" in Zeph 3:14–16 and Zech 2:10, from a prophetic, eschatological perspective. Thus the "daughter of Zion" prefigured the future mother of Jesus. The scene of the annunciation (Luke 1:26–38) does present an announcement of Jesus' birth, expressed in classic terminology, but it is even more so a narrative of Mary's calling to be the mother of the "Son of the Most High," to

---

[67] See Grelot, *Jésus de Nazareth, Christ et Seigneur,* 2:455–97. Clearly, the infancy narratives in Matthew and Luke were composed after Jesus' resurrection, since they presuppose a retrospective reflection on his early years in light of his resurrection, which more fully revealed the mystery of his being. The two evangelists apply to him, from the beginning of his life, texts from the First Testament that clarify the purpose of his coming into the world.

whom the Lord will give "the throne of his ancestor David" (Luke 1:32). Thus Jesus is identified as the Messiah. There is then an announcement of the virginal conception, in response to the question that Mary, who is only engaged (Luke 1:27), asks: "How can this be, since I am a virgin?"[68] (Luke 1:34). The child will be conceived by the creative activity of the Holy Spirit and will therefore be known as the "Son of God" (Luke 1:35). This essential fact could not have been predicted in the Scriptures, because it was entirely unanticipated (but "nothing will be impossible with God," as Gabriel says in Luke 1:37, in an adaptation of Gen 18:14 [cf. Jer 32:27]). For the same reason, there could not have been any prefiguration of the virginal conception of Jesus.[69]

The songs of Mary (Luke 1:46–55) and Zechariah (Luke 1:67–79) are woven together out of scriptural allusions,[70] among which we

---

[68] We need to appreciate exactly what Mary is saying here. She only specifies that she "does not know a man" because she is a virgin but has been told she will have a child. She is not referring to a prior vow of perpetual virginity.

[69] Certain historians of religion, who feel that this account must be explained as another imaginary creation myth, have sought parallels in Greek and Egyptian mythology (cf., e.g., Harpocrates = Horus the Child). However, we must actually understand this account of Jesus' birth by beginning with his resurrection from the dead, which revealed that he was the Son of God in the most profound sense. From there we must ask how he needed to be equipped for the public ministry that culminated in his death and resurrection, and specifically whether Mary and Joseph, who were responsible for his moral and religious upbringing, would not have needed some sign that indicated the unique character of the child whom they were to bear and raise. The virginal conception was, above all, a sign to help them understand their special vocation within the realization of God's plan. They both needed this sign to understand the entirely unique vocation that they were being given. Those who do not believe in the resurrection of Christ and the divine sonship of Jesus will consider his virginal conception a fabrication of Christian mythology. We must respond to such people by once again beginning at the end of his life. The virginal conception of Jesus did not become part of the common revelation until after the doctrines of Christ's resurrection and divine sonship were established. If we do not begin with these doctrines, we will only be wasting our time in useless disputes.

[70] See the discussion of these texts, as well as the song of Simeon, in Grelot et al., *La liturgie dans le Nouveau Testament,* 239–72.

may note a reference to God fulfilling the covenant oath that he swore to Abraham (Luke 1:72–73; cf. Gen 15:18; 17:4; 22:16–18). As for John the Baptist, he is said to fulfill the oracles of Mal 3:1 (Luke 1:76) and Mal 4:2 (Luke 1:78). But Luke is also thinking of the work of the risen Christ from a more transcendent perspective when he says that God will fulfill, in an entirely unforeseen way, the oracle of Isa 9:2 (Luke 1:79).

The promised child will be "Christ the Lord," a title that connects the messianic oracles with a new reality that could not have been imagined previously: the "Savior," the "son of David," will also participate in the "Lordship" of God (cf. Luke 2:11). But in what sense? Luke writes from a perspective in which salvation has been accomplished by the death and resurrection of Jesus. This salvation includes Israel, but it is offered to every nation, as we hear in Simeon's song (Luke 2:32). Here Luke is alluding to Isa 42:6 and 49:6, two oracles that have had only a figurative meaning up to this point, but which have now been "fulfilled." Thus Jesus, through his life on earth and his death on the cross, and through his salvific action as the Risen One, reveals the deeper meaning of those things that, in the First Testament, were figurative: events, institutions, and the symbolic texts that were already using these events and institutions as images.

The Language of Ecclesiology

Although the story told in the First Testament centers on certain figurative persons, the story itself is of a specific human community that established precise institutions for itself. The New Testament also appeals to these as prefigurations. The prophetic promises had already projected them into the future of the people of God, and the later apocalypses gave them an "eschatological" character. In the New Testament they become an essential source of symbolic expressions for the language of ecclesiology, but they are not the only source, because the Christian experience itself supplied some further materials. We will consider these at the end of this section.

The Church of God

The Greek word *ekklēsia* most often translates the Hebrew *qahal,* which originally designated the cultic assembly of the people of Israel.

This meaning is preserved in Acts 7:38, where *ekklēsia* is used to refer to the "congregation in the wilderness." But there are also places in the First Testament where the word is used in more of a "New Testament" sense, as in the references in Psalms to "assemblies" where God receives praise and thanksgiving (Ps 22:23, 26 [ET 22:22, 25]; 26:12; 35:18; 40:10 [ET 40:9]; 68:27 [ET 68:26]; 149:1). Jesus himself uses the term only on two occasions (Matt 16:18; 18:17), and in both cases the evangelist has worded his sayings in a way that ultimately reflects later Christian usage.[71] In the book of Acts the word *ekklēsia* is sometimes used with its civil meaning (Acts 19:32, 39, 40). Everywhere else, however, it refers to the people of God gathered together to pray and to hear the word of God. Thus it can refer to a local church, "the church of God that is in" such and such a place (1 Cor 1:2; 2 Cor 1:1; 1 Thess 1:1; 2 Thess 1:1). The word can also be used in the plural (e.g., Gal 1:2; 2 Thess 1:4; 1 Tim 3:5; 3 John 6; Rev 1–3 [12x]; 22:16).

This does not mean that there was only one *ekklēsia* in each of the cities in which Paul founded churches; assemblies met in private meeting places,[72] typically in houses big enough to hold a large num-

---

[71] The apologetic in use since the eighteenth century insists that Jesus actually used the word "church" (*ekklēsia*) in these two sayings recorded by Matthew, in order to prove that "Jesus was the founder of the church." This is a purely defensive argument, offered against those who would see the church in sociological terms as a human creation. In fact, the church, as a cultic assembly gathered around Christ, is the result of his resurrection, which it celebrates each time it gathers to observe the Lord's Supper. Nevertheless, it is possible that Jesus' words to Peter (Matt 16:18), as well as the confession of faith that precedes them ("You are the Christ, the Son of the living God"), are statements that were originally made after Jesus' resurrection. By reporting them at the point where Peter's confession, "You are the Christ," is recorded in Mark, Matthew would be connecting Jesus' promise to Peter with the faith that Peter's words express. That would be authentic New Testament theology, not defensive apologetics.

[72] In Paul's day and in the centuries that followed, right up until Constantine, the church had no legal identity within the Roman Empire. Its members could only hold private meetings, which were monitored more or less closely by the imperial police. Thus the homes of members were the only place where believers could gather. This was true even in Jewish territory, in Galilee and Judea, where the synagogues were reserved for Sabbath-day meetings. For the use of the word *ekklēsia* see the articles in K. L. Schmidt, *TDNT* 3:501–36; J. Roloff, *TWNT* 10:1127–31; and

ber of believers (Rom 16:5; 1 Cor 16:19; Phlm 2). In one sense, this is a continuation of the First Testament model, but the Jewish name for prayer assemblies, "synagogue," is retained only in Jas 2:2. Instead, the emphasis is placed on the new cultic act that has Christ at its center: in Acts 20:7–11 we discover that the culmination of these meetings was the Lord's Supper (which is described there as the "breaking of bread," as in Acts 2:46; Luke 24:30, 35).

The People of God

Thus the cultic assemblies of the New Testament were in continuity with those of the First Testament. However, the death and resurrection of Jesus gave them a new form. They retained their fundamental character as gatherings in which God was worshiped and the Scriptures were read, but now this was done in light of the mystery of Christ, and the remembrance of his death and resurrection replaced the former sacrifices. They were still intended for the "people of God," but now this people was also reshaped and redefined.[73]

Nevertheless, we should not think of the church of Jesus Christ as a new "people of God" that is substituted for the old one. Israel, the people of God by virtue of the covenant that God made with them at Sinai, is still called to be the first member of the faithful community; this calling has become a reality for those Jews who have believed the good news of Jesus Christ, the Son of God, who died and was raised on the third day. This is the thrust of Peter's speech in Acts 2:14–36. Now, however, members of every nation may become part of the "people of God" if they put their faith in the risen Christ, according to the Scriptures. Hence Isa 66:18 predicts the gathering of "all nations and tongues." Texts such as Zech 14:16–18 give us a glimpse of this universal convocation of nations, just as the oracle in Isa 2:2–4 depicts all nations going up to the Temple Mount to worship God.

J. Roloff, *EDNT* 1:410–15. In French see P. Ternant, "Eglise," *VTB* 323–35. The *EDNT* article provides a bibliography.

[73] See the articles by H. Strathmann and R. Meyer, "λαός" *TDNT* 4:29–57 and H. Frankemölle, "λαός" *EDNT* 2:339–44, with an extensive bibliography. In French see P. Grelot, "Peuple," *VTB* 979–92.

These figurative descriptions have now become a reality through the preaching of the gospel to the nations. The fact that Peter and Paul divided up the work of evangelization—the former going to the Jews, the latter to the Gentiles (Gal 2:7–8)—does not mean that Israel has been dispossessed of its heritage. Nevertheless, that same heritage now is offered to members of the nation of Israel and to those of every other nation, if they will believe the good news of Jesus Christ. Why have most Jews not come to believe? This is a mystery that Paul himself was the first to agonize over (Rom 9:6–11:24). Those who have not yet believed, he writes, remain "beloved, for the sake of their ancestors" (Rom 11:28), and he expects that ultimately they all will embrace the gospel (Rom 11:23, 26). In the meantime, however, the gospel must be preached to all nations![74]

The New Covenant

It was through the institution of the covenant that Israel became the "people of YHWH" (Exod 24). There was, nevertheless, a continuity between this covenant,[75] which was connected with the gift of the law, and the covenant that the traditions traced back to Abraham and the other patriarchs (Gen 15; 17:1–8). Jesus made specific reference to the covenant to explain the meaning of his death. In the authentic saying preserved in 1 Cor 11:25 and Luke 22:20 Jesus refers directly to the covenant as he circulates the cup among his followers at the Last Supper: the blood he will shed in his passion will be "the blood of the new covenant" (Luke) or "the new covenant in my blood" (1 Corinthians). There is a direct verbal correspondence

---

[74]This is the meaning of Rom 11:15, 28–32. Thus it appears that within the plan of God the Jews are meant to remain a distinct people, with their religion based on the Sinai covenant, until all nations have heard the gospel. But naturally there is a distinction, among the Jews as well as among the nations, between those who welcome the gospel and those who willfully reject it. The gospel is welcomed by a personal act of faith in a salvation that comes by grace, but no one can say how this grace is distributed by God. From the sociological point of view, this welcome can be expressed by an entire people, or by a believing "remnant" that may go unnoticed because of the indifference of the masses.

[75]See the articles on *diathēkē* by J. Behm and G. Quell, "διατίθημι, διαθήκη," *TDNT* 2:104–34; H. Hegermann, "διαθήκη," *EDNT* 1:299–301, and J. Giblet and P. Grelot, "Alliance," *VTB* 28–38.

with an oracle of Jeremiah that speaks of the future of the people of God as the day of the new covenant (Jer 31:31–34). The prophet acknowledges that the covenant has been broken by the people's radical abandonment of the law (Jer 31:32), but he promises that in the future there will be a "new covenant" and that the law will be written on their hearts (Jer 31:32–34). In what Jesus says about the cup he does not mention the law; it is the covenant of which he is the mediator that will seal the relationship between God and humanity. Nevertheless, it does not abolish the law;[76] rather, it re-centers it on the "first commandment" and the "second commandment, which is like it" (Matt 22:34–40; Mark 12:28–34). In Luke's Gospel this second commandment is illustrated by the parable of the Good Samaritan (Luke 10:25–37).

Should we conclude that the Sinai covenant was a "figure" of the new covenant? The term is not quite accurate, since Jesus did not abolish the Sinai covenant by anything he said, nor did he do so by concluding a new covenant in his own blood at the Last Supper. Rather, we should understand that God has been developing a single covenant with humanity throughout the historical dispensation of salvation: from the covenant with Noah to that with Abraham, and from the Sinai covenant with the people of Israel to a universal covenant that was announced in the prophetic texts and finally inaugurated by Jesus. However, this covenant operates on a different basis from a covenant with a people or a nation: it is extended to all people by means of faith in Christ. Thus it would be inaccurate to limit its effects to those who have put their faith in him: it is, by its very nature, a universal gift. Nevertheless, we become conscious of it only through faith in Christ: the gospel is the announcement of this covenant, and its announcement is entrusted to apostles who thus become "ministers" of it (2 Cor 3:6). Through this new covenant God achieves the "reconciliation" of people with himself,[77] and the

---

[76] See P. Grelot, "Loi," *VTB* 667–80. For Paul's thoughts on the law given at Sinai see cols. 677–78.

[77] See L. Roy, "Réconciliation," *VTB* 1075–78. There is a more detailed discussion in P. Grelot, *Péché originel et redemption, examinés à partir de l'épître aux Romains: Essai théologique* (Paris: Desclée, 1973); the seventh chapter (pp. 263–325) is entitled "De l'existence déchirée à l'existence réconciliée" ("from a broken life to a reconciled Life").

message that Jesus entrusted to the apostles makes them ministers of this reconciliation (2 Cor 5:18–20). The reason that a new covenant was needed, beyond the old, was that sin held all people in its grip; their deliverance was "purchased" by the death of Jesus, and that death sealed the new covenant.

No New Testament writing explains this better than does the Epistle to the Hebrews.[78] This letter depicts Jesus as the "mediator" of the new covenant (Heb 9:15), in fulfillment of an oracle from Jer 31:31–34 that is quoted in its entirety in Heb 8:8–12 and again, partially, in Heb 10:16–17. In his explanation of this the author draws a parallel between the ratification ceremony for the Sinai covenant (Heb 9:19–20) and the death of Christ, who shed his blood for us: he offered himself as a sacrifice to "bear the sins of many" (Heb 9:28, quoting Isa 53:12). Juxtaposing biblical references, the author combines an allusion to the ratification ceremony with a reference to the Day of Atonement, when the high priest entered the sanctuary with the blood of the sacrifices (Heb 9:1–10). He does this to argue that Christ has entered into the heavenly sanctuary "with his own blood" to "purify our conscience from dead works" (Heb 9:11–14). Thus the Sinai covenant failed—even though it was operative for a time— because of human sin; this is why Christ "offered his body" (Heb 10:10), thus sanctifying sinners in a way that the rites of the first covenant could not. The shedding of blood, which occurred both at the ratification ceremony (Heb 9:19–20) and on the Day of Atonement (cf. Heb 9:12–13), was the prefiguration of the act by which Christ shed his blood for us.

The former rituals could only bring people "a shadow of the good things to come" (Heb 10:1); it was a "shadow" (*skia*) in comparison with the reality of the salvation that Christ obtained for us. This teaching has to do with the rituals observed under the regime of the former covenant. Like the sanctuary in which they were practiced, they were only reproductions (*antitypa*) (Heb 9:24) and imitative figures (*hypodeigmata*) of a transcendent model (*typos*) (Heb 8:5). The model of the temple existed in heaven (Heb 8:5, cf. Exod

---

[78] The terminology of the Epistle to the Hebrews is not identical to that of the apostle Paul on this point, since it is influenced by Alexandrian allegorism. For the difference between the two terminologies see Grelot, *La Bible, Parole de Dieu*, 265–67.

25:40); the death of Jesus, which took place in history, was the model for the sacrificial rituals. By wiping away sin through his sacrifice, Christ "abolished [*anairei*] the first in order to establish [*stēsē*] the second" (Heb 10:3). This is a reference neither to the Sinai covenant nor to the law in its moral aspect, but only to the rituals in which the Jews had provisionally put their confidence. These rituals were figurative, but the figure was erased by the reality when it finally came: the shadow (*skia*) gave way to the active image (*eikōn*) (Heb 10:1).

Thus we see that those things that the first covenant could not achieve—those things that were promised in the new covenant that Jeremiah announced—were fully accomplished by the death of Jesus Christ and his entry into glory by the resurrection. At the same time, the promises that were still tied to a figurative "economy" were accomplished, in order to bring salvation to humanity.

The Relationship of Christ and the Church

The church is thus the "new humanity" that Christ purchased by his blood during his sojourn here on earth. By his death, Christ "broke down the dividing wall" between the Jews and the people of other nations, and "abolished the law with its commandments and ordinances, that he might create in himself one new humanity in place of the two . . . and might reconcile both groups to God in one body through the cross" (Eph 2:14–16). This body is none other than the body of Christ himself: "in the one Spirit we were all baptized into one body—Jews or Greeks, slaves or free" (1 Cor 12:13), men or women. The church, with the functions that it fulfills in the name of Christ, is nothing other than the body of Christ itself (cf. Rom 12:4–5). This fact could not have been prefigured in the First Testament, because it is not the result only of Christ's coming to earth, but ultimately the fruit of his death and resurrection, both of which were unforeseen.[79]

---

[79] The discussion in 1 Cor 12:12–27 is not simply a development of the analogy attributed to Menenius Agrippa ("the members and the stomach"). The word "body" is used in direct reference to the reception of the body of Christ in the Lord's Supper. This point is made in Grelot, *Péché originel et redemption,* 288, with an important reference to L. Cerfaux, *La Théologie de l'Église suivant saint Paul* (n. 66).

A text in the Epistle to the Ephesians depicts Christ, in passing, as the husband of the church,[80] in order to derive a moral lesson for husbands: "Husbands, love your wives, just as Christ loved
the church and gave himself up for her" (Eph 5:25). Paul did not
create this symbol to reinforce the point he wanted to make, even
though it is a particular emphasis of his (in Col 3:19 he similarly
teaches, "Husbands, love your wives"). Instead, marriage as a
symbol of the covenant relationship between God and his people
goes back to the prophetic corpus (Hos 2:4–23; Jer 2:2; Ezek 16;
Isa 54:1–10). Ezekiel actually uses it to announce that there will be
a new covenant (Ezek 16:59–63). By the time Paul takes up
this same symbol, the new covenant has been inaugurated through
the death of Christ; thus he is able to appeal to it in a homiletical
passage as a conventional theme, without having to explain it.
There is, however, something original in Paul's usage: the image of
the covenant is transferred from God to Christ. It is through
Christ that God has effectively realized his covenant—or, in
symbolic terms, his marriage—with his people. This is not a
new people substituted for the old, but a people renewed by the
grace of salvation and by its extension to all nations. We should not
speak of the prophetic texts just cited as prefigurations in the strict
sense, but they did contain, implicitly, a veiled announcement of
what God would finally achieve through the coming of his Son to
earth. However, the depiction of the people of God, or of their
capital, the city of Jerusalem, as a "bride" was indeed a prefiguration of the church as such. Now that this figure has been "accomplished," it can be applied to the domestic relationship between
husband and wife, a relationship that now constitutes and remains
a very eloquent symbol of the commandment to love that is
expressed here by the verb *agapan*. Is this commandment not
essential to the gospel (cf. 1 Cor 13; Rom 13:8–10), according to
Jesus' own teaching (Mark 12:28–33 and parallels; John 13:14; 15:12,
17; 1 John 3:16)?

The image of marriage as a symbolic representation of the relationship between Christ and the church, which is the new human-

---

[80] See M.-F. Lacan, "Époux, Épouse," *VTB* 366–70, which concludes
with a discussion of the theme in the New Testament.

ity, occupies a significant place at the end of the book of Revelation. In its closing scenes we are beyond time, in the "new heaven and a new earth" (Rev 21:1). "(T)he bride, the wife of the Lamb" (Rev 21:9b), who has "made herself ready" for her marriage (Rev 19:7), is "the holy city Jerusalem coming down out of heaven from God" (Rev 21:10). Here we can recognize an image borrowed from the book of Isaiah (Isa 54:5–10). But as in the Pauline texts, the image of the husband has been transferred from God to the "Lamb as if it had been slain," whom the author shows in his heavenly glory after his resurrection. The figurative character of Jerusalem[81] inspires the image of the city, except that now it is transferred to the "new earth" that will appear at the end of time, in keeping with the eschatological conventions of Jewish apocalypses. The people of God are being envisioned beyond time, after the resurrection of the dead and the Last Judgment (briefly depicted in Rev 20:12–13), thanks to an image that can be applied to the church, into which they are now gathered.

In the meantime, however, the church is locked in a struggle with the powers of evil, symbolized in Revelation as the mythical "beast"[82] who operates on earth through agents such as "the great whore," to whom the author gives the figurative name "Babylon the great, mother of whores and of earth's abominations" (Rev 17:5). It is clear that the author sees Rome the persecutor behind this biblical figure that he develops at length (Rev 17–18). The historical hostility of the Babylonian Empire toward the people of the first covenant thus becomes a prefiguration of this new pagan, persecuting empire. What was true in the time when Revelation was written has remained true throughout the centuries: the church of Christ, in which the plan of God is being fulfilled, has always clashed with human powers that are an earthly incarnation of the empire of evil. It was not by accident that Hitler's regime, which was devoted to the old German paganism, modernized into the "myth of the twentieth century," first attempted to annihilate the Jewish people, with whom the plan of God had begun in history,

---

[81] See M. Join-Lambert and P. Grelot, "Jérusalem," *VTB* 585–92. The entire closing portion of Revelation (Rev 21–22) depicts the marriage of the new Jerusalem and the Lamb, now glorified.

[82] See in ch. 3, "Texts in the New Testament" pp. 95–97.

and then attacked Christianity itself. This was just the latest manifestation, in our own day, of a battle to the death that has been raging since Antiochus Epiphanes in 167–164 B.C.E. and the persecution of Christians in the Roman Empire. And the battle is not over yet, because the gospel has not yet been preached to all people in every nation of the world.

5
Relational Symbols

How can we speak of our relationship with God? It is part of our *interior* experience. God understands this relationship completely, but our understanding of it is partial as best, and is difficult to put into words. Faith can give us some assurances, but the reality lies in a twilight that is difficult to see into. We can speak of our relationship with God only by analogy to our relationships with other people, or perhaps to our relationship with the world, but even these analogies obscure as much as they reveal. Any philosophical definitions that we attempt would necessarily exclude that which we know by experience in the life of faith. How can we describe this experience? The two Testaments are somehow able to do this, but it is important that we recognize the conventions to which their vocabulary is subject. An analogy to relationships between people provides the essential elements of this vocabulary, although the Scriptures often need to move beyond the limits of these relationships in order to suggest the indescribable. Indeed, the analogy ultimately is insufficient because its appeal to various elements drawn from the experience of family and social relationships only serves to underscore the shaky nature of all comparisons between us creatures and our Creator. Thus we will have to pursue our inquiry in two stages. In the First Testament those who believed in the divine revelation were able to respond to God's initiative and enter into a conscious relationship with him. Then Jesus came, within this very framework, but his relationship with God had a new dimension, one that showed the way to the experience of Christian faith, which we will examine in the apostolic writings. The Gospel of John invites us to enter into the same experience as that of Jesus himself when it presents a "rereading" of that experience in light of his identity as the Risen One.

RELATIONSHIP WITH GOD IN THE FIRST TESTAMENT

Is it really proper to speak of the *Old* Testament? From the time that God first revealed himself, even though it may have been only in a preliminary way in the times of the patriarchs and of the Sinai covenant, the relationship that people could have with God *by faith* acquired a form that is still found today within the Christian faith. This is not the arbitrary invention of modern theology; the apostle Paul himself, in the Epistle to the Romans, uses the faith of Abraham as a prototype for the Christian faith (Rom 4:3). Paul says that the promise of salvation that God made to Abraham is a free gift that is available to all those who "share the faith of Abraham," who is the "father of us all" (Rom 4:16). This "faith of Abraham," as it is understood from the Scriptures, was the first expression of an interior experience that continues today in the experience of Christians. But how are we to trace it in the texts? It seems that it is expressed by verbs of relating that describe the search for, or the nearness of, the invisible God, and by expressions that speak of seeing or hearing God. Even though God is beyond such sensory experiences, the texts describe his action within human hearts and thereby enable us to perceive what life can be like with God or near God. A careful consideration of such texts will make clear, bit by bit, what life can be like when it is lived in relationship with God, even if his essential being necessarily remains veiled.

Expressions of Desire

The Search for God

The search for God is a primary aspect of the life of faith in the First Testament.[1] It is particularly emphasized in the calls to prayer

---

[1] See the short article "Chercher" ("Search"), *VTB* 162–65. More extensive information may be found in the articles by Siegfried Wagner, "בָּקַשׁ

that are found throughout Psalms. Thus it is something very close to the experience of Christian faith, given that the prayers of the psalms provided the foundation for the church's prayers. The same theme is found frequently in the prophetic books. Amos says, "Seek the LORD and live" (Amos 5:6), while Hosea says, "It is time to seek the LORD" (Hos 10:12) (the verb is *darash* in both cases). Isaiah complains about the people of Judah, "They do not seek the LORD" (Isa 9:13). In the "Message of Consolation" we hear, "Listen to me . . . you that seek the LORD" (Isa 51:1 [with the verb *biqqesh*]). In the apocalypse of Isaiah we find this double formulation: "My soul yearns for you in the night; my spirit within me earnestly seeks you" (Isa 26:9 [with the verbs *'awwi* and *shakhar* in the Piel]).

We may now consider the prayers in Psalms. The search for the Lord, with the same two verbs *darash* and *biqqesh,* is mentioned seventeen times, with certain variations in which it is God's commandments or precepts that are sought (Ps 119:82, 94, 123). The idea recurs in Wisdom of Solomon (which was written in Greek) with the verb *zētein,* both in the sense of seeking God (Wis 1:1; 13:6) and in the sense of seeking the personified Wisdom of God (Wis 6:12; 8:2, 18), which ultimately amounts to the same thing. In short, seeking God is an essential aspect of religious faith. But how can we actually "seek" God, whose presence must necessarily be disclosed only to our sensibilities and our understanding? The expression is not, strictly speaking, a symbol, but it does transfer to our interior experience an activity that we usually pursue with regard to the objects and people of this world.

Waiting for God

The same thing may be said about waiting for God. In the Psalter the verb most frequently used to render the idea of "waiting" in general is the root *qawah* (22x in the Qal; 3x in the Piel). A survey of the Psalter reveals that the verb is used 11 times in the Piel and 2 times in the Qal to say that one is waiting specifically for the Lord—for example, "Wait for the LORD, be strong, and let your heart take courage" (Ps 27:14), and "I waited patiently for the LORD" (Ps 40:1

---

biqqēsh בַּקָּשָׁה *baqqāshāh,*" *TDOT* 2:229–41 and "דָּרַשׁ *dārash* מִדְרָשׁ *midhrāsh*" in *TDOT* 3:297–207 which provide bibliographies for the First Testament.

[using the infinitive-indicative construction]). But in what does this waiting consist, and how might God manifest his presence or his intervention? The *Bible de Jérusalem,* in all of its editions, uses the word *espérer* ("hope"). Psalm 40 constitutes a cry for help, which God answers by "inclining" to the one who is calling out to him. But whether we think of it as "waiting" or as "hoping," the action in view here is that of turning to God to ask for a favor or for help. In Ps 130:5–7 the verb *qiwwah* is used in parallel with *kholel;* these verbs typically are translated by "wait" and "hope," respectively. What the psalmist is waiting or hoping for is not God himself, but rather the manifestation of his activity. The psalm continues, "For with the LORD there is steadfast love, and with him is great power to redeem [*pedut*]" (Ps 130:7b). The Greek version of this psalm uses a term that will become part of the vocabulary of redemption in the New Testament (*lytrōsis* in Luke 1:68; 2:38; *lytron* in Mark 10:45; Matt 20:28). Waiting hopefully presumes that one has a relationship with God that is rooted in faith, even if that faith itself may not see everything with perfect clarity.

Seeing God and Being Seen by God

The verbs "seek" and "wait" are not, properly speaking, reciprocal: they apply only to the state of people before God; they are verbs of "desire." By contrast, the verb "see"[2] can be applied both to people and to God. Nevertheless, if we limit its meaning to that of our ordinary experience, we cannot apply it to God in the same way that we apply it to ourselves.

It is self-evident to suggest that God "sees," but even this is actually an understatement, since God, by his very nature, sees everything, unlike the idols, who "have eyes but do not see," in the words of the classic taunt that appears in Ps 115:5 and elsewhere. Nevertheless, the ancient biblical traditions make use of this verb as an anthropomorphism to highlight God's omniscience. Thus we read in Gen 11:5, God "came down to see" what people were doing in building the tower of Babel (cf. Gen 18:21). We encounter the same

---

[2] See the article "Voir" ("See") in *VTB,* and the articles (with bibliographies) by A. Jepson, "חָזָה *chāzāh,*" *TDOT* 4:280–90 and by H. F. Fuhs, "רָאָה *rā'âh,*" *TDOT* 13:208–42.

thing in some of the stories in Exodus (e.g., Exod 2:25; 3:7, 9; 4:31). In other cases, God himself says, "I have seen this people" (Deut 9:13). The psalmists frequently implore God to see their condition; although we usually translate the underlying Hebrew word as "consider" in these contexts, it is the same verb *ra'ah:* "See my affliction and my trouble" (Ps 25:18).

Can this verb *ra'ah,* or its synonyms such as *khazah,* be applied to people who see something of God? We need to distinguish between two cases, that of prophetic vision or something similar, and that of ordinary sight, for which the verb is used in a general sense. Should we call ancient vision-narratives "prophetic" when they speak of seeing God (or the "angel of God")? We may, if we wish to emphasize the way in which their authors depicted their ancestors' familiarity with God. In that case, we may find such visions in Genesis, such as Jacob's at Bethel (Gen 28:10–19), although it was in a dream, and at Penuel, where he said, "I have seen God face to face, and yet my life is preserved" (Gen 32:30). But in Exodus, when Moses said to God, "Let me see your glory," God replied, "you cannot see my face; for no one shall see me and live" (Exod 33:18–20). However, when we hear that Balaam's donkey saw the angel of YHWH on the road (Num 22:23), we realize that we are reading a fable. Even the cases of Judg 6:22–23 and 13:22 must be appreciated according to the conventions of legends that have been preserved with the goal of edification but cannot critically be considered history.

The case is entirely different with the calling of prophets and the narratives that describe their experience of calling. Prophets are not mystics who derive personal satisfaction from their visions; rather, they receive visions because they have a mission to fulfill and a message to convey. Let us consider several significant cases.[3]

The calling of Isaiah is a characteristic example. It is dated: "In the year that King Uzziah died, I saw the LORD sitting on a throne, high and lofty" (Isa 6:1). The rest of the vision describes the heavenly worship of God, who is depicted in royal imagery. However, the vision has a specific goal—to commission the prophet—and so his lips are purified, so that he can proclaim the word of God (Isa 6:6–13). The narrative in 1 Kgs 22:17 similarly presents a vision of

---

[3] See in ch. 2 "Corporeal Representations of God" (p. 28).

Micaiah son of Imlah: "I saw all Israel scattered on the mountains," but YHWH manifests himself only through a spoken word (1 Kgs 22:17b). The calling of Jeremiah (Jer 1:4–19) is related essentially in terms of God's words, but we see from the way Jeremiah describes what happened—"the LORD put out his hand and touched my mouth" (Jer 1:9)—that he was having a vision. The rest of the account explains that Jeremiah then saw symbolic objects that conveyed a message: the branch of an almond tree and a boiling pot that tilted away from the north (Jer 1:11–16). However, it was no longer God himself who was being seen.

The opening vision in Ezekiel (Ezek 1:4–28) has all the appearances of being a literary development of the vision in Ezek 10:1–5, 18–21 (these last verses being a secondary addition). But to what extent does the detailed description of the "divine chariot" in Ezek 1 correspond to an actual vision? Ezekiel speaks like a poet who wants to suggest the presence of an indescribable God ("this was the appearance of the likeness of the glory of the LORD" [Ezek 1:28]): the presence of God lies beyond anything that can be said about it.[4] Nevertheless, Ezekiel describes himself as having visions: the Spirit carries him away to the temple in Jerusalem to see the sins that are being committed there and the punishment that will result (Ezek 8:1–11:12). But how much of what we read in these chapters represents literary license? It is clear, for example, that the "vision" of the dry bones in Ezek 37:1–14 is a literary construction. May the case not be the same for the visions that are described at length in Ezek 40–48? These include a "vision" of the Lord returning to the temple (Ezek 43:4–9).

Thus Ezekiel thus prepares the way for a literary genre in which the interpreted vision plays an essential role in expressing the prophetic message. Zechariah, after the return from the Babylonian exile, makes frequent use of this device (Zech 1:7–6:8): his eight "visions" communicate his message. This had already been the case much earlier with the five visions of Amos (Amos 7:1–8:8; 9:1–4); but three of them, we should note, say that the prophet saw the Lord

---

[4] See my detailed study of this first chapter of Ezekiel, "L'imagerie des quatre Vivants," in *Études sémitiques et samaritaines offertes à Jean Margain* (ed. C.-B. Amphoux, A. Frey, and U. Schatter-Rieser; HTB 4; Lausanne: Zèbre, 1999), 241–50.

himself in action (Amos 7:4, 7; 9:1). Since these vision reports serve to convey a message, it is difficult to say exactly how the prophet saw God. The role of literary convention is clearer in the book of Daniel, in the case of its dream reports (Dan 2; 4) and the visions that are described and explained in Dan 7; 8; 10:1–12:4. In these apocalyptic chapters the role of literary fiction is evident, as it is in the passages in the book of *Enoch* that make use of the same convention. Outside of Isaiah and a few passages in Jeremiah and Ezekiel, however, it is rarely the case that God himself is seen: the expressions that Ezekiel uses show that God is above anything that human language can say about him. On the other hand, it is clear that God knows and sees everything that people do, whether good or evil. God's presence is on a level other than that of earthy and cosmic realities.

Hearing God and Being Heard by God

Within the symbolic language that is being used, God, by definition, hears people's voices (Gen 21:17), their groaning (Exod 2:24), their murmuring (Exod 16:7), their cries (Exod 22:23), their words (Deut 1:34), their complaining (Num 11:1), and so forth.[5] Since this is simply a given of the faith, it is not surprising to see repeated references in Psalms to the Lord, who "has heard" such and such a prayer (e.g., Ps 6:8–9; 18:6), as well as appeals to God to "listen" (e.g., Ps 4:1; 17:1, 6; 27:7). Hearing and listening are expressed by the same Hebrew verb *shama'*. In Greek the verb most often used is *akouō*. Hence the urgent prayers "Hear, O LORD, when I cry aloud" (Ps 27:7) and "Give ear, O Shepherd of Israel!" (Ps 80:1).

But the people of God, for their part, are urged to listen: "Hear, O my people, while I admonish you!" (Ps 81:8). The people who receive the word of God must "listen" and "hear" just as they want God to. But how does the word of God come to them? By the voice of his messengers, Moses and the prophets. Thus we find the verb *shama'* repeatedly in the book of Deuteronomy. We are familiar with the text that became a profession of faith for the nation of Israel and

---

[5] See C. Augrain's article "Écouter" ("Listen"), *VTB* 309–10, which gives the principal references; in the same volume the article "Entendre" ("Hear") refers back to it. For the Hebrew see U. Rüterswörden, "Shama'," *ThWAT* 8:255–79.

later for the Jewish people: "Hear, O Israel: the LORD is our God, the LORD alone" (Deut 6:4). The verb is used just as frequently when the word of God comes to Israel through the prophets. This explains the frequency in Jeremiah, for example, of the exhortation "Hear the word of the LORD" (e.g., Jer 2:4; cf. 3:13; 5:21; 11:2, 4; 13:15; 17:20). However, even though the prophet repeats this exhortation over and over again, it does not achieve its goal: "I warned . . . them persistently, . . . saying, 'obey my voice.' Yet they did not obey or incline their ear" (Jer 11:7–8). As a result, God tells the people through Jeremiah, "I will not listen when they call to me" (Jer 11:14). Thus it is not so much a dialogue that we find throughout the book of Jeremiah as a refusal to dialogue. This sums up the history of Israel, a history characterized throughout by the preaching of the word of God as an appeal and as a threat, but also as a promise.

As the prophet looks farther ahead to the future, he becomes even more insistent and speaks to the nations themselves to announce the fulfillment of God's plans: "Hear the word of the LORD, O nations . . . 'He who scattered Israel will gather him' " (Jer 31:10). But will the nations hear this proclamation any better than did Israel, which did not listen to the voice of its Lord? The entire drama of Israel's history turns on this question, which Isaiah summarizes in a phrase spoken in the name of God himself: " 'Keep listening, but do not comprehend; keep looking, but do not understand.' Make the mind of this people dull. . . ." (Isa 6:9–10). The problem of hardened hearts recurs with such frequency that Jesus takes up Isaiah's phrase to describe the situation of his own hearers (Matt 13:14–15 and parallels). Listening, hearing and understanding, recognizing the voice of God when he speaks—this is the perpetual difficulty, because our hearts are hardened.

Being Thirsty

There is a bodily thirst, such as Israel suffered in the desert (Exod 17:3; Deut 8:15), but there is also another kind of thirst: the thirst for God.[6] "I will send a famine on the land; not a famine of

---

[6] See D. Kellermann, "צָמֵא *sāmē*," *TDOT* 12:405–9, an article that also discusses Semitic parallels. For the Greek see J. Behm and G Bertram, "διψάω, δίψος," *TDNT* 2:226–29, which indicates the principal passages in the Septuagint.

bread, or a thirst for water, but of hearing the words of the LORD" (Amos 8:11). Should we understand this oracle as a threat or as a promise? However we understand this particular oracle, the psalmists take up the same theme in a very positive sense: "My soul thirsts for God, for the living God" (Ps 42:2). The psalmist, a Levite, is bemoaning the fact in exile he is far from the temple: God is far away, and for that reason he thirsts for God. The mystics later would describe the same kind of spiritual "desert" experiences that the psalmists knew: "O God, you are my God, I seek you, my soul thirsts for you; my flesh faints for you, as in a dry and weary land where there is no water" (Ps 63:1). This is an extreme expression of desire. In the book of Sirach it is divine Wisdom that creates this kind of inner desire: "Come to me, you who desire me. . . . Those who eat of me will hunger for more, and those who drink of me will thirst for more" (Sir 24:19, 21). Would not Jesus Christ himself come and satisfy such desires?

Loving

"Love" is the supreme relational verb.[7] We understand love first from relationships between people. In Hebrew the verb *'ahav* is by far the one used most frequently to speak of love; the most usual Greek translation is *agapan*. The Hebrew noun for love, *'ahavah,* is most often translated by *agapē* in the Septuagint. But do the verb and the noun have exactly the same nuance, when they describe the unequal relationship between people and God, as when they describe the relationship between two people? When we speak of God loving, it is not a case of pure symbolism, but we should recognize that the love of God for people is not of the same order as that of people who are responding to God's love. We should always emphasize the fact that the initiative in love is God's. Is not even the desire that people feel for God the expression of a prior attraction that has come from God himself? In short, love is an unequal relationship in which God always has the initiative.

---

[7] See C. Spicq, *Agapè: Prolégomènes à une etude de théologie néo-testamentaire* (StudHel 10; Louvain: E. Nauwelaerts, 1955), and Spicq's subsequent work *Agapè dans le Nouveau Testament: Analyse des textes* (3 vols.; Études bibliques; Paris: Gabalda, 1958–1959). On the theme of love see above in ch. 2 "God's Emotions" (pp. 36–37).

In the First Testament the earliest traditions do not yet speak of this initiative of God toward Israel. The verb has a weaker sense in passages such as 2 Sam 12:24–25, which says that "the LORD loved Solomon" and that the prophet Nathan gave him the name "beloved of YHWH." Here "love" signifies favor and goodwill. The theme of love in the stronger sense is actually first introduced in the prophetic corpus by Hosea, who uses a rarer verb, *rakhem* in the Piel, which indicates "pity" and "mercy" that are inspired by a tender love; the Greek correctly translates this with *elein* (Hos 1:6, 7; 2:4, 23 [2:6, 25 MT]). In the course of the allegory in which marriage becomes the symbol of the covenant that God has made with his people (Hos 2), this verb appears in Hos 2:4, 23 (2:6, 25 MT), and a word derived from it appears in Hos 2:19 (2:21 MT). It is associated with *khesed* to proclaim the "mercy" of God in the new covenant. It is actually the "lovers" of the adulterous wife (the false gods that Israel served) who are named here with the root *'ahav.* This same verb is used in a more typical way, however, in Hos 3:1 to show the paradoxical love that God still has for his people. Here the prophet is an allegorical representative of God himself: "The LORD said to me again, 'Go, love a woman who is loved by another[8] and is an adulteress, just as the LORD loves the people of Israel, though they turn to other gods." Here it is clear that God's love for his people is being described by the usual verb, *'ahav.*[9]

Hosea's symbolic marriage is a figure for the covenant that God has made with an unfaithful people. In the same way, the passage that compares Israel to a son whom God has "called out of Egypt" (Hos 11:1–6) says that God led Israel with "bands of love [*'ahavah*]." Thus love can be used very effectively to characterize God's relationship with his people, since he loves them no matter what. However, the term is not so accurate for the people's relationship with God, since they keep having adulterous affairs. When such infidelities happen, can God's love turn to hate? This is precisely what is said in Hos 9:15 and Jer 12:8, if we take the verb *sane'* literally (but we should bear in mind that in Mal 2:16 God, using this same verb, says that he hates divorce!). We need to take into account a linguistic fact that bears on how we should interpret this expression: Hebrew has

---

[8] The NRSV reads "who has a lover," but this translation is in keeping with the internal logic of the text.

[9] See above, (pp. 30–32, 36–37).

no word for any feeling between "love" and "hate." In our own language we would say that while God does not hate anyone, God can only feel a strong aversion toward evil conduct.

What does God expect of his people in return for his love? Obedience to his commandments and faithfulness to his covenant. This is already clear from the allegory in Hosea, but it is perhaps in Deuteronomy that the point is made with the greatest insistence. It reminds the people how God has loved them from the start: "the LORD set his heart in love on your ancestors alone" (Deut 10:15; cf. 23:5). But in response, the command to love God is heard repeatedly, beginning with the text that became the fundamental profession of faith for the Jews: "Hear, O Israel: the LORD is our God, the LORD alone. You shall love the LORD your God with all your heart, and with all your soul, and with all your might" (Deut 6:4–5). The same expression recurs, directly or indirectly, 10 more times in the same book. It is also found in Josh 22:5; 23:11, in Jer 31:3, 20, and frequently in Psalms (Ps 18:1; 31:23; 97:10; 116:1; 12x in Ps 119) in reference to God's commandments. It is also found a dozen times in Sirach and Wisdom of Solomon.

This brief survey is sufficient to show that in the First Testament God's love for people through the vehicle of the chosen nation, and the commandment for all people to love God in return, are expressly in evidence. It is therefore absurd to contrast a First Testament "law of fear" with a New Testament "law of love," as a strange ignorance of the Scriptures has led some to do. The conclusion we must draw from our survey is that God's love for people, which was shown first toward those he whom chose to be the original repository of his revelation, is of an absolutely unconditional character, while the love that God has received in return has been much more unreliable and has been spoiled by multiple infidelities. However, we also know that the end of the story has not yet been written, and that love will triumph in the end.

Symbolic Descriptions of the Relationship with God

The human relationship with God, particularly among the chosen people, often is described by expressions that go unnoticed in a cursory reading of the Scriptures because of the simple language that they employ: "to be with" or "to be near." A brief investigation will enable us to pick out several texts in which the relationship with God is described in this way. Such phrases can be considered metaphorical, because clearly they are not intended to be understood literally. But perhaps it would be better to describe them as specific way of suggesting symbolically what the relationship with God is like.

Being with God

The use of the Hebrew particle *'im* ("with"), translated in Greek by *meta* (or, less often, by *syn*), almost goes unnoticed in the phrases where it occurs. However, we should pay particular attention to this particle when it precedes the word "God," because it then points to the existence of a relationship with God and tells us something highly significant about those who are in such a relationship. We first encounter this construction in one of the most ancient passages in Genesis. In the list of the patriarchs who lived before the flood, only one is described as righteous, the seventh: "Enoch walked with God. . . . all the days of Enoch were three hundred sixty-five years. Enoch walked with God; then he was no more, because God took him" (Gen 5:22–24). The verb "walked" refers here to the manner in which he conducted his life. This brief notice probably is a summary of a much longer legend.[10] The number of years that he lived is the same as the number of days in a solar year, which is a sign of his perfection. This legend was elaborated at length in the priestly circles that produced the sacred history to which Gen 6 belongs. A "Book of Enoch," written in Aramaic, was found among the writings of the priests at Qumran. The important thing for us to note here, however, is that Enoch's exemplary personal conduct is described by the phrase "he walked *with* God."

In the ancient traditions of Israel, preserved in the books from Genesis through Kings, the presence of God beside those whom he loves and helps is indicated by the expression "to be with." God

---

[10] See my article "La légend d'Hénoch dans les Apocryphes et dans la Bible," *RSR* 46 (1958): 5–16, 181–210. This study shows that the legend of Enoch, which is the subject of only a brief allusion in Genesis, contains many elements borrowed from Mesopotamia and connected with the solar cult there. This explains why the biblical patriarch is said to have lived 365 years.

promises Isaac, "I am the God of your father Abraham; do not be afraid, for I am with you" (Gen 26:24). Similar expressions are found in, for example, Gen 26:28; 28:15; 31:5; 39:2 (with the particle *'et*); 48:21; Exod 3:12. The customary blessing is "May YHWH be with you" (e.g., Exod 10:10), and the characteristic divine promise is "I will be with you" (e.g., Deut 31:23; Josh 1:5). This is a promise of God's presence. It recurs in the prophetic books. In Isa 7:14 the child whose birth will be a sign represents such promise that it is said he will be named Immanuel, meaning "God-with-us." Similarly, the promise that God will help the people when their enemies invade "Immanuel's land" is expressed in the words "God is with us" (Isa 8:10). The same expression is found in Jeremiah (Jer 1:8; 15:20; 30:11; 46:28 [always with the preposition *'et*]), in Amos 5:14; Ezek 34:30; Hag 1:13; 2:4, and with the preposition *'im* in Psalms (Ps 46:7 [46:8 MT]; 91:15). God's presence is the source of confidence in difficulty (Ps 23:4; 54:4). Psalm 73, which takes up the problem of evil, culminates in this declaration: "Nevertheless I am continually with you. . . . Whom have I in heaven but you? And there is nothing on earth that I desire other than you" (Ps 73:23, 25). In short, "being with God" is a unique source of confidence, joy, and desire because it is also an essential rule of conduct.

Acting in God's Presence

This expression is obviously metaphorical, since the presence of God is universal. However, the language makes use of this metaphor in order to insist that God is nearby[11] when deeds are carried out solely with God in mind and when faith thus makes the believer fully aware that God is looking on. Two Hebrew expressions are used in this case: *qadam*[12] and *lifney*[13] (which means literally "before the face of"). The former refers more to the nearness of God, while

---

[11] The "proximity" of God is indicated by the adjective *qarob,* "nearby," derived from the root *qarab.* See R. E. Gane and J. Milgrom, "קרב *qārab,*" *TDOT* 13:135–48, which includes a bibliography.

[12] See T. Kronhold, "קדם *qādam,*" *TDOT* 12:511–15, which includes a bibliography.

[13] The article by H. Simian-Yofre, "פנים *pānîm,*" *TDOT* 11:589–615 includes a section dedicated to the semi-prepositions *lifney, 'al-peney, mippeney* (pp. 608–14). The usage and meaning of each of these terms is analyzed by H. Simian-Yofre.

the latter indicates the presence of a witness to the deeds that people are performing.

Let us consider several examples of the first case. In the Message of Consolation we hear, "I will bring near my deliverance swiftly, my salvation has gone out" (Isa 51:5). This is a promise of the nearness of God. Thus we hear shortly afterwards, "Seek the LORD while he may be found, call upon him while he is near" (Isa 55:6). The Servant of YHWH is able to say, "He who vindicates me is near" (Isa 50:8). Deuteronomy assures the believer, in order to invite obedience, "the word is very near to you; it is in your mouth and in your heart" (Deut 30:14). The psalmists speak in the same way of their spiritual experience: "the LORD is near to the brokenhearted" (Ps 34:18); "Surely his salvation is at hand for those who fear him" (Ps 85:9); "Yet you are near, O LORD, and all your commandments are true" (Ps 119:151); "the LORD is near to all who call on him" (Ps 145:18). Even if these are standard formulas, they express a sentiment shared by all who pray.

Now let us consider some cases where people are aware of being in God's presence. We read in Exodus that Moses spoke "to the LORD" (Exod 6:12) and that the people "drew near to the LORD" (Exod 16:9). Leviticus specifies repeatedly that cultic acts are to be performed "before the face of the LORD" (*lifney*, used characteristically for rituals). The formula recurs in Deuteronomy, but there it is applied to other kinds of acts as well: the people "stood before the LORD" (Deut 4:10), they "wept before the LORD" (Deut 1:45), they are to "rejoice before the LORD" (Deut 12:12), and it is "before the LORD" that they are to carry out all of the liturgical acts described in the book, such as eating the meat of sacrifices (Deut 12:18) and other sacred meals (Deut 14:23, 26) and celebrating the liturgical festivals (Deut 15:20; 16:11). It is "before the LORD" that the Levites carry out their duties (Deut 18:7) and that trials are conducted (Deut 19:17). All acts of generosity are done "before the LORD" (Deut 24:13), while acts that defile are "abhorrent before the LORD" (Deut 24:4). Finally, it is "before the LORD your God" that Israelites are to make a profession of faith when offering the firstfruits of the harvest (Deut 26:5–10).

The expression is found less often in the prophetic books, as in Isa 9:3, "they rejoice before you." However, it does occur somewhat frequently in Psalms. Regarding God's judgment, we hear, "Rise up, O LORD! Do not let mortals prevail; let the nations be judged before you" (Ps 9:19). The experience of crying out to God is described in these terms first by David: "In my distress I called upon the LORD; to my God I cried for help" (Ps 18:6); and then by the psalmist who is praising the law of God: "Let my cry come before you, O LORD; give me understanding according to your word" (Ps 119:169). Another psalmist's testimony says, "you have upheld me because of my integrity, and set me in your presence forever" (Ps 41:12). In a prayer for the king one of the petitions asks, "May he be enthroned forever before God" (Ps 61:7). In Psalm 68, whose internal logic is sometimes difficult to follow, we hear, "let the righteous be joyful; let them exult before God" (Ps 68:3), and, "the heavens poured down rain at the presence of God" (Ps 68:8). God the judge is described in similar language: "Then shall all the trees of the forest sing for joy before the LORD; for he is coming, for he is coming to judge the earth" (Ps 96:12–13); "let the hills sing together for joy at the presence of the LORD, for he is coming to judge the earth" (Ps 98:8–9). Finally, in the long psalm that praises the law we hear, "Let my supplication come before you; deliver me according to your promise" (Ps 119:170).

Thus the believing Israelite was aware of being in the presence of God at all times, and particularly during prayer and on occasions of worship. We need to appreciate that it is only in a certain sense that someone can be in or out of God's presence, because that presence is universal. Nevertheless, this is one way to express a relationship with God, by analogy to the relationship one has with other people. Eventually these believers would invite all of creation to enter into this relationship, as in Ps 148. Human beings, however, remain the praying voice within creation.

JESUS THE JEW AND OUR RELATIONSHIP WITH GOD

We have a record of Jesus' inner life only in the Gospels. They show that Jesus was very cautious about what he confided to others. For example, he customarily went off by himself in order to pray (Mark 6:46; Matt 14:23; Luke 9:28; cf. John 6:15). We see this particularly in Gethsemane after the Last Supper (Mark 14:36; Matt 26:36,

39, 42; Luke 22:41, 44). As a result, the words of very few of his prayers have been preserved. Nevertheless, we are sure that when he spoke to God, it was with an unprecedented intimacy. He did not say, as was customary in Judaism before him, "Our Father," but simply "Father"[14] (Matt 11:25–26 = Luke 10:21; Mark 14:36, where the Greek word *Patēr* is accompanied by the original Aramaic *'Abba*). The same formula is preserved in Greek in Luke, in Jesus' prayer from the cross (Luke 23:34, 46), and in two prayers quoted in John (John 11:41; 17:1, 5, 11, 21, 24, 25). It is true that in John's Gospel all of Jesus' words are being reread and recomposed after the fact in order to express the theological reflections of the evangelist. This is why, in that Gospel, as controversies between Jesus and the Jewish leadership are being described, the title "Father" frequently is given to God, and the title "Son" to Jesus. Is this significant in light of the verbs whose use we noted and the relational expressions we considered in the texts of the First Testament?

Expressions of Desire

Because Jesus likely studied the Scriptures in the synagogue school at Nazareth and heard them read and preached each week as he was growing up, it is entirely appropriate for us to look for echoes of the verbs of "desire" that we highlighted in the texts of the First Testament in his sayings and in the conduct of his life. At the same time, however, we must consider what the Gospel texts say about Jesus' contemporaries' attitude toward him, as this is also significant for the present inquiry.

Seeking

The title of this section intentionally does not limit its content to the search for God.[15] In effect, Jesus was familiar with all of the texts in the prophets and the psalms that bear on this theme, and in the case of the psalms, he had prayed them with other Jews in the synagogue. He knew them from birth, and as he grew in "wisdom

---

[14] On "Father" and "Son" see above, pp. 47–49, 127–28).

[15] The essential references are in P.-M. Galopin and J. Guillet, "Chercher," *VTB* 162–65. For this theme in the First Testament see above, p. 150).

and in years, and in divine and human favor" (Luke 2:52), he was raised as a "seeker of God." Thus this is a point that the Gospel traditions do not need to insist on.

The Synoptic Gospels. Here we never read about Jesus seeking for something, but he clearly told his hearers that they should seek (the verb is *zētein*). In Matthew his teachings in this regard are summed up in one statement: "But strive first for the kingdom of God and his righteousness, and all these things will be given to you as well" (Matt 6:33). This conclusion comes after a warning against excessive concern over the material things of life (Matt 6:25–32) and an invitation to trust in God's providence. The parallel text in Luke (Luke 12:22–31) puts a similar emphasis on confidence in God's providence to supply one's material needs in life: "For it is the nations of the world that strive after [*epizētousin*] all these things, and your Father knows that you need them. Instead, strive for his kingdom, and these things will be given to you as well" (Luke 12:30–31). The "kingdom of God" and the "righteousness of God"— these are the essential things to have, and it is God who gives them. To seek them is to seek God himself. This is why it is said, "Search, and you will find; knock, and the door will be opened for you. . . . If you, then, who are evil, know how to give good gifts to your children, how much more will your Father in heaven give good things to those who ask him!" (Matt 7:7, 11).

Some of the parables illustrate this search for God, his kingdom, and his righteousness. For example, there is the parable of the merchant who is in search of fine pearls: when he finds a pearl of great value, he sells all that he has in order to buy it (Matt 13:45–46). The kingdom of heaven is this fine pearl. However, the parable of the woman who searches throughout her house for a coin that she has lost (Luke 15:8–10) has an entirely different meaning. This time it is the lost sinner, represented by the missing drachma, who is being sought. The woman rejoices when she finds it, in the same way that "there is joy in the presence of the angels of God over one sinner who repents." People should indeed seek God, but it is God himself who has first begun to seek them, because the tendency to go astray has brought evil and its troubles into their lives. So how does God go about seeking us? The parable of the Father and the Two Sons enables us to appreciate one aspect of the way in which God does this: the father, who symbolizes God, waits patiently until his son's experiences of failure and suffering bring him back home, and then the father welcomes his son with open arms (Luke 15:11–32). But there is more to the reality of God seeking us than this parable discloses, because God did not await the return of his sinful children without doing anything; instead, he sent his own Son to earth to bring us back onto the right path. The whole story of the gospel can be seen to underlie this simple tale.[16]

It is actually John (to whose Gospel we will turn shortly) who shows best how Jesus, who was sent by the Father, came seeking sinners. He did not do this on his own initiative, because, as he said, "I seek to do not my own will but the will of him who sent me" (John 5:30). "My food," he said elsewhere, allegorically, "is to do the will of him who sent me" (John 4:34). The way in which his life ended showed, paradoxically, what that will was. A phrase from the Gospel of Luke summarizes it succinctly: "the Son of Man came to seek out and to save the lost" (Luke 19:10). But how was that to be done? On this point, the four Gospels agree. The Son, who was sent by the Father, ran into resolute opposition to his mission. On Jesus' final visit to Jerusalem, while he spent each day teaching in the temple, "(t)he chief priests, the scribes and the leaders of the people keep looking for a way to kill him" (Luke 19:47). This is not what the crowds wanted; as Matthew notes, after relating the parable of the murderous tenants in the vineyard, which the Jewish authorities realized that Jesus had told against them, "(t)hey wanted to arrest him, but they feared the crowds, because they regarded him as a prophet" (Matt 21:46). Mark notes this same design in several places: "they kept looking for a way to kill him" (Mark 11:18); "They wanted to arrest him" (Mark 12:12). Matthew writes similarly that Judas "began to look for an opportunity to betray him" (Matt 26:16), and Luke makes similar observations on three occasions (Luke 19:47; 20:19; 22:2).

John's Gospel. It is here that the conflict between Jesus and his opponents is presented most insistently. This Gospel describes Jesus

---

[16] I discuss this question in *Jésus de Nazareth, Christ et Seigneur: Une lecture de l'Évangile* (2 vols.; LD 167, 170; Paris: Cerf, 1997–1998), 1:370–74 (see especially p. 373). We can see Jesus' practical conduct reflected in that of the father in the parable, but we should not identify Jesus with any of its characters.

going to Jerusalem not just once for a final Passover, but on several occasions: for an unnamed festival (John 5), for the Feast of Tabernacles (John 7–9), for the Feast of Dedication (John 10), and for the final Passover (John 12). And on each occasion the evangelist notes that Jesus' opponents "were seeking all the more to kill him" (John 5:18), "tried to arrest him" (John 7:30), and "tried to arrest him again" (John 10:39), until they concluded definitively, "You do not understand that it is better for you to have one man die for the people than to have the whole nation destroyed" (John 11:50).

From that point the conflict proceeds to its climax. The Sanhedrin—or at least the part of it loyal to Caiaphas, the high priest—takes charge of operations. Guided by the apostate disciple who has "betrayed" Jesus, a small armed band comes to arrest him in the Garden of Gethsemane. The exchange is well known: Jesus asks, "Whom are you looking for?" They reply, "Jesus of Nazareth." Jesus answers, "I am he. . . . If you are looking for me, let these men go" (John 18:4–7). Jesus did not seek to flee.

Jesus' last prayer is also well known, which was his prayer at the Last Supper, and on the cross, and in eternity:[17] "Father, the hour has come; glorify your Son so that the Son may glorify you, since you have given him authority over all people, to give eternal life to all whom you have given him" (John 17:1–2). Thus Jesus sought not his own glory, but that of the one who sent him (John 7:18). And that glory was obtained, paradoxically, by his death on the cross.

Waiting

Here we will look at those texts in the Gospels that offer Greek renderings of the Hebrew verb *qawah,* which we examined earlier. While these texts are not numerous, they clearly have to do with a hope based on the prophetic promises.

There are, first of all, three passages unique to Luke in which contemporaries of Jesus are said to have been inspired by this hope. In the infancy narratives the aged Simeon is said to have been "looking forward to for the consolation of Israel" (Luke 2:25). After Jesus' death on the cross, two men went to Pilate to ask for his body so that

---

[17] See Grelot, *Jésus de Nazareth, Christ et Seigneur,* 2:253–61 (especially pp. 254–55).

they could bury it; Luke mentions only one of them, Joseph of Arimathea, but specifies that he was "waiting expectantly for the kingdom of God" (Luke 23:51). John describes him as a secret disciple of Jesus (John 19:38) and explains that Nicodemus accompanied him. Clearly he was among those who were inspired by the Jewish hope that was founded on the Scriptures. He was not like the servant in the parable who took advantage of his master's absence to mistreat his fellow servants, and whose master returned on a day when he was not expecting him (Matt 24:50)! In short, the Jews were divided about Jesus, but there were always some who were waiting for him (Luke 8:40).

This was because his words and actions necessarily made people of goodwill wonder whether he was the fulfillment of their hopes, and he could only encourage them. He had them in mind when he told the parable about the servants who were awaiting the return of their master: "be like those who are waiting for their master to return from the wedding banquet, so that they may open the door for him as soon as he comes and knocks. Blessed are those servants" (Luke 12:36–37). John the Baptist and his disciples were among them. This is why the disciples of John came to Jesus and asked, "Are you the one who is to come, or are we to wait for another?" (Matt 11:3 = Luke 7:19–20). "The one who is to come" is a clear allusion to the prophetic promises that predicted the Messiah. Jesus was indeed the one whom Israel was waiting for, but his mission as the Messiah would be accomplished in a way entirely different from the one that the Scriptures appeared to indicate.[18] There are surprises in the realization of God's plan!

"Seeing": What and How?

The verb "see" can refer to two very different kinds of perception: ordinary sight and supernatural vision. Both are mentioned in the Gospel texts, and both have their place in the revelation of which Jesus is the mediator. But we will not be considering those cases where the idea of seeing is used in a metaphorical sense, as when Jesus, contradicted by Peter when he first announced his imminent sufferings and death, rebuked him by saying, "you are setting your

---

[18] See in ch. 4 "Messiah of Israel" (pp. 126–27).

mind not on divine things but on human things" (Mark 8:33 = Matt 16:23 [with the notion of "envisioning"]).

Visions. Jesus does not seem to have had visions frequently.[19] Nevertheless, the Gospels do record several visions, both those that people around Jesus had (such as Zechariah and Mary in the infancy narratives) and those that Jesus himself had, most notably when he was baptized by John and during his transfiguration. What do these visions tell us about our relationship with God?

The visions reported in the infancy narratives have to be literary compositions, since all of the eyewitnesses had died before Luke began his work. This does not mean that they cannot be history in a real sense, but we should note that Luke has composed these narratives purposefully, basing them on earlier traditions and writing them up in the style of the Greek Bible, with numerous allusions to Genesis and Judges and to the messianic oracles of the classical prophets. This is not the place to analyze them in detail;[20] let us simply recall the two essential visions, those of Zechariah and Mary. In both cases, the divine intermediary is the angel Gabriel (cf. Dan 9:21). Both accounts have a christological purpose: the first appeals to Mal 4:5–6 to explain the role of John as a precursor of Jesus, while the second reveals to Mary her personal vocation to be the mother of Jesus, describing the role and the status that her child will have. These narratives obviously were composed from the perspective of a clear doctrinal understanding of Jesus Christ after his resurrection.

Every account of a vision presupposes a direct relationship between God and the person who receives the vision. But is the word of God communicated through actual sights and sounds, or is the communication, rather, an interior one? We can hardly settle that question here. However, whether the vision itself is sensory or not, the essential thing is the interior communication that results from it: Zechariah's expectation of John the Baptist's birth, and Mary's personal vocation to be the mother of a child who would be the "Son of God" (Luke 1:35) in a way that no one had ever been

---

[19] See Grelot, *Jésus de Nazareth, Christ et Seigneur,* 2:433–97. I intentionally take up these chapters from the Gospels *after* the resurrection of Jesus because these memories of his childhood are recorded in light of it.

[20] Ibid., 1:114–20.

before. The fact that Mary accepted this vocation as her own free act is something the evangelist insists on (Luke 1:38), and in an essential expression of his storytelling art he then includes four songs in the narrative (Luke 1:46–55, 68–79; 2:14, 29–32).

But there are also accounts of visions that Jesus himself had. How do these help us to know Jesus better and to understand his relationship with God? Mark and Matthew say specifically that it was Jesus who saw the heavens opened at the time of his baptism; Luke's account is so individualized that the crowds around him are not even brought into the picture. John is the only evangelist who says that John the Baptist saw the vision (John 1:32–34). But we may legitimately ask how John was able to see "the Spirit" descending upon Jesus, since the Spirit is, by definition, invisible, without any voice speaking to declare that Jesus was God's Son (as in the Synoptics) or Chosen One (as in John). The narrative in John seems to be a secondary composition by comparison with the Synoptics, and particularly with Mark. Thus it was Jesus who received the vision.

The vision expresses, in carefully chosen symbolic terms, the nature of his relationship with God. God is presented clearly as "Father," and his words make allusion to three Scripture texts, quoted from the Greek version: "you are my son" (Ps 2:7), "my beloved son" (cf. Gen 22:2), "with you I am well pleased" (cf. Isa 42:1). The meaning of these words is clear: as the Messiah, Jesus is the "Son of God" (in the sense of Ps 2); his filial relationship to God is of the same order as Isaac's to Abraham (theologians would say that it was "of the same nature"); he is the "Servant of the Lord" that the book of Isaiah spoke about. We should not think that Jesus himself related the spiritual experience that he had when he was baptized by John; rather, the biblical tradition is presenting a summary of the inner experience that crystallized the sense he had, from the beginning of his mission, of his relationship with God. He was "God's Son" in an essential sense, and he had a messianic vocation, but he was to be like the "Suffering Servant." The words that express this relationship are accompanied by a vision that shows that Jesus will be filled with the Spirit of God: the heavens "open" (Matthew and Luke) or are "torn apart" (Mark), and the Spirit descends upon him in the form of a dove. According to a rabbinical commentary on

Gen 1:1, "The Spirit of God hovered over the waters" of creation as
the dove hovers over its young.[21] Thus the "new creation" (cf. Isa
65:17) is beginning with Jesus.

In the scene of Jesus' transfiguration (Mark 9:2–8), three disciples participate in the same vision as does Jesus, who talks to
Moses (= the Law) and Elijah (= the Prophets). Luke adds that they
were "speaking of his departure [= death],[22] which he was about to
accomplish at Jerusalem" (Luke 9:31). The heavenly light that surrounds him announces in advance that he will enter into the glory of
God, after his resurrection from the dead.[23] From this time on, the
evangelists note, Jesus repeatedly referred to his imminent sufferings
and death, and to the fact that he would be raised "on the third day"
(Matthew and Luke) or "after three days" (Mark),[24] a conventional
designation for the "day of the consolation of the dead," following
the traditional interpretation of Hos 6:2.[25]

Other than this, while the Gospel texts insist at more than one
point that Jesus spent long hours in prayer, they do not portray him
as a mystic or a visionary. We can understand Jesus' temptation[26]
(Matt 4:1–11 and parallels) without assuming that it involved a vision
of Satan. And when we read that Jesus said, after the seventy-two
had returned from their mission,[27] "I watched Satan fall from heaven

---

[21] Ibid., 1:116, with a quotation from the second-century rabbi Simeon ben Zoma, in *b. Hagigah* 15a.

[22] See W. Bauer, F. W. Danker, W. Bauer, W. F. Arndt, and F. W.
Gingrich, *Greek-English Lexicon of the New Testament and Other Early
Christian Literature* (3d ed.; Chicago, 1999), 350, which cites parallels for
the use of this euphemism in Wis 3:2; 7:6, and in Philo and Josephus.

[23] See A. Feuillet and P. Grelot, "Lumière," *VTB* 684–90. There is a
discussion of "Le Christ transfiguré" in cols. 688–89. See also Grelot, *Jésus
de Nazareth, Christ et Seigneur,* 1:413–20.

[24] Grelot, *Jésus de Nazareth, Christ et Seigneur,* 1:408–10. See there p.
409 n. 1 for an explanation of how the "third day" is to be understood in a
nonchronological sense. Cf. P. Grelot, *L'Espérance juive à l'heure de Jésus*
(11th ed.; Jésus et Jésus-Christ 6; Paris: Desclée, 1994), 134, 187.

[25] This point is discussed in P. Grelot, "La résurrection du Christ et
son arrière-plan biblique et juif," in P. de Surgy et al., *La résurrection du
Christ et l'exégèse moderne* (LD 50; Paris: Cerf, 1969), 28, 38–39.

[26] See P. Grelot, "Les tentations de Jésus," *NRTh* 117 (1995): 501–16.

[27] For more details see P. Grelot, "Étude critique de Luc 10, 19," *RSR*
69 (1981): 87–100.

like a flash of lightning" (Luke 10:18), we should recognize that the verb "see" is being used in a colloquial sense to express the inner certitude of Jesus: the proclamation of the good news of the reign of God and the signs that have accompanied this proclamation (Luke 10:9) are bringing about the victory of God over every form of evil.

"Seeing" the Acts and Deeds of Jesus. We should also note the places where the verb "see" is used to describe an otherwise ordinary action on the part of the disciples that becomes significant after the resurrection as a foundation for the gospel witness. None of the traditions collected in the four Gospels have been placed there arbitrarily. A passage in the book of Acts summarizes in a few words exactly how they have been chosen. When the high priest forbids them to speak any more about Jesus, Peter and John reply, "we cannot keep from speaking about what we have seen and heard" (Acts 4:20). What the disciples have "seen" is not simply the material acts and deeds of Jesus during his ministry, but also, and especially, the recognition that these were "according to the scriptures," in the light that his resurrection appearances shed on all of his earthly activity: "The God of our ancestors raised up Jesus, whom you had killed by hanging him on a tree. God exalted him at his right hand as Leader and Savior that he might give repentance to Israel and forgiveness of sins. And we are witnesses to these things, and so is the Holy Spirit whom God has given to those who obey him" (Acts 5:30–32). The witness to the resurrection of Jesus is even more important than the witness to what Jesus did during his ministry, because the resurrection provides the key to interpreting everything else.

But the disciples "saw" Jesus after his resurrection in a different way from the one in which they saw him during his public ministry.[28] Peter's speech in Acts 10:36–43 emphasizes this: "We are witnesses to all that he did both in Judea and in Jerusalem. They put him to death by hanging him on a tree; but God raised him on the third day and allowed him to appear, not to all the people but to us who were chosen by God as witnesses, and who ate and drank with him after he rose from the dead" (Acts 10:39–41). Thus the visual witness is to two different categories of real facts: those that everyone

---

[28] See above, pp. 131–37. The subject is treated in detail in Grelot, *Jésus de Nazareth, Christ et Seigneur,* 2:373–413.

was able to see, and those that God reserved for a small number of witnesses whom he called to make this extraordinary announcement. For Jesus, the "world to come" arrived when God snatched him from the power of death. All of the other events of his life, right up to his death on the cross, took place in public view. However, a small number of privileged witnesses were brought into a living relationship with him when "God exalted him at his right hand" (Acts 5:31).

Thus the sight of what Jesus did in plain view of everyone during his earthly ministry was already a revelation of what God wanted to do through his supreme envoy. It was, paradoxically, part of God's plan for this envoy, in his capacity as the "Suffering Servant," to be killed by those "hanging him on a tree" (Acts 5:30–35). But when God raised him from the dead, he opened up the "world to come" for him and introduced into history the mysterious presence of his own plan. This was the meaning of the good news that was preached from that time on. No longer would the risen Christ let himself be seen by those who would believe in him (cf. John 20:29), but they would have the assurance of his presence and the benefit of "the forgiveness of sins and the gift of the Holy Spirit" (Acts 2:38) so that they could "save [themselves] from this corrupt generation" (Acts 2:40).

There is one more way in which the verb "see" is used. It has to do with the end toward which the plan of God is moving. We should take literally the words that Jesus spoke to the high priest during his interrogation: "You will see the Son of Man seated at the right hand of Power and coming on the clouds of heaven" (Matt 26:64; cf. Mark 14:62; Luke 22:69). This will be the gathering of the elect announced in Jesus' eschatological discourse (Mark 13:26–27; Matt 24:30–31; more briefly, Luke 21:27). It will be the great day of judgment (Matt 24), but also it will be the fulfillment of the promise to the pure in heart that "they will see God" (Matt 5:8),[29] this God whom no one here below may see (Exod 33:20).

The Verb "See" in the Johannine Writings. We may pass quickly over the book of Revelation, noting simply that in this book, we find accounts of visions (with the verbs *horan/eidon* or *blepein*). The

---

[29] Regarding this expression see P. Grelot, "Voir Dieu: Le ciel, l'Enfer, le Purgatoire," *Esprit et vie* 108 (1998): 241–46.

author is writing that which he has seen (Rev 1:11, 19; cf. 19:17; 21:1–2, 22; 22:4, 8).

In the Gospel and First Epistle of John, however, the verb "see" is used on multiple occasions, with many different potential meanings. "(W)e have seen his glory" (John 1:14). Does that refer to the earthly life of the Word-made-flesh, or to the resurrection appearances of Christ? The glory of the risen Christ is a prism through which the evangelist considers all of the acts and deeds of Jesus. He asserts explicitly that in principle, "No one has ever seen God"; but if "it is God the only Son . . . who has made him known," this is because he is forever "close to the Father's heart" (John 1:18).

The intimate relationship between the Son and the Father allows the evangelist to put this astonishing saying in the mouth of Jesus: "Not that anyone has seen the Father except the one who is from God; he has seen the Father" (John 6:46). This is why "to see the Son" and especially "to believe in him" opens the way to "eternal life": the Son will "raise . . . up on the last day" those who believe (John 6:40). Was it in anticipation of the life to come that Jesus said to Nathaniel, "you will see [*opsesthe*] heaven opened and the angels of God ascending and descending upon the Son of Man" (John 1:51)?[30] And when he was speaking with Nicodemus, why did Jesus say, "*we* speak of what we know and testify to what we have seen [*heōrakamen*]" (John 3:11)? Is it Jesus who is speaking here, or is it the evangelist, as in his first letter: "what we have seen with our eyes [*heōrakamen*], what we have looked at [*etheasametha*] and touched with our hands, concerning the word of life . . . we declare to you what we have seen and heard" (1 John 1:1, 3).

In the same way, in a polemical discourse that reveals who he is, Jesus is able to say, "I declare what I have seen in the Father's presence" (John 8:38). And a little later, in reference to Gen 17:17, he says, "Abraham rejoiced that he would see my day; he saw it and was glad" (John 8:56). What kind of sight is Jesus talking about? A prophetic sight, which his interlocutors were not in a position to

---

[30] The allusion to Gen 28:12 is clear, but how should we understand the phrase *epi ton huion tou anthrōpou:* "upon the Son of Man," who thus would be likened to the ladder to heaven, or "above the Son of Man"? The translators are divided.

appreciate.[31] Still later in the Gospel, Jesus says to Martha, regarding Lazarus, who is in the tomb, "Did I not tell you that if you believed, you would see the glory of God?" (John 11:40). The resurrection of Lazarus would be the manifestation of that glory, but the "seeing" that is promised to Martha refers to the vision of faith that will be able to discern the meaning of the event, beyond sensory perception. The same verb can also be understood as a reference to prophetic sight. How else can we understand the evangelist's reflection on the Jews' failure to believe in Jesus, in which he cites two passages from the book of Isaiah (Isa 53:1; 6:9) and then comments, "Isaiah said this because he saw his glory and spoke about him" (John 12:41)? An attitude of faith, moreover, bestows a kind of vision of the most invisible mystery: "whoever sees me," Jesus says, "sees him who sent me" (John 12:45). As he is speaking privately with his disciples, he tells them, "If you know me, you will know my Father also. From now on you do know him and have seen him" (John 14:7). When Philip says, "Lord, show us the Father, and we will be satisfied," Jesus replies, "Whoever has seen me has seen the Father. . . . Do you not believe that I am in the Father and the Father is in me?" (John 14:8–10).

We will return to this significant formula "to be in." These words touch directly on the mysterious relationship between Jesus and God. As for the rest of the conversation with the disciples, it is dominated by the perspective of Jesus' death and resurrection. "In a little while the world will no longer see me, but you will see me" (John 14:19; cf. 16:16). "So you have pain now; but I will see you again, and your hearts will rejoice" (John 16:22). Then everything that Jesus has said comes to pass: he is killed, but on the third day he appears to his disciples—but Thomas is missing. Thomas thus plays the role, in this drama, of the unbeliever: when the other disciples tell him, "We have seen the Lord," he wants not just to see the risen Christ, but to touch him. He insists, "Unless I see the mark of the nails in his hands, and put my finger in the mark of the nails and my hand in his side, I will not believe" (John 20:25). Jesus appears a week later and offers him the opportunity that he has

---

[31] See Grelot, *Jésus de Nazareth, Christ et Seigneur,* 2:67, where there is a discussion of *Jub.* 16:19, to which this passage seems to allude.

asked for, adding, "Do not doubt but believe." But it is enough for
Thomas to see him, and he confesses his faith: "My Lord and my
God!" Jesus replies, "Have you believed because you have seen me?
Blessed are those who have not seen and yet have come to believe"
(John 20:27–29). To believe that Christ has risen from the dead is, in
some way, to see him inwardly.

The Acts of the Apostles. There are countless ordinary uses of
the verb "see" in the Acts of the Apostles, which we need not review
here. But in Acts 2:25 a quotation from Ps 16:8 is put in the mouth
of the risen Christ, "I saw the Lord always before me," and in Acts
2:27, "you will not let . . . your Holy One experience corruption"
(from Ps 16:10). Thus "see" has a further meaning.[32] To see God,
and not to see the corruption of the tomb, are two aspects of
the risen Christ's condition. In the same way, in Acts 7:55 Stephen,
as he is being stoned to death, sees "the glory of God and Jesus
standing at the right hand of God." Thus he is being trans-
ported into the invisible world. When Saul of Tarsus was con-
verted, this man who would become the apostle Paul was blinded
to the point that he "could see nothing" in this world (Acts 9:8).
Nevertheless, he had "seen the Lord," who spoke to him (Acts
9:27); he saw "the Righteous One" (Acts 22:14), and Paul himself
tells us what the Lord said to him when he had this vision of the
resurrected Christ (Acts 22:18). To defend his vocation as an
apostle, he challenged the Corinthians, "Have I not seen Jesus our
Lord?" (1 Cor 9:1).

The vision of faith is different from the kind of vision that was
granted to Paul in this experience. In 1 Cor 13:12 he writes, "now we
see in a mirror, dimly, but then we will see face to face," in the
beatific vision of eternal life. It is this vision that the believer desires:
"we look not at what can be seen but at what cannot be seen; for
what can be seen is temporary, but what cannot be seen is eternal"
(2 Cor 4:18). Here two different kinds of realities are being contrasted: one is of the earth, and the other is of God. One we can
"see," and the other we "hope for" (cf. Rom 8:24). This hope draws
us toward the One who "dwells in unapproachable light, whom no

---

[32] I discuss this text in *Le mystère du Christ dans les Psaumes* (Jésus et
Jésus-Christ 74; Paris: Desclée, 1998), 79–81.

one has ever seen or can see" (1 Tim 6:16). The resurrected Christ lives in that light, and our faith brings us into fellowship with him even as we live here on earth: "Although you have not seen him," Peter writes to the churches of the Diaspora, "you love him, and even though you do not see him now, you believe in him and rejoice with an indescribable and glorious joy" (1 Pet 1:8). This joy is the anticipation of seeing God "face to face," as Paul says.

Hearing and Listening

As in the First Testament, the verbs for "hearing" and "listening" are used quite often in the New Testament. This is not surprising, since the message of the gospel is transmitted by the spoken word.

The Sayings of Jesus. We will consider these here and then take up the words of those who first proclaimed the gospel. "Listen!" This is what a speaker challenges his audience to do, and it is something that we find both Jesus (Mark 4:3 and parallels) and his apostles (e.g., Acts 2:22) saying. There is a particular nuance to this challenge, as it refers to more than just listening materially to what is going to be said: it means "(l)isten and understand" (Matt 15:10). The listener's heart needs to be open to the meaning of the word of God that is about to be proclaimed. This is what the voice from heaven meant when it told the three apostles, at the time of Jesus' transfiguration, "This is my Son, my Chosen; listen to him!" (Luke 9:35; cf. Mark 9:7; Matt 17:5). The words of Jesus were the word of God itself, as Matthew insists in his chapter of parables (in which Jesus complains of the people that "hearing they do not listen" [Matt 13:13]). They were the "word of the kingdom" (Matt 13:19): "many prophets and righteous people longed . . . to hear what you hear, but did not hear it" (Matt 13:17). The attitude that a listener adopts while the word is being heard determines that person's situation before God. This fact is seen implicitly in the narratives in the Synoptics, and it is the lesson of the parable of the Sower, in which four different categories of listener are distinguished (Luke 8:10–15 and parallels). John insists on the point even further: "anyone who hears my words and does not keep them [i.e., 'The one who rejects me and does not receive my word'] . . . has a judge" (John 12:47–48). To hear the word but not pay attention to it incurs the judgment of God.

This is because "the word that you hear is not mine, but is from the Father who sent me" (John 14:24).

The Apostolic Writings. Jesus taught how important it was to listen attentively to the word of God, and it was just as important for salvation in the days of the apostles. The proclamation of the gospel extended the preaching of Jesus by adding to it the double fact of his death and resurrection. This is why the verb "hear" saturates the book of Acts. On the day of Pentecost, when Peter gave the very first gospel message, the visitors to Jerusalem exclaimed about the apostles, "in our own languages we hear them speaking about God's deeds of power" (Acts 2:11). "(W)hen they heard" Peter's message, "they were cut to the heart" and asked what they must do, and so repented and were baptized (Acts 2:37–41). Thus the preaching of the word of God was transformed by the object of the gospel: Christ Jesus himself became its center. To "hear" this word is to open oneself up to the grace of God that brings salvation. Thus the author of the book of Hebrews, himself a preacher of the gospel, can take up the text of Ps 95 and give it a wider application: "Today, if you hear his voice, do not harden your hearts" (Heb 3:7–8). Hearing the word accomplishes nothing for those who are not "united by faith" with those who listen (cf. Heb 4:2).

In the First Epistle of John the verb "hear" is given yet another meaning, to describe the apostolic message to which the recipients must hold firmly. "As you have heard that antichrist is coming, so now many antichrists have come" (1 John 2:18). And so it is essential that what they have heard from the beginning abide in them (1 John 2:24). The author summarizes the content of this message (1 John 3:11). Thus perseverance in obedience to the word that has been received becomes a condition of salvation.

The Book of Revelation. We need not examine all of the occurrences of the verb "hear/listen" in Revelation. "Hearing" and "seeing" are, in this literary genre, linguistic conventions that introduce the message that the author wants to transmit to the recipients. Thus the verb *akouō* occurs 46 times in the book; it is paired with the verb "to see," which appears 24 times. Nevertheless, we must recognize the message that is being conveyed through these literary conventions. The author has not invented any of the things that he introduces in this way: "I, John, am the one who heard and saw these things" (Rev 22:8). What he says does not come from his own imagination: he says what he has been commissioned to say. And even though he constantly speaks from an eschatological perspective, his message is nothing other than the gospel itself, which is the bearer of revelation and the invitation to hope.

Being Thirsty

This can refer to human suffering, expressed in hunger and thirst. The apostle Paul experienced such suffering (1 Cor 4:11; 2 Cor 11:27). Love for neighbor must not be indifferent to this kind of human suffering. The facts of hunger and thirst are a summons to charity, even toward our enemies; the apostle Paul teaches this principle by quoting from the book of Proverbs (Rom 12:20; cf. Prov 25:21–22). On the day of judgment the Son of Man will consider anything done to give food or drink to "the least of these who are members of my family" as having been done for him (Matt 25:34–40).

There is, however, another kind of thirst. The psalms speak of "thirsting after God." In the same way, in the John's Gospel, Jesus says intriguingly to the woman of Samaria, "those who drink of the water that I will give them will never be thirsty" (John 4:14a). What water is he talking about? "The water that I will give will become in them a spring of water gushing up to eternal life" (John 4:14b) The intriguing allusion is clarified a bit by Jesus' declaration on the "great day" (the last day) of the Feast of Tabernacles: "Let anyone who is thirsty come to me, and let the one who believes in me drink. As the scripture has said, 'Out of the believer's heart shall flow rivers of living water'" (John 7:37–38). We recognize that the thirst in question here is the same "thirst after God" spoken of in Ps 42:5 and Isa 55:1. Now, however, Jesus makes a mysterious promise about how this thirst can be satisfied, which the evangelist explains: "he said this about the Spirit, which believers in him were to receive" (John 7:39). The gift of the Spirit will satisfy this thirst by making God present directly to the believer. It does not matter that the "scripture" to which the text refers is very difficult to identify.[33] The important thing is the meaning that Jesus himself gives to it.

---

[33] For a more detailed discussion see P. Grelot, *Dieu, le Père de Jésus Christ* (Jésus et Jésus-Christ 60; Paris: Desclée, 1994), 314–16.

The evangelist also records Jesus saying on the cross, "I am thirsty" (John 19:28). Does this saying have a symbolic meaning? The soldiers rush to offer Jesus a sponge soaked in a vinegary drink (John 19:29–30), and the evangelist notes that the Scripture thus was fulfilled, in a likely allusion to either Ps 69:21 or Ps 22:15. But may John also be infusing the saying with a hidden symbolism? Possibly. What might Christ have been thirsty for when he was dying, in relation to humanity, for which sacrificed himself? This is a fitting question for spiritual meditation.

Loving

This time we are not faced with a metaphor that we need to explain. There are only two things that the verb in question can refer to: human love or divine love.[34] As we observed earlier, the Hebrew verb *'ahav* had already been translated constantly by *agapan* in the Greek Bible. The New Testament writers prefer to use *agapan* and *agapē* rather than *philein* and its derivatives. Nevertheless, the two verbs are very close in meaning, as we see from the fact that in the phrase "the disciple whom Jesus loved," *agapan* is used in John 13:23, but *philein* is used in John 20:2. Thus we should not base any interpretations on the difference in nuance between these two verbs.

How, then, should we translate Jesus' words to Peter, and his three responses, in John 21:15–17, where both *agapan* and *philein* are used and seem to be distinguished from one another? We could translate Jesus' original question, *agapas me,* as "Do you love me?" and Peter's response, *philō se,* as "I love you very much," meaning that the third repetition of the question, in which Jesus also uses *philein,* could be translated, "Do you indeed love me very much?" (to which Peter replies, "You know everything; you know that I do"). But even if this analysis is correct, it does not resolve the general question posed by the verb "love" in the New Testament.

The Love of God. Why should we speak of loving as something that God does? Because the expression symbolically explains God's action in terms of something that we can understand from human

---

[34] Ibid., 139 (with a bibliography in the note). See also C. Wiener, "Amour," *VTB* 46–56. See above in ch. 2 the discussion on love in marriage in "The Symbol of Marriage" (pp. 40–42).

experience. Nevertheless, we must not attribute to God the same limits on the ability to love that apply to humans.

Paul expresses, in his writings, the understanding that it is love that has determined God's providential conduct. He says of the Jews, "as regards election they are beloved" (Rom 11:28). Paul actually encourages the Corinthians to give to the offering for the relief of the poor in Jerusalem by telling them, "God loves a cheerful giver" (2 Cor 9:7), but he also writes that believers are "God's chosen ones, holy and beloved" (Col 3:12). The author of the Epistle to the Hebrews quotes Prov 3:12 (LXX) to remind his readers that "the Lord disciplines those whom he loves" (Heb 12:6).

Is in the Johannine corpus, however, that we hear the most about God's love. In 1 John 4:8 we find the lapidary phrase "God is love," after which it is explained, "God's love was revealed among us in this way: God sent his only son into the world" (1 John 4:9). "In this is love, not that we loved God but that he loved us"—a fact in which John finds the fundamental motive for love between people (1 John 4:10–11). In the Gospel of John it is Jesus himself who speaks of this love, of which he is the primary object: "The Father loves the Son and has placed all things in his hands" (John 3:35; cf. 5:20). Jesus tells his disciples, "The Father himself loves you, because you have loved me" (John 16:27). He gives thanks for this in his last prayer (John 17:23) and then expands the perspective even further: "you loved me before the foundation of the world. . . . so that the love with which you have loved me may be in them, and I in them" (John 17:24, 26). Here we are entering into the mystery of the love that is in God himself. It is through Jesus that this love of God is made known to the world.

The Love of God Shown through Jesus. As the Son of God, Jesus is the manifestation of the Father to humanity. As a result, every time a text describes a sentiment of love in him, God is in the background. This is true of, for example, the episode in which the rich young ruler asked Jesus what he needed to do to inherit eternal life (Mark 10:17–22). As Jesus listed the commandments to be observed, the man replied, "I have kept all these since my youth." Then, Mark notes, "Jesus, looking at him, loved him" (Mark 10:21). Clearly, this was something that Jesus felt in his heart. Unfortunately, the man went away sad (Mark 10:22). We can feel the same sadness in

Jesus as he then looks around at the crowd and speaks to his disciples
(Mark 10:23–27). God's love for humanity is expressed through the
feelings of Jesus, as John notes in several places. Jesus was aware of
the love that the Father had for him as he put his life on the line to
fulfill God's plan (John 10:17). And the evangelist is not embarrassed
to mention, when Jesus went to raise Lazarus from the dead, the particular love that Jesus had for the family in Bethany (John 11:3, 5, 36).

It is particularly in the final chapters of his Gospel that John
highlights this love: "Having loved his own who were in the world,
he loved them to the extreme" (John 13:1).[35] In the conversation
between Jesus and his disciples after the Last Supper the verb "love"
is used 26 times, and the noun "love" appears 6 times. But now
everything is mixed together: the love of the Father and the love of
Jesus, love for the Father and love for Jesus, and the mutual love
among those whom Jesus has loved. "As the Father has loved me, so
I have loved you; abide in my love. If you keep my commandments, you will abide in my love, just as I have kept my Father's
commandments and abide in his love" (John 15:9–10). "This is my
commandment, that you love one another as I have loved you"
(John 15:12). "No one has greater love than this, to lay down one's
life [*psychē*] for one's friends. You are my friends if you do what I
command you" (John 15:13–14). And a little later Jesus says, "I am
giving you these commands so that you may love one another"
(John 15:17). And again, to explain that the Father will grant anything that is asked in his name, he says, "for the Father himself loves
you, because you have loved me and have believed that I came from
God" (John 16:27).

Does the verb "love" have the same meaning in all of these
statements? It is clear that the love of the Father for the Son, and of
the Son for the Father, is on quite a different level from the mutual
love that the disciples may have for one another. Even though Jesus
is human, he remains the Son, and so his love for his disciples, which
leads him to "give his life" (or to "give himself") for those he loves,
communicates to us the love of God himself. This love infuses us to

---

[35] There are different opinions about how *eis telos* should be translated
in John 13:1: "to the extreme" or "to the end." I have chosen the translation
that gives a superlative meaning to the verb "love": "to the extreme." See
Grelot, *Jésus de Nazareth, Christ et Seigneur,* 235.

the extent that we can receive it in order to emulate it ourselves. Thus the commandment to love one another becomes a call to do something beyond our usual human capacity: "love one another as I have loved you" (John 15:12). The love that Jesus shows his disciples through the gift of his person and his life is, in itself, a divine love. When his disciples emulate this, they are going beyond what Jesus said was the "second great commandment" in the law (Mark 12:31; Matt 22:39; cf. Lev 19:18; Matt 19:19). They are giving love for neighbor a new dimension that makes it a participation in the love that has come from God to Jesus Christ and then, from him, to those who, as his disciples, participate in his own life.

Thus Jesus establishes the connection between the unsurpassable love that God is in himself (1 John 4:8), with which he loves his Son, and the simply human love that the commandment in Leviticus prescribes. We should note that if this commandment is taken literally, the neighbor was only a fellow Israelite (Lev 19:18); other people were "resident aliens" who were simply not to be abused (Lev 19:33–34). Jesus, however, extends the notion of "neighbor" in his reply to the lawyer who asked him, "And who is my neighbor?" (Luke 10:29). Jesus responded by telling the parable of the Good Samaritan, which describes a foreigner who obeyed the commandment to love, after two respectable people—a priest and a Levite—had ignored it (Luke 10:30–37). Thus the love that Christ commands is not simply the mutual love that exists within the believing community; it is universal. "We know love by this, that he [Jesus] laid down his life [*psychē* = Aramaic *nafsheh,* equivalent to the reflexive pronoun, "himself"] for us—and we ought to lay down our lives [same definition] for one another" (1 John 3:16).

Clearly, these texts are not symbolic and ambiguous in meaning. We now have a part in the love of God, who "is love," through the mediation of Jesus, who is at the same time "the Son" to God and a human brother to all of us.

Symbolic Expressions of Our Relationship with God

Some ordinary-looking expressions caught our attention in the First Testament because they could actually take on, in certain contexts, an amazing meaning. These expressions were "to be with" and "to act before" God. The New Testament takes up these same expressions and actually adds another: "to be in." However, in the New Testament a new factor has been introduced: the mediation between God and those who believe in him by Jesus Christ, through the life he lived among them until his death on the cross, and then by his immediate presence with those who have come to believe in him since his resurrection from the dead.

To Be with God or with Christ

This phrase is used many times in the New Testament with the same significance as in the First Testament, most often with the Greek preposition *meta,* but sometimes also with the preposition *syn* (particularly in compound verbs).[36]

The Gospel Narratives. In the Synoptic Gospels it is said significantly that the disciples "were with" Jesus during his life and his mission, as in Mark 3:14 (cf. 5:18), where being a disciple is described as "being with" Jesus (cf. Mark 14:67; 16:10; Matt 26:38, 40, 69; Luke 8:1, 38 [where Jesus turns down a man's request to "be with" him]; 22:28, 56). In John's Gospel the formula is used not just for Jesus (John 7:33; 13:8, 33; 14:9, 25; 15:27; 16:4; 17:12); it also describes the Father, who "is with" Jesus (John 8:29; 16:32), and even the Spirit, whom the Father will send at Jesus' request (John 14:16). Nicodemus says that he knows that God "is with" Jesus (John 3:2). In quotations from the First Testament, typically it is God who "is with" someone; for example, the prediction of the birth of Emmanuel is said to have been fulfilled by Jesus because the name "Emmanuel" means "God with us" (Matt 1:23). But what does the expression mean in the parables? In the parable of the Prodigal Son, when the father says to the elder son, "you are always with me" (Luke 15:31), this refers to the life that they have in common. But in the short parable about the friends of the bridegroom having him "with" them, who is this bridegroom (Mark 2:19; Matt 9:15; Luke 5:34)?

Often when the expression "to be with" is used in the Gospel tradition after the resurrection of Jesus, it suggests a presence just like the one described at the end of Matthew: "And remember, I am

---

[36] On the meaning of *meta* see the article by W. Radl, *EWNT* 2:1018, and of *syn* see the article by W. Elliger, *EWNT* 3:697–702.

with you always, to the end of the age" (Matt 28:20). Beyond this, when it is occurs in the words of Jesus, it can refer to salvation itself: "Whoever is not with me is against me" (Matt 12:30; cf. Mark 9:40, where "me" is replaced by "us"). The formula of First Testament, in which it is God who is "with" someone, is also found in the New Testament. For example, the angel's greeting to Mary in Luke 1:28 uses it. It also occurs in the book of Acts (Acts 7:9; 10:38). In Acts 18:9–10, however, it is the risen Christ who says to Paul, "Do not be afraid . . . for I am with you."

Paul's Letters. Here the wish, often expressed in the First Testament, that God would "be with" someone reappears occasionally (Phil 4:9; 2 Cor 13:11; Rom 15:33). But when Paul speaks of "the Lord," it is clear that he is referring to Christ (2 Thess 3:16; Phil 4:23; 2 Tim 4:22). His references to "the grace of our Lord Jesus Christ" (Rom 16:20; 1 Cor 16:23; Phil 4:23; 2 Thess 3:18) clarify those passages in which "grace" alone is mentioned (Eph 6:24; Col 4:18; 1 Tim 6:21; 2 Tim 4:22; Titus 3:15). The phrase "to be with" essentially refers to the presence of the risen Christ with his disciples in the church, in keeping with what is said at the end of Matthew (Matt 28:20). But beyond this, the phrase also refers to the way in which the Christian sacraments enable those who receive them to share in essential aspects of the mystery of Christ, who died and rose again. Paul says that this is true of his death (Rom 6:8; Col 2:12), of his resurrection (2 Cor 4:14 [with mention of the final resurrection]; Col 2:12; 3:1), and of our present participation in the new life that he gives (2 Cor 13:4; Col 2:12). In short, those who believe in Christ come to share, through faith, in all of the successive aspects of his mystery.

The Book of Revelation. The book of Revelation adds to all of this the idea of participating with Jesus at his table (Rev 3:20) and in his eternal reign (Rev 3:21; 20:4, 6), after sharing in his victory (Rev 17:14). The book reaches a joyous culmination in which God-with-them "shall be their God" (Rev 21:3, an allusion to Isa 7:14; 8:8, 10, the text taken up in Matt 1:23 to announce the birth of Jesus). Thus the way the disciples "were with" Jesus becomes a symbolic anticipation of the way believers will "be with" Christ eternally as he plays his full role of mediator between God and redeemed humanity.

"To Act Before"

In Hebrew "before" often means "in the presence of." In Greek *pro* is a simple preposition, while *emprosthen* is a complex one that often translates the Hebrew *lifney*,[37] as in the quotation from Mal 3:1 in Matt 11:10 and Luke 7:27. As we noted earlier, the messenger who was sent "before God," John the Baptist, becomes a messenger sent "before Jesus." Let us consider some further significant texts. "Everyone therefore who acknowledges me before others, I will also acknowledge before my Father" (Matt 10:32; Luke 12:8 [with a variation in the formula]). Here the reference is to what Jesus will do on the day of judgment before the Father. Matthew 18:14 says, literally, "It is not the will *before your Father* that one of these little ones should be lost." Clearly, the text here is Hebraized, since obviously it is referring to the will of the Father himself. By contrast, in Matt 25:32 it is before the Son of Man in glory that all the nations will be gathered for judgment. And we should not overlook the episode from Jesus' passion described in Matt 27:27–30. Even though the soldiers were beating and mocking Jesus, they said to him, "Hail, King of the Jews!" Behind their mockery we can see Jesus' true royalty shining through, to such an extent that a believer may paradoxically recognize the soldiers' act of kneeling "before him" (Matt 27:29) as an act of homage rendered to Christ the King.

In John's Gospel we are struck immediately by the tribute that John the Baptist pays to Jesus: "After me comes a man who ranks ahead of me because he was before me" (John 1:30, reprising 1:15). What John says about his position relative to that of Jesus makes sense only if Jesus possesses something other than a temporal priority. This fact is confirmed by John 3:28, where John bears witness to Jesus once again by reminding his own disciples that he has said, "I am not the Messiah," and adding, "but I have been sent ahead of him." John tells a short parable to explain the situation: he compares Jesus to the bridegroom and calls himself the "friend of the bridegroom" (John 3:29). The other uses of the word *emprosthen* in the Gospel of John only concern Jesus indirectly, as in John 10:4, where he compares himself to the shepherd who "goes before" of his sheep.

---

[37] See, briefly, the articles on ἔμπροσθεν by A. Kretzer, *EDNT* 1:446, and on πρό by W. Radl, *EDNT* 3:150. *VTB* does not discuss these prepositions.

Moving to the book of Acts, we may note the traditional biblical expression in the angel's words to the centurion Cornelius:
"your prayer has been heard and your alms have been remembered
before God" (Acts 10:31). And regarding John the Baptist himself,
we read in Acts 13:24, "before his coming John had already proclaimed a baptism of repentance to all the people of Israel." Here
the word *prokēryxantos* and then the phrase *pro prosōpou tēs eisodou*
clearly show that Jesus himself is the principal object of the
statement.

We may also highlight several texts in the Pauline corpus where
the priority of Christ is asserted. Colossians 1:17 says, "He himself is
before [*pro*] all things, and in him all things hold together." Ephesians 1:4 says of Christ, "he chose us in Christ before the foundation
of the world." We should remember that that creation was an act of
God himself. We hear in Titus 1:2 of the "eternal life that God, who
never lies, promised before the ages began," and in 2 Tim 1:9–10 of
the grace "given to us in Christ Jesus before the ages began." James
5:9 warns us that "the Judge is standing at [*pro*] the doors." This is a
reference to God, unless it refers to the Lord whose coming has just
been announced (Jas 5:7). In 1 Pet 1:19–20 Christ Jesus is described
as the "lamb without defect or blemish . . . destined before the foundation of the world." In all of these texts God is not mentioned
directly as the one before whom an action takes place, but things
nevertheless take place at a time that depends entirely on God, and
God is the one who makes them happen.

"To Be In"

The First Testament does not provide many examples where
"God" is preceded by the particle *b-* (the Greek equivalent is *en*).
When this does occur, the meaning is "with," as in Ps 60:12 (59:14
LXX): *be'elohim na'aseh khayil* (Greek: *en tō theō poiēsomen dynamin*),
"with God we shall do valiantly." In the First Testament the preposition does not have the meaning "in," understood symbolically,
but the New Testament provides several important examples of
this usage.[38]

---

[38] For a good discussion of the significance of the preposition *en* see
the article by W. Elliger, *EWNT* 1:1093–96.

The Pauline Corpus. The phrase occurs numerous times Paul's letters, but many of these are in repeated formulas: "in the Lord" or "in Christ Jesus" or "in the Spirit." Paul's thought is dominated by this presence, to which he refers constantly to qualify his own acts or those he wants carried out by the believers to whom he is writing.

Let us consider some examples in which God and Christ are associated by the expression that we are considering. Both of Paul's letters to the Thessalonians are address to "the church of the Thessalonians in God the Father and [in] the Lord Jesus Christ" (1 Thess 1:1; 2 Thess 1:1). But Paul also writes "in the Lord" in 1 Thess 3:8; 5:12; 2 Thess 3:4; "in Christ Jesus" in 1 Thess 2:14; 5:18; "in the Lord Jesus" in 1 Thess 4:1; and "in the Lord Jesus Christ" in 2 Thess 3:12. These examples, taken from Paul's earliest letters, demonstrate that this is his characteristic style. These are almost stock phrases, being used to show how everything should be done from the moment one enters into the Christian life. Thus it should not surprise us to encounter the formula "in the Lord" constantly in the greetings that Paul includes at the end of the Epistle to the Romans. Its final chapter was sent with a copy of the letter to the believers in Ephesus,[39] where Paul knew many people (cf. Rom 16:2, 8, 11, 12, 13), but Rom 16:22 is a salutation from the scribe Tertius.

The First Epistle to the Corinthians provides examples of many things that should be done "in Christ" or "in the Lord." In him believers "are sanctified" (1 Cor 1:2); "grace of God that has been given" to them (1 Cor 1:4); they are "brothers and sisters" in him (1 Cor 1:26–30); in him Timothy is Paul's "beloved and faithful child" (1 Cor 4:17); "whoever was called in the Lord as a slave is a freed person," while "whoever was free when called is a slave of Christ" (1 Cor 7:22); because Paul is an apostle, the believers in Corinth are "the seal of [his] apostleship in the Lord" (1 Cor 9:1–2); in the Lord "[their] labor is not in vain" (1 Cor 15:58); and it is in the Lord that Paul sends his final greeting (1 Cor 16:19). It is only in the brief discussion in 1 Cor 12:9–13 that the phrase takes on a different

---

[39] This opinion is shared only by some commentators. J. Fitzmyer rejects it in his commentary in the Anchor Bible series. But I do not see how Paul, who had left Ephesus less than a year before, could have known so many people in Rome, where he had never been. Would the believers in Ephesus have had the time to relocate to Rome in such great numbers?

nuance: there it is said that it has been "in the Spirit" or "in the one Spirit" that the Corinthians have received spiritual gifts. In the Second Epistle to the Corinthians, however, Paul uses the formula only twice: he asserts that he speaks the word of God "in Christ . . . standing in [God's] presence" (2 Cor 2:17), and he appeals to the principle "Let the one who boasts, boast in the Lord" (2 Cor 10:17). In Galatians Paul says only once, "I am confident about you in the Lord" (Gal 5:10), but this is not an offhand comment; Paul is saying that by the Lord's grace the believers in Galatia will be able to judge faithfully between him and his opponents.

The expressions "in the Lord" or "in Christ" or "in Christ Jesus" occur frequently in Philippians (10x) and in the other Prison Epistles (Col 3:18; 4:17), especially in Ephesians (Eph 1:15 and 8 other times) and even in the short letter to Philemon (Phlm 20). The expression "in Christ Jesus" is also found in the Pastoral Epistles: 2 times in 1 Timothy, 9 times in 2 Timothy. We see from these examples what an important place the awareness of Christ occupied in Paul's thought and spirituality. This is evidence of the apostle's personal attachment to his Lord, of whom he said, "[H]e loved me and gave himself for me" (Gal 2:20).

The Johannine Writings. It is here that perhaps we find the phrase used in the strongest theological sense. There is only one occurrence in Revelation: "Blessed are the dead who from now on die in the Lord" (Rev 14:13). This is a reference to a union with Christ that even death itself cannot break, and that issues in eternal life. The First Epistle of John associates God with Christ in a single formula that describes the Christian life: because "the Son of God has come and has given us understanding so that we may know him who is true"—the only true God—"we are in him who is true, in his Son Jesus Christ" (1 John 5:20). Thus we should not be surprised to see John's Gospel teaching, in several significant contexts, that the essence of the Christian life consists of an awareness of this fact.

John's Gospel begins with a prologue that immediately repeats the expression "to be in" 3 times, to provide a glimpse into the paradox of the incarnation. We are struck by these phrases as we encounter them in this hymn to the incarnate Word: "He was in the world, and the world came into being through him" (John 1:10); "He came to what was his own" (John 1:11). This was the Word made flesh. But there is another side to the mystery: "It is God the only Son, who is in [*eis*] the Father's heart,[40] who has made him known" (John 1:18)— the invisible God. There is no contradiction here: this is how the Father has revealed himself to the world, through his Son becoming human.

Let us move ahead in our understanding of the relationship between the Father and the Son. Let us hear Jesus respond to those who have accused him of blasphemy because he has made himself "God's Son" (John 10:36). The accusation was, more precisely, "you, though only a human being, are making yourself God" (John 10:33). Is that what Jesus really claimed? "God" was, effectively, for the Jews as for Jesus himself, the name of the Father.[41] Jesus appeals to his works, which are the very works of the Father, "so that you may know and understand that the Father is in me and I am in the Father" (John 10:38). The mutual immanence of the Father and the Son constitutes the foundation of the divine unity. Jesus says the same thing to his disciples in their conversation after the Last Supper. Philip says to Jesus, "show us the Father" (John 14:8). Jesus replies, "Do you not believe that I am in the Father and the Father is in me?" (John 14:10). The formula is repeated in John 14:11, where Jesus invites the disciples to believe at least in the works that he has done, since he has explained, "the Father who dwells in me [*en emoi menōn*] does his works" (John 14:10). In addition to the verb "be" we now have the verb "dwell," indicating the continual presence of God.

Thus we need to investigate the uses of the verb "dwell" (*menein*) in order to complement what we have learned from studying the formula "to be in." In his Gospel John uses the verb *menein* quite frequently (40x), both in a literal sense and in a symbolic one. When used symbolically of God or of Christ, the word takes on an existential meaning: it indicates the permanent presence of its sub-

---

[40] The preposition *en*, "in," referring to the place where someone is, does not appear here, but rather *eis*, which indicates a direction. Thus the statement could be paraphrased as "the only Son, who is turned toward the Father's bosom."

[41] In John 20:17 it is Jesus himself who says to the disciples that he is going "to my Father and to your Father, to my God and to your God." Thus "the Father" is the personal name of God.

ject in the person who is its object. We also must take into account the twenty-four uses of the verb in the First Epistle of John. Generally, we can set aside those cases where it indicates a local residence. However, it does not seem to be said arbitrarily that the two disciples of John, having learned where Jesus was dwelling, followed him and dwelled with him that day (John 1:35–39). The evangelist is also careful to note when and for how long Jesus "stayed" with certain people or in certain places (e.g., John 4:40; 7:9; 11:6). Even more significant are Jesus' statement that the Father "dwells" in him (John 14:10; also his invitation to his disciples to "abide" in his love, just as he himself "abides" in the Father's love [John 15:9–10]). In the light of Jesus' resurrection we are able to understand the application that he makes of his parable of the Vine and the Branches and appreciate the meaning of his statements, "Abide in me as I abide in you" (John 15:4), and "Those who abide in me and I in them bear much fruit" (John 15:5). In the same way, it is after the resurrection of Jesus that we are able to understand the precise meaning of his saying in John 6 about the bread that is his body and the wine that is his blood: "Those who eat my flesh and drink my blood abide in me, and I in them" (John 6:56).

John's first letter is written from the same perspective. The anointing received from Christ "abides" in believers and "teaches [them] about all things" (1 John 2:27); it thereby permits them to "abide in him" (1 John 2:27–28). And whereas "(w)hoever does not love abides in death" (1 John 3:14), "(a)ll who obey his commandments abide in him, and he abides in them" (1 John 3:24; cf. 4:12, 15, 16). Clearly, the verb is not being used in a locative sense here, nor is it being use metaphorically. It is describing a reality beyond words that, for the believer, is of an existential nature: it is a reciprocal relationship whose sole mediator is Christ, who died and rose from the dead. This relationship enables the believer to participate in the intimacy that exists between the Son and the Father. Before this mysterious reality, one can only remain in contemplative silence and seek to respond to love with love.

Thus expressions that otherwise would be very ordinary take on unexpected dimensions in the contexts in which they appear in the Bible. In these contexts they disclose invisible realities: "No one has ever seen God. It is God the only Son, who is close to the Father's heart, who has made him known" (John 1:18).[42] One might indeed ask why such simple expressions in the New Testament—common verbs and frequently used prepositions—should be the subject of such detailed investigation. The reason is that even though they are not likely to attract attention during a cursory reading, they actually express very powerfully the relationship between us and God, or between us and Christ in the unity of the Spirit. There are other symbolic expressions that describe this relationship in their own way, but in the end, the essential thing is to live with Christ and, through him, with God; to be in him and, through him, in God, in the unity of the Spirit, who is the bond of love between the Father and the Son. When we are in this situation, we understand best why we call God "Father" when we pray. All of the other symbolic names that we give to God—"king," "judge," and so on—find their existential content in the name "Father." The relationship that we have with God through prayer and devotion cannot be expressed in words. The deeper our faith, however, the more fully we are able to understand it.

The Relationship Broken and Restored

This understanding of the relationship that God wants to have with us presents a marvelous ideal, but there is an obvious problem with it: the relationship can be broken all too easily by our own bad will, or at least by our weakness and our inclination to do wrong and fall into sin. Thus our relationship with God is broken. How can the relationship be renewed? It cannot happen through our own initiative. In the Epistle to the Romans Paul explains what goes on inside of us: "I do not do the good I want, but the evil I do not want is what I do" (Rom 7:19). This is because, right from the beginning, Sin—the power of evil personified—has been in the world and has controlled us (cf. Rom 5:12–13). God, however, has dealt with this catastrophic situation by sending Christ into the world, as Paul explains: "where sin increased, grace abounded all the more" (Rom

---

[42] The translation of the phrase containing the verb *exēgēsato* in John 1:18 is much debated. The Vulgate renders it "he has told about him," but this draws our attention to what has been said about God rather than to God himself. Another possible translation is "he has let us know of his interest (in us)."

5:20). How do we experience this intervention of God on the existential level of our relationship with him?

The answer to that question is best understood in terms of the principle of "reconciliation": "we were reconciled to God through the death of his Son" (Rom 5:10). Paul also understands this principle to be the key to his own ministry as an apostle. In Christ, God has made each of us a "new person"; "All this is from God, who reconciled us to himself through Christ, and has given us the ministry of reconciliation" (2 Cor 5:18). In Christ, "God was reconciling the world to himself, not counting their trespasses against them, and entrusting the message of reconciliation to us" (2 Cor 5:19). This is a very concrete depiction of the relationship between God and humanity. When there is a quarrel between two people, it is quite unusual for the offended party to take the initiative to restore the broken relationship, but that is exactly what happens here. It is God who has taken the initiative—and at what a price!—to restore our relationship with him, even though we were the ones who offended him, on a transcendent level. As we seek to understand what God has done for us in these relational terms, we realize that his mercy is beyond our imagining, since the means by which we were reconciled to God was the coming of Jesus "in the flesh" to suffer a painful and unjust execution. These were the lengths to which God's love for us was willing to go.

From the Being of God to the Being of Jesus

I have given this slightly enigmatic title to a group of symbolic expressions that describe the being of God and of Christ within the context of a relationship with humanity. What "way" or "ways" lead to God and bring us into relationship with him, and how is this metaphor transformed in the New Testament? How does the truth of God manifest itself, and what is the role of Christ Jesus in revealing it? How can we understand the life that we experience here on earth as something that Christ, and God himself, also experience, and thus as something that can be imparted back to us in completely unexpected ways? One might say that the way, the truth, and the life are just images. Nevertheless, it is precisely these images that can express the meaning of God's being and of Christ's being, and of defining our relationship with God in Christ.

The Way

The way, or the path, is not a metaphor that is applied to God himself; rather, it speaks of our journey toward him.[43] The image does not have exactly the same meaning in the two Testaments: the New Testament gives it a new and unanticipated meaning.

Here on earth, we are on a journey, but toward what destination, and by what paths? Our lives can end in failure, in death, and even in hell if we do not follow the right path. What roads lead to God, at the end of a blessed life? The Bible's answer is clear: we must walk in the way(s) of the LORD (cf. Ps 119:1; 128:1). The premise is that people are always facing a choice between two routes that lead in opposite directions: that of "the righteous," which is "like the light of dawn," and that of "the wicked," which is "like deep darkness" (Prov 4:18–19). The former leads to life (Prov 6:23), while the latter ends in perdition (Ps 1:6) and death (Prov 12:28). God himself marked out the path that leads to him by giving Israel the law: "Happy are those . . . who walk in the law of the LORD" (Ps 119:1). This is the way that leads to life (Bar 3:13–14). Thus we must choose between these to paths, these two ways of living.

Jesus did not change this general principle, but he did specify the way in which the law needed to be understood in order to be "fulfilled" (Matt 5:17). He did not contradict the law that was given at Sinai, but he did not hesitate to demonstrate its limits. He had not come to abolish the law, but to perfect it, to "take it to the limit": "You have heard that it was said . . . but I say to you . . ." (Matt 5:21–47). The gospel is the proclamation of a new rule of conduct (*halakah*), of a new way of life. Thus it is appropriate, as we learn from the book of Acts, that in its early days Christianity was known as "the Way" (Acts 9:2; 19:9, 23; 22:4; 24:14, 22). This is because, in the end, the way that leads to God is personified by its only mediator, Jesus Christ. In the Gospel of John Jesus defines himself in a saying that describes his role as mediator: "I am the way,

---

[43] For the Hebrew see K. Koch, "דֶּרֶךְ *derekh*," *TDOT* 3:270–93; F. J. Helfmeyer, "הָלַךְ *hālakh*," *TDOT* 3:388–403. For the Greek see M. Völkel, "ὁδός," *EDNT* 2:491–93 (with a bibliography based on W. Michaelis, "ὁδός," *TDNT* 5:42–96). In French see A. Darrieutort, "Chemin," *VTB* 159–62.

and the truth, and the life. No one comes to the Father except through me" (John 14:6). This saying, which uses the specific expression "I AM,"[44] leads us to consider the two other terms that characterize the role that Jesus plays, as a truly human person, in opening the way for a relationship between humanity and God.

The Truth

The theme of truth is not unique to the New Testament.[45] The Hebrew word 'emet characterizes truth as a stable and solid reality (it is derived from the verb 'aman). Truth is connected with God's faithfulness and steadfastness ('emunah): God is faithful to his promises and to his covenant. This is why God's law is characterized by truth (Ps 19:9; 119:86, 138, 142, 151, 160). Thus we are able to trace the theme of truth through the texts that praise God's teachings.

This theme naturally recurs often in the New Testament. It appears some 30 times in the Pauline corpus, for example, to describe the teaching that has come from God and been transmitted by the apostle. In the Synoptic Gospels, however, truth is mentioned relatively rarely, although when Jesus' enemies were trying to trap him, they flattered him by saying, "We know that you . . . teach the way of God in accordance with truth" (Mark 12:14; Matt 22:16; Luke 20:21). In the Gospel of John, however, the theme appears very frequently, both in the sayings of Jesus and in the reflections of the evangelist. Jesus defines his own words as truth (John 8:40, 45, 46), and in the end, he defines himself not just as "true" but as Truth itself: "I am the way, and the truth, and the life" (John 14:6). Thus Jesus is the unique mediator between God and humanity, the one who brings us to the knowledge of God. The revelation of Jesus as the truth transforms it from an abstract concept that could be

---

[44] I offer a brief discussion of the expression "I am" in *Jésus de Nazareth, Christ et Seigneur*, 2:112, but I do not discuss this specific text.

[45] All of the derivatives of the root 'aman are discussed in A. Jepsen, "אָמַן 'āman," *TDOT* 1:292–323 (with a bibliography). For the Greek *alētheia* and related words see H. Hübner, "ἀλήθεια," *EDNT* 1:57–60, with a bibliography based on *ThWNT* 1:233–51. In French see I. de la Potterie, "Vérité," *VTB* 1338–35. De la Potterie also authored the excellent book *La Vérité dans saint Jean* (2 vols.; AnBib 73, 74; Rome: Biblical Institute Press, 1977).

misunderstood as a purely intellectual matter into an essential aspect of our relationship with God, who is "living truth."

The Life

The third thing that Jesus affirmed about himself was, "I am the life."[46] The First Testament insists that life is a gift from God. This is why he is called "the living God" (e.g., Dan 6:20, and in a great many other places, especially in Jeremiah [e.g., Jer 12:16; 16:14–15; 23:7–8; 23:36; 38:16; 44:26; 46:18]). And this is why his most desirable promise is that of life, even life after death. This is symbolized in Ezek 37:11–14 but spoken of literally in Dan 12:2–3; 2 Macc 7:23, 36; Wis 5:15. This life in the "world to come" is "eternal life" (Dan 12:2), and thus it is a participation in the eternity of God himself. But what does this have to do with the relationship between God and humanity?

We find the answer in the New Testament, which teaches that Jesus Christ is the mediator of this life. By his death and resurrection he became the "Author of life" (Acts 3:15). This is why the new life of the Christian is "hidden with Christ in God" (Col 3:3). The proclamation that new life has been given to us in Christ is found throughout the Pauline corpus, but it is in the Johannine writings that the theme appears most insistently. Jesus describes himself as the "living bread" (John 6:51) and says, "whoever eats me will live because of me" (John 6:57). The context indicates clearly that what is in view here is "feeding on" the body of the resurrected Christ. His mediation effectively transmits life to us: "Whoever believes in the Son has eternal life" (John 3:36; cf. 3:15–16). The communication of eternal life, which is the very life of God, is the fruit of Christ's mediation, through the relationship that we enter into with him by faith.

Jesus himself explained why this is so when he said, "I am the way, and the truth, and the life" (John 14:6). This is the very definition of his being, not from the perspective of his personal relationship with God—in that connection he is "the Son"—but from the perspective of the relationship that we can have with him through

---

[46] See H. Ringgren, "חָיָה chāyāh," *TDOT* 4:324–44. For the Greek see L. Schottroff, "ζῶ, ζωή," *EDNT* 2:105–9, who draws on the article *zaō* and its derivatives in G. von Rad, G. Bertram, R. Bultmann, "Ζάω," *TDNT* 2:832–75. In French see the collaborative article "Vie," *VTB* 1348–53.

his death and resurrection. The words "way, truth, life" are not used just as a series of empty metaphors; they are, in symbolic language, the very definition of his relationship with us as the mediator of our salvation. There is nothing beyond this that we could add to this chapter on the use of existential or relational symbols in the language of the two Testaments.

6

The Meaning of Scripture:
Literal Exegesis and Symbolic
Exegesis

O ur study of the symbolic language of the two Testaments now leads us to consider a question that relates to exegesis but has implications for theology. What is the value of observing the symbols that abound in the language of the biblical writings, if not to draw out their implications for Christian faith?[1] The biblical texts, because they are the "word of God," continue to speak to us today about God and about Jesus Christ, from the perspective of the "mystery" that they bear witness to and reveal. There is certainly enough to keep us busy if we study them from a historical-critical perspective, examining in detail all of the problems that they raise in this regard: who wrote them, and when; how they were composed and transmitted; how the events they narrate are to be "reconstructed" historically; and so forth, drawing on all of the disciplines that are necessarily required to address such questions. But would all of this really establish the meaning in light of which they were written, preserved, and interpreted, to the extent that the plan of God has so far

---

[1] Let me say again that reading the biblical texts from the perspective of faith in no way prevents us from reading them critically as well. Nevertheless, we must stand against the pretensions of a totalitarian rationalism. Indeed, faith requires us to use our intelligence fully, both in the literary analysis of texts and in evaluating their exact relationship to historical "facts." Faith enables us to understand these "facts" from a point of view whose outlines reason can legitimately appreciate, but which it can never replace by its own resources alone.

unfolded? To speak of the "plan of God" is to situate our inquiry on a different plane from that on which professional historians work; it is to enter the domain of theology. The very nature of the Bible requires that we do so, but it does indeed bring us onto a different plane; we move from the "historical" to what I have elsewhere[2] called the "historic,"[3] which is open to interpreting events and institutions from the perspective of Christian faith.

An interpretive reading of the Scriptures is always concerned with the "historic." This is true in the church, as it was true of Judaism beforehand. This is why the church's teachers elaborated rules for exegetical method that sought to determine not the *meaning* of biblical texts, but the *meanings* of Scripture. Can we today identify a relationship between that approach, which formerly regulated Christian exegesis of the two Testaments, and the appreciation for symbolic language that has guided our inquiry to this point, and that has even enabled us to sort the examples we have identified into specific categories? Before attempting to answer such a question, we need to remind ourselves what the doctrine of the *meanings* of Scripture was and how it developed through various stages, and also consider what became of it with the advent of critical studies in biblical exegesis. I have discussed these issues at great length elsewhere.[4] The official documents of the Catholic Church have also dealt with them at various times, beginning with the encyclical *Divino afflante Spiritu*[5] in 1943.

---

[2] See P. Grelot, "La résurrection de Jésus et l'histoire: Historicité et historalité," in J. Guillet et al., *Dieu l'a ressuscité d'entre les morts* (Les quatre fleuves 15–16; Paris: Beauchesne, 1982), 145–79 (see especially 158–62).

[3] [I have used the term "historic," which refers to what is historical but also significant within history, to translate the author's term *historial,* which he contrasts with *historique* ("historical").—Trans.]

[4] See P. Grelot, *Sens chrétien de l'Ancien Testament: Esquisse d'un traité dogmatique* (Bibliothèque de théologie 1, Théologie dogmatique 3; Tournai: Desclée, 1962), 16–76; idem, *La Bible, parole de Dieu: Introduction théologique à l'étude de l'Écriture sainte* (Bibliothèque de théologie 1, Théologie dogmatique 5; Paris: Desclée, 1965), 238–91.

[5] The encyclical *Divino afflante Spiritu* was published on September 30, 1943, and confirmed by a declaration of the Pontifical Biblical Commission, *Sancta mater Ecclesia,* on April 21, 1964. It was reaffirmed and amplified by the dogmatic constitution *Dei Verbum* of November 18, 1965. A detailed presentation of the method outlined in these documents may now be found in *The Interpretation of the Bible in the Church* (Vatican City:

Thus I will offer only a brief review, in order to situate the question I have just raised within the context of the inquiry we have conducted into the symbolic language of the two Testaments.

I must, nevertheless, assert an essential fact: the primary principle of biblical textual interpretation, from the perspective of Christian faith, is the contemplation of Christ Jesus in the totality of his "mystery." It was from this perspective that the doctrine of the meanings of Scripture was elaborated, from its very beginning. We have just examined the question of symbolic language from this same perspective, and it must be from this perspective as well that we explore the possible relationship between these two exegetical approaches. In the logic of medieval theologians (which is still valid today), successfully determining the truth value of a text (its "formal object *quod*") depended on the point of view that one adopted in order to examine that text and determine its meaning (its "formal object *quo*"). I will be guided by this logical principle as I inquire into the doctrine that the ancient theologians held of the *meanings* of Scripture and into the way that exegetes today understand the critical *meaning* of texts, and as I investigate the relationship that an appreciation for symbolic language might have with both of these approaches.

THE MEANINGS OF SCRIPTURE IN THE
THEOLOGICAL TRADITION

Why should we speak of the *meanings* of Scripture, in the plural, rather than of the *meaning* of the biblical texts, in the singular? It is essentially a matter of distinguishing the areas in which these texts have implications and in which they can help clarify certain questions: those of the mystery of Christ, of life in the church, of practical morality, and of life after death. Certain texts may touch on several of these questions. Thus the distinction between several possible *meanings* of Scripture was a purely pragmatic consideration for ancient interpreters. Beginning in New Testament times, two different ways

Libreria Editrice Vaticana; Washington, D.C.: United States Catholic Conference, 1993). A discussion of the meaning—and meanings—of the inspired Scriptures is found on pp. 69–76 of the French edition of this publication (Paris: Cerf, 1994). These official teachings do not forbid further investigation of the question under consideration.

of reading the texts began to emerge. Jewish scholars, who spoke Semitic languages (Hebrew and Aramaic), followed fixed rules of interpretation[6] based on those that Hillel had established and that Rabbi Ishmael, in the second generation of the Tannaim, then developed. Greek-speaking Jewish and Christian readers, however, tended to follow the allegorical method elaborated by Philo of Alexandria.[7] Among the Greek fathers, Origen elaborated a theory of the meanings of Scripture around 225 C.E. in *Peri arkon*,[8] which served as a manual for the allegorical exegesis practiced by the Alexandrian fathers. In the school of Antioch,[9] Diodorus of Tarsus, in a lost treatise on the difference between allegory and *theoria*, established the basis of a method that could separate the "spiritual meaning" of a text from the letter in which it was concealed, even as he emphasized the historical character of the text. We should recognize, however, that theoreticians of exegetical method were rare in Christian antiquity. Augustine's *De doctrina christiana*[10] draws implications from a general exposition of Christian doctrine for the method of scriptural interpretation that should be used in preaching, but it does not

---

[6] See H. L. Strack and G. Stemberger, *Introduction au Talmud et au Midrash* (trans. M.-R. Hayoun; Paris: Cerf, 1986), 37–55. This volume describes Hillel's seven rules, the sixteen rules of Rabbi Ishmael, and the thirty-two rules (*middoth*) of Rabbi Eliezer.

[7] See the chapter on Philo of Alexandria by R. Arnaldez in *Le monde grec ancien et la Bible* (ed. C. Mondésert; Bible de tous les temps 1; Paris: Beauchesne, 1984), 37–54.

[8] Curiously, *Le monde grec ancien et la Bible* has no chapter on Origen, but it does have one on Celsus (pp. 171–93), even though Celsus is known only through Origen's *Contra Celsum*. On Origen himself see H. Crouzel, *Origène* (Paris: Lethielleux; Namur: Culture et vérité, 1985), 91–120, "L'interprétation de l'Écriture." A French translation of *Peri arkon* is available in the Bibliothèque augustinienne: *Traité des principles* (Paris: Desclée de Brouwer, 1976).

[9] See Grelot, *Sens chrétien de l'Ancien Testament*, 39 (with some older bibliographic references in n. 7).

[10] See the analysis of this work by M. Moreau in *Saint Augustin et la Bible* (ed. A.-M. La Bonnardière; Bible de tous les temps 3; Paris: Beauchesne, 1986), 253–85. Augustine was willing to rely on the seven rules of Tychonius, a Donatist bishop, which he discusses in his Book III (cf. Moreau, p. 267). The vocabulary used by Ambrose (cf. pp. 392–400), Hillary (pp. 517–20) and Jerome (pp. 538–50) was rather fluid, although Jerome did insist on the value of the literal meaning, as the Antiochenes did.

really provide any systematic rules for exegesis. In the Latin church the commentaries of Ambrose and Hillary are written in the tradition of Origen.

It is only in the seventh century that we first encounter a presentation on interpretive method, Hugo St.-Victor's *Eruditio didascalica*.[11] All of the meanings of Scripture rest on its literal sense (which Hugo calls the "corporeal" or "historical"). On this are built three spiritual senses: the allegorical, the tropological (or moral), and the anagogical. These meanings reveal the "sacrament of scripture," as Hugo explains in his *De sacramentis christianae fidei*.[12] In this method, however, Christian doctrine often is projected onto texts rather than deduced from them. It is not until the thirteenth century that we find a rational method of interpretation that is free from generalized allegory, in the work of Thomas Aquinas.[13] Thomas distinguishes the "literal sense" or "meaning of the texts" from the "spiritual sense" or *sensus rerum,* the "meaning of the things." The "things" in question here, the *res* of Scripture, are to be understood within the history of the plan of God. The word is being used in the sense of the ancient Latin expression that designated what we call "history": *res gestae,* or *res* for short; the unfolding of the historical experience was called the *cursus rerum.* Thus the *sensus rerum* is determined by theological reflection on historical events and what they bring in their wake: institutions, personalities, and transformations of the various components of individual and social life. In doctrinal matters Thomas states as a principle that the literal sense is the only one capable of proof, but he understands this *littera* as that intended by the transcendent author of all of the canonical Scriptures: God himself, who used the human authors as his instruments,[14] in

---

[11] For a brief discussion of this work see Grelot, *Sens chrétien de l'Ancien Testament,* 54–57. The *Eruditio didascalica* is reproduced in PL 176. See the discussion by J. Chatillon in *Le Moyen Âge et la Bible* (ed. P. Riché and G. Lobrichon; Bible de tous les temps 4; Paris: Beauchesne, 1984), 180–83.

[12] *De sacramentis* is reproduced in PL 176, 183. See J. Chatillon, in Riché and Lobrichon, *Le Moyen Âge et la Bible,* 178–80.

[13] *Summa theologica* Ia, q. 1a, a. 10; *Quodlibet* VII, q. 6, a. 14–16; *Commentary on St. Paul's Epistle to the Galatians,* ch. 4, lesson 7. See Grelot, *Sens chrétien de l'Ancien Testament,* 58–60; idem, *La Bible, parole de Dieu,* 234–38.

[14] Grelot, *La Bible, parole de Dieu,* 61–71.

the same way that the individual speech of the prophets transmitted the word of God. It was only much later, with Richard Simon and Spinoza at the end of the seventeenth century, that an appeal to literary and historical criticism came to characterize exegesis.

After that point, the theory of the meanings of Scripture had to be transformed in order to accommodate the demands of critical inquiry. This was not done easily, since it was necessary to move from an understanding in which the texts were defined as the "word of God" to an interpretation that sought to place itself within the historical perspective from which the human authors wrote, and to take into account their cultural setting and the historical situation in which they lived. When the "literal sense" is defined in this way, it clearly involves all of the areas that Thomas related to the "spiritual sense." To what extent, therefore, can we move beyond "literality," defined as the authors' intentions and the circumstances in light of which they wrote, to see farther than their explicit intention, which was limited by their historical situation? We can do this if we take into account an essential fact of the faith: the historical development of God's plan, first throughout all of the First Testament, and then in the absolutely unique fact of Jesus, the ultimate revealer of the Father, the Son of God, who died on the cross and who rose from the dead. In light of Jesus, all of the First Testament can be "reread" from a new perspective, and the literal meaning of its texts is "fulfilled" in a way that could not have been foreseen at the time when they were composed. This is the way the New Testament authors cite the First Testament texts, as anticipatory witnesses of Christ Jesus and all of his mystery. These authors themselves bear witness to the mystery of Christ only to the extent, and in the way, that their own perspectives permit, but their works nevertheless clarify and complete one another and attest to the divine revelation in its totality.

Thus we do not abandon the "literal sense" of the texts, but we do accept a testimony to a deeper level of their meaning, giving it a fullness that the First Testament authors would not have suspected in advance, even if their witness to the divine plan as it unfolded remained open to further developments in the future. This is why the question of a *sensus plenior*[15] arises even within the discussion of

---

[15] Ibid., 312–27.

the "literal meaning" of the texts, particularly those of the First Testament. Christ Jesus, considered within the total unfolding of his mystery, becomes the key to interpreting all of the texts that preceded him, announced his coming, and prepared the way for it, and that served as a "pedagogy of faith" for the people who received the word of God through the intermediaries that he sent: prophets, sages, psalmists, and all of the other sacred writers.[16]

At the same time, such a Christian reading of the texts, while it does not ignore any of the books that made up this divine pedagogy, is nevertheless radically different from the traditional Jewish reading of the letter of the texts, which followed a different criterion of interpretation: the Torah of Moses. (We need not concern ourselves here with the fact that biblical criticism later would invite the Torah, or "Pentateuch," itself to be seen as the product of a historical development.) The texts of the Law, taken as a whole, provided an interpretive principle to which all of the other books were subjected, and the hope of Israel, which was founded on the prophetic promises, remained focused on a future Messiah who was depicted according to the letter of the prophetic texts (even though these sometimes seemed not to agree with one another). This is how the Scriptures were being understood at the end of the long story that the New Testament—or rather, the apostolic tradition to which it bears witness—brought to a close.

In the theological tradition of the church, which is an extension of the foundational tradition of the apostles, the meaning of Scripture can be recognized as an organic whole, despite the literary and historical diversity of its books. This is the perspective of Christian exegesis and of contemporary church teaching, and it is from this perspective that the question of symbolic language in the Bible can be reexamined, to help us determine whether we should speak of the *meaning* or the *meanings* of Scripture. How can literal exegesis and symbolic exegesis not only be harmonized, but actually further one another's work, to make the fullness of Christ's mystery in all of its aspects better understood?

---

[16] I have attempted to give an example of a Christian interpretation of a First Testament book in *Le mystère du Christ dans les Psaumes* (Jésus et Jésus-Christ 74; Paris: Desclée, 1998), which includes several quotations from select commentaries by the ancient church fathers.

BIBLICAL EXEGESIS AND THE INTERPRETATION
OF SYMBOLS

In order to identify the variety of symbols used in the language of the Bible, I practiced a consistently literal exegesis of its texts. Indeed, it is initially on the literal level that the use of different types of symbols plays a role within the language of the Bible. Nevertheless, we must offer an immediate qualification: moving from the First Testament into the New Testament requires us to reinterpret a great number of symbols. This is less true of the second category of symbols, which I have called "mythical." The symbolism of heaven and hell, the personifications of Death and Sin, are hardly things that the entrance of Jesus Christ into human history would modify, except that the "heavenly" presence of God is now accessible to us through the mediation of the risen Christ.

The coming of the Son of God into our world, the coming of the Word of God in the flesh, is a revelatory reality that has nothing symbolic about it except the words that are being used to describe it. The verb "come" is used symbolically to describe the mission of Jesus: "I have come to call not the righteous but sinners" (Mark 2:17 and parallels); "I have come in my Father's name" (John 5:43); and so forth. Besides the coming of the Son into the world, there is the promise of another coming, that of the Spirit (e.g., John 14:26; 15:26; 16:13). There will also be a second coming of Christ in glory, "when the Lord Jesus is revealed from heaven with his mighty angels" (2 Thess 1:7). The verb "descend" is also used to describe the same reality: "No one has ascended into heaven except the one who descended from heaven, the Son of Man" (John 3:13). In the same way, the verb "send" indicates the mission of Jesus specifically in conjunction with his "descent" from heaven.[17] It is in the Gospel of John that we hear Jesus speaking most often about the Father sending him (e.g., John 3:17). We understand what this means, in no small part, by analogy to the ancient prophets, who were sent by God to bring his word to his people. However, the unique situation of the Son, who was sent by the Father, gives this language a new sig-

---

[17] *VTB* has no articles on the verbs "venir" ("come"), "descendre" ("descend"), "envoyer" ("send"); for this last verb see the article on "apôtre" ("apostle"), *VTB,* 71–75.

nificance in light of the unprecedented relationship that the Son has with the Father. The symbolic title "Father" that is sometimes given to God in the First Testament (e.g., Isa 64:8) does not have the depth that Jesus alone revealed in it when he addressed God as *Abba*. Thenceforth, God would be the "Father of our Lord Jesus Christ" (2 Cor 1:3). Since the resurrection of Jesus, "heaven" is no longer just the symbolic location of the presence of God; it is the symbolic location of the presence of Christ in glory.

What changes least in symbolic significance is the meaning attributed to hell as the "place" of evil, of death, of the devil and his minions, of sin as an evil power, and of damnation far from God. Although it is said that Jesus "descended to hell" after his death (1 Pet 3:19; Rom 10:7), this means only that he went among the dead, not that he suffered damnation like the rich man in the parable in Luke 16:19–31. The phrase signifies that his experience of death was a real one.[18]

As we have noted, in the New Testament "mythical" symbols do not lose their original meaning. Nevertheless, the coming of Jesus and his death and resurrection give them a new dimension that we may describe as "existential": we now understand these symbols in relation to Christ, who died and rose from the dead, and with whom we can now have a personal relationship by faith. But there are three other categories of symbols: analogical, figurative, and existential. Has the coming of Jesus modified these symbols in some way?

---

[18] Although the image of hell is a mythic one (there is a "descent into hell" previously attested in Akkadian literature for the goddess Ishtar), this does not mean that the theme is without significance in the New Testament. The application of the imagery to Christ confers a new meaning upon it. In Rev 1:18 it is said that Christ, who "was dead" and who now "is alive," has "the keys of Death and of Hades." This means that he is the master of both. In Acts 2:24–31 the quotation of Ps 15:8–11 LXX (ET 16:8–11) emphasizes that God did not "abandon" Jesus' soul "to Hades." This depicts the resurrection as an ascent from the realm of the dead. This is why Col 1:18 can describe him as the "firstborn from the dead." The First Epistle of Peter takes up this theme in two places, 1 Pet 3:19–20; 4:5–6. Both texts are obscure; it appears that the author is suggesting that the gospel was preached to the dead who had "descended into hell" before Jesus, to invite them to salvation. Both texts are discussed at length by J. Chaine in "Descent du Christ aux Enfers," *DBSup* 2:395–431 (cols. 410–31 discuss the New Testament, with extensive reference to patristic and medieval commentaries).

Jesus and the Analogical Symbols in the Bible

Family Analogies

As we examined the analogical symbols of the two Testaments, we noted that symbols based on family experience take on a dimension in the New Testament that could not have been foreseen in the First Testament. The fatherhood of God, which was understood in a purely analogical sense as an expression of his goodness toward humanity, took on a new meaning from the moment that Jesus addressed God by saying, "Abba! Father!" When the New Testament writers described Christ as the "only begotten" (*monogenēs*),[19] effectively calling him God (John 1:14, 18; 3:16, 18; 1 John 4:9), this was a symbolic expression of the same order. (This "begetting" does not suppose any feminine principle, by contrast with human experience.) In the same way, the symbolic titles "Father" and "Son," given to God and Jesus in his human incarnation, take on an unforeseen meaning, by comparison with the title "Father" given to God in the First Testament and, even more so, by comparison with the adoptive title "Son" given to the king of Israel, to the people as a whole, or to the righteous. The sonship of Jesus is of an entirely different order; it puts him on the level of God himself.

This does not mean that adoptive sonship cannot be granted to other members of the human race. Paul says this expressly, using the word that means "adoptive sonship," *huiothesias* (Gal 4:5; Rom 8:15, 23). However, he specifies that this status is granted to us by the mediation of Jesus Christ (Eph 1:5). It depends on the fact that baptism unites us to him, making us "members of his body" (e.g., Rom 12:5). This is no longer the same thing as the adoptive sonship that the Israelites were granted under the old covenant (Rom 9:4). This was given to them in anticipation of the coming of Christ; but Israel as a community did not yet constitute the "body of Christ," even though the redemptive grace of Christ could have reached in advance to those within this community who were righteous.

The implication is that as we reread the texts of the First Testament in the light that the New Testament casts retrospectively onto

---

[19] See the article on *monogenēs* by J. A. Fitzmyer, "μονογενής," *EDNT* 2:439–40, which draws on F. Büchsel, "μονογενής," *TDNT* 4:737–41.

them, we are able to give the symbolic words that they contain a sur-
charge of meaning, which gives them a significance that could not
have been foreseen within the historical situation in which they were
composed.[20] God already *was* the "Father" in the sense that the coming of Jesus Christ gave to that word; but this had not yet been
revealed: it was only the coming of Christ into human history, by a
mysterious dispensation of God's plan, that gave this fullness of
meaning to an expression whose use was already preparing the way
for the doctrinal language of the New Testament. But in saying this,
are we departing from the literal meaning of the texts? If we accept
Thomas's definition, in which God himself is the author of the
texts[21] because he inspired the sacred writers, we are keeping strictly
to the literal meaning. But if we adopt the definition that modern
critics use in their interpretation of the Bible, we have actually
moved to a higher level of meaning, the *sensus plenior*,[22] and we are
projecting it retrospectively onto texts whose literal meaning has
already been explained by biblical criticism.

Does what we have said about the name "Father," by which
God is known, apply equally well to the name "Mother," which is attributed to the community? Yes, as long as we acknowledge that we
move to a different level when we pass from the First Testament into
the New Testament. In the texts of the First Testament Jerusalem is
given the title "Mother" because it is equated with or explicitly

---

[20] The Qur'an's criticism of the title "Father" given to God in the
Gospels is the result of a complete misunderstanding of the meaning being
given to the word. The Qur'an equates the notions of "the Father" and "the
Son" in the New Testament with the imagery of the divine triad that was
worshiped in pre-Islamic Arabia: a father-god, a mother-goddess, and a
son-god. The New Testament, however, is teaching nothing of the kind.
Within Judaism the title "Father" that was given to God designated an
adoptive paternity, which left God in his proper place of absolute uniqueness. In the Gospel texts the change in the way this language is understood
comes exclusively from the fact that Jesus addressed God by calling him
'Abba ("Father"), a term that presupposed an astonishing and unprecedented familiarity. But Jesus distinguished formally between "*your* Father
who is in heaven" and "*my* Father," speaking of him in a *relational* sense,
understandably departing from the humility that he showed on other
occasions.

[21] Grelot, *La Bible, parole de Dieu*, 312.

[22] Ibid., 314–27.

called the "wife" of God (Isa 54:1, 5; Ps 87:5; 149:2), in keeping with a
convention of the time by which cities and communities were personified and spoken of in the feminine. It was from this same perspective that the national community of Israel was depicted as
the "wife" of YHWH by virtue of the covenant that God had made
with it. In the New Testament, however, the metaphor finds new
grounds: it is as the "body of Christ" that the church, the community to which all believers belong as children, is the bride of Christ
(Eph 5:22–25; Rev 19:7; 21:2, 9). The church is also the mother of
believers, since it is the personification of the new humanity (Rev
12), the mother of Christ (Rev 12:5) and of all believers (Rev 12:17).
Thus the set of symbols is transformed as the realization of God's
plan progresses within human history.

Jesus' entrance into that history as the Son of God in human
form transformed the symbols that had been developed within the
First Testament, in the context of a culture in which symbolism was
already an accepted type of religious language. These symbols were
not adopted arbitrarily; they are deeply rooted in the human psyche.[23]
However, we should recognize the successive stages through which
they passed in the course of their development: (1) that of the universal religious language in which they are rooted; (2) that of the language of the First Testament, in which they are reconditioned by
monotheism and the strictures of the covenant that God made with
the people of Israel; and (3) that of the New Testament, in which
Jesus' earthly life and his death and resurrection bring about a radical
mutation, transforming the symbols into Christian ones. Christian
symbolism itself can undergo cultural adaptations appropriate to the
contexts into which the gospel is received, but it must remain funda-
mentally faithful to itself. This may create difficulties in certain places,
depending on the cultures that were present before the gospel came,
but these are problems that should be studied within the context of
evangelization itself. Because we are talking about symbols based on
family life, the solutions to these problems can be implemented only
by those who are sharing the gospel with the people of those places.

---

[23]There is a brief discussion of this in P. Grelot, *Péché originel et
rédemption, examinés à partir de l'épître aux Romains: Essai théologique*
(Paris: Desclée, 1973),18 n. 2 (with reference to the works of Carl Jung;
these are what Jung calls "archetypes").

Social Analogies

The First Testament bequeathed certain symbols to the New Testament: God as judge, as king, and as warrior, with the powers of heaven and the angelic host at his side. Did the coming of the Son of God into human history, in the person of Jesus of Nazareth, change these symbols in some way? As Jesus carried out his historical mission here on earth, right up to his death on the cross, he claimed none of these titles for himself. The "Son of Man," as Jesus used the phrase, was a person just like any other, except that he had been given a special mission to proclaim the good news of the reign (or kingdom) *of God*. Even in terms of this kingdom, he did not draw a distinction between himself and others; in his teachings he spoke of God as king alone, in a way that his hearers could understand because of their familiarity with the First Testament. Even in his eschatological discourse (Mark 13 and parallels), his depiction of the final judgment (Matt 25:31–46), and his response to the high priest during his trial (Mark 14:62; Matt 26:64; Luke 22:69), he spoke objectively of the Son of Man in his glory, identifying him with the Davidic Messiah, but never explicitly claiming the title for himself. It was enough for him to assert his filial relationship with God. But in what sense? In Luke 20:36, in the course of his discussion with the Sadducees about the resurrection of the dead, he said explicitly that in the world to come the resurrected righteous would be equal to the angels because they would be "children of God." However, the Jewish authorities said that he deserved to die "according to the law" because he "claimed to be the Son of God" (John 19:7). Luke reports that a similar conclusion was reached at Jesus' trial (Luke 22:70–71). But Mark 14:61 and Matt 26:63 say that Jesus was silent and did not explicitly claim this Messianic title for himself.[24]

---

[24] An "objective" reading of Matt 16:16–17 would suggest that Jesus affirmed Peter's messianic confession, "You are the Christ, the Son of the Living God." Nevertheless, we should not overlook the fact that the parallel text in Mark has only the words "You are the Christ" (the Messiah), and that Jesus immediately commanded his disciples not to tell anyone this, because the claim would have been interpreted in the customary political sense that the word "Messiah" had for Jews of the time. It was only after his resurrection that Jesus was recognized as the Messiah in a completely different sense.

The Gospel narratives are "rereadings" of Jesus' life, written after the fact from the perspective offered by his resurrection from the dead, and thus from the perspective of the "world to come," in which his divine sonship was revealed in all of its fullness. From that perspective, as the "Son" he is directly associated with God—with "the Father," as John would say—in the exercise of his functions as king, judge, and victor over the powers of evil. This association leads to a new set of symbols that refer to Christ directly: by means of a figurative interpretation they transfer to Christ in glory what the texts of the First Testament said about the future Messiah. Now we can ask again how its social analogies are to be applied to the man Jesus, who became the "Messiah in glory" by his resurrection. It is through him that the God of Israel will manifest his reign over humanity, his saving justice, his irrevocable judgment against human sin, his campaign against all the manifestations of evil and his ultimate victory over them. All of this takes place on an entirely different plane from the one on which, from the perspective of the First Testament, the "wars of YHWH" and the battles of Israel's kings were fought, and from the one on which, from a prophetic perspective, the future Davidic Messiah would engage in combat. We should now consider these same symbolic themes in light of the "figurative" meaning of the texts.

Jesus and the Figurative Symbols in the Bible

As we saw earlier, the prefigurations of Christ and his mystery, and those of his church, underwent a historical development within which we can distinguish two periods. First there was the historical experience that led to the founding of the Israelite community and its institutions; then came the time when the disasters that the nation experienced led the prophets to reflect on its past and to project the great events of its history and the major institutions of its society into a future that at first was unspecified, but then was fixed by eschatology at the "end of time."

This is where things stood in the days of Jesus. Hopes for the future were alive, but in many different forms within Judaism, depending on what major events, important people, social institutions, and prophetic texts were in view. The latent opposition of different currents of thought within Judaism accentuated the diversity in the way that the hoped-for future was represented, at this time when Roman domination had cost the nation its political liberty, but not its institutional religious, cultural, linguistic, and legal autonomy. The Jews enjoyed this autonomy wherever they lived, whether in their established communities in Babylon, in the Parthian Empire; in Judea and Galilee, in their historic homeland; or in the "Dispersion" on all the shores of the Mediterranean: in Egypt, Greece and Macedonia, Asia Minor and Syria, Cyrene, and Italy, all the way to Rome itself.

To what great experiences of the past did these Jews turn in order to depict the future, and what institutions did they hope to restore, by what means, and under whose leadership? All of these details were much disputed by those familiar with the scriptural texts. The events of the exodus provided an obvious model for deliverance from political servitude, and there was no disagreement about reestablishing free institutions in the land of the ancestors. But how were these things to be achieved? By a miracle of God, or by the force of arms? The Sadducees were content to maintain the continuity of worship in the temple, but also there were activists who dreamed of a revolt that would throw off the yoke of the enemy from the Jewish people. Did not the book of Joshua record the success of a holy war? And did not the image of the great king David project onto the future horizon the restoration of an independent kingdom that would revive the greatness of the past? The great diversity of prophetic texts allowed interpreters of Scripture to imagine the future in many different ways.[25] The Pharisees held that, above all, the "law of Moses" should be observed as the rule of life for Israel. The common people, who were fervently attached to the faith, were captivated by the great images of the coming of the royal Messiah and the final resurrection. But how would these things take place, and when?

When Jesus, a humble artisan from Nazareth in Galilee, began his preaching ministry, initially he could have been seen as continuing

---

[25] We should note that the same diversity of interpretations continues among both believing and unbelieving Jews today. The founding of the State of Israel has really changed nothing in this regard, even though this state appears to be a modern-day version of the "national homeland" that was reestablished by the Persian Empire after the exile of the Jews to Babylon.

the work of John the Baptist, whom the tetrarch Herod Antipas had arrested. However, the prophetic allure of his "good news of the reign of God" inevitably raised the question in people's minds, "Who is this, and what role does he intend to play among the Jewish people?" Was he a prophet, like those of old (cf. Mark 8:28; Matt 16:14; Luke 9:19)? Or could he be the longed-for Messiah? The disciples who followed him were prepared to hope that he would play the role of liberating Messiah for his people (Mark 8:29). But Jesus, for his own part, did not accept this politico-religious perspective, to which the activists were ready to rally. On the contrary, he foresaw that his preaching of the reign of God soon would meet with failure and that he himself would suffer a personal catastrophe: all three Synoptic evangelists agree that on three separate occasions he made this somber prediction (Mark 8:31; 9:31; 10:32–34 and parallels).[26]

Things happened exactly as Jesus predicted. His theological dispute with the Pharisees and the outrage over the scandalous act that he perpetrated in the temple, despite the religious police who were supposed to maintain good order there (Mark 11:15–17 and parallels), could only have led to the plot that was hatched by the high priest and his circle to get rid of this troublemaker.[27] Jesus was put on trial before the Roman prefect Pontius Pilate, and he was mercilessly crucified. Had the hopes that he raised in the hearts of his disciples been permanently extinguished? No, because an entirely unanticipated event then took place that clarified everything that Jesus had done to that point: starting on the "third

---

[26] To be sure, the reports of these predictions were written up after the fact. We can easily recognize in the third (Mark 10:32–34) a summary of Jesus' passion. Thus we should not look for a verbatim reproduction of Jesus' words in any of them. Nevertheless, it is too simple to reject the authenticity of these texts by considering them to be cases of *vaticinium post eventum,* "prophecies" of events already past. The triple repetition of the prediction shows that the Gospel tradition retained the memory of the insistence with which Jesus returned to this somber perspective on the future.

[27] I made this point in *Jésus de Nazareth, Christ et Seigneur: Une lecture de l'Évangile* (2 vols.; LD 167, 170; Paris: Cerf, 1997–1998), 2:121, 124. Clearly, the responsibility for this decision to do away with Jesus does not rest with all Jews, but only with those who were responsible before the Roman authorities for maintaining order in Judea.

day"—the day of the "consolation of the dead," according to one version of the Jewish hopes that was based on an interpretation of Hos 6:2[28]—Jesus showed himself alive to chosen witnesses (Acts 10:40–41). He was alive, but not with the life of this "present world"; rather, by the will of God, whom he called his "Father," he had entered into the "world to come." Thus he inaugurated a new stage in the unfolding plan of God.

After this, all of the prophetic promises had to be reread from a new perspective. The hope that had been founded on these promises, and on a figurative interpretation of the great events and major personages of the past, had to be reinterpreted from the perspective of his resurrection from the dead. This resurrection itself represented a promise that all those who had put their faith in the good news of the reign of God would themselves be raised from the dead in the future. Jesus had been the "Son of God" since birth, and he was called this explicitly at the beginning of his ministry of proclaiming the good news, when he was baptized by John. He had fulfilled his mission as the "Servant of the Lord" right to the end, when he became the "Suffering Servant." But even his death led only to his enthronement in glory as the Son of Man, as predicted by Daniel (Mark 14:62 and parallels; Acts 7:56). Afterwards, on the day of Pentecost, his followers received the Holy Spirit, who sent them throughout the world to proclaim the good news. As a result of all this, they began to recall the events of Jesus life in order to understand how they had fulfilled the Scriptures. Drawing on a new understanding of the figurative events and institutions of the past, they reread the Scriptures in order to construct, by means of their preadapted expressions, a presentation of his mission as the Messiah in glory. In this way, they departed from the common approach to reading that the Jewish scribes practiced.

Indeed, Jesus' followers no longer read the Scriptures the way the Jews did. The Jews were attached to a literal observation of the

---

[28] I have explained the meaning of this expression, which is connected with the text in Hos 6:2, in an article published in P. de Surgy et al., *La Résurrection du Christ et l'exégèse moderne* (LD 50; Paris: Cerf, 1969), 46–47. I take up the question again, with supporting references, in *L'Espérance juive à l'heure de Jésus* (11th ed.; Jésus et Jésus-Christ 6; Paris: Desclée, 1994), 134, 187–88, 234.

law, which was understood according to the oral tradition, and they were concerned with the immediate implications of the prophetic promises. For the apostles and the other heralds of the good news, however, the figurative principle of interpretation used by the prophets permitted a new description of the redemptive work of Jesus: his death had been a sacrifice, and he had served as a mediator. Thus he had brought forgiveness of sin to those who believed in him, and he had bestowed on them the promised Holy Spirit. This was a new way of presenting God's plan, and indeed a new way of understanding God himself. Under these conditions, what became of the figurative interpretation of the events and people that the ancient prophets had considered to be veiled prefigurations of the anticipated salvation? It was transformed in light of the resurrection of Jesus: he had opened the way to the "world to come," not yet in the experience of this earthly life, but in a firm hope that even now gave its possessors an advance experience of what was to come. The Torah itself underwent a certain transformation as it was re-centered on the commandment to love (Rom 13:8–10), but its legal precepts regarding Israelite society became quiescent.

The figurative meaning of the people and institutions of the First Testament is applied in this way not to the earthly life and ministry of Jesus, but to his position and functions as Christ in glory. His "mystery" is presented in biblical language, through the transposition of texts that refer to the people, institutions, and rites of the past. The covenant founded on the sacrifice that Jesus' death represents is identified with the new covenant of Jer 31:31–34. The royal Messiah who was expected on the basis of the prophetic promises is identified with Christ in glory, through a total transposition of his functions: they are understood to be carried out in the realm of the "world to come," which is already present secretly in the church and, through it, within history itself.

This transposition of ancient realities, and of the texts that record them, is observable not only in Paul's descriptions of Christ's glory, in Revelation, and in the Epistle to the Hebrews, but also in the infancy narratives in Matthew and Luke.[29] In the way Christ's

---

[29] This is why I discussed the infancy narratives in Matthew and Luke *after* the resurrection of Christ in *Jésus de Nazareth, Christ et Seigneur,* 2:433–97.

messianic vocation is announced those narratives, the characteristics of his future situation are depicted as already present in seminal form. At the same time, his divine sonship is clearly portrayed. This is notably the case in the episode in which his mother's vocation is revealed (Luke 1:26–38)[30]. We can see from this that these infancy narratives are not "historical" in the sense in which modern criticism understands this word. Nevertheless, they are based on solid traditions, and they reflect the reality of these traditions even as they bring out, by means of the biblical allusions that they project onto the "facts," their "historic" meaning, by which I mean their meaning within the unfolding of the divine plan. The texts that are used in these allusions sometimes are considered in their enlarged literal sense—in their *sensus plenior*—and sometimes adapted, for better or for worse, to the circumstances that they are intended to illustrate. This is the case for, for example, the quotations of Hos 11:1 in Matt 2:15, and of Jer 31:15 in Matt 2:18, and of the unlocatable text in Matt 2:23. A detailed study of these quotations shows how the evangelist understood the "conformity to the scriptures" that he constantly attributes to the events he relates, but it also shows how easily he could slip from using texts in their *sensus plenior* to adapting them more or less arbitrarily; the difference needs to be recognized on a case-by-case basis.

The most interesting example in the New Testament of christological rereading is that of the biblical quotations and allusions in the Epistle to the Hebrews.[31] How can this Christian author show how two aspects of Christ's work, his sacrifice and his high priesthood, were in conformity to the Scriptures, when no messianic text among the prophetic oracles attributes these to the Davidic Messiah? For Christ's high priesthood, he calls upon the description of

---

[30] Ibid., 2.461–71. The narrative of the annunciation is not merely a "birth announcement," as is often claimed when it is compared with the analogous narratives that appear in the books of the First Testament; rather, it is the narrative of a vocation. It shows the unique role that Mary will play in the unfolding of the divine plan. On the virginal conception see my comments there on pp. 466–70.

[31] I have called attention to this point in, among other places, *Corps et sang du Christ en gloire: Enquête dogmatique* (LD 182; Paris: Cerf, 1999), ch. 7, "Le sang du Christ dans l'épître aux Hébreux."

Melchizedek in Gen 14:18 and Ps 110:4, applying these texts to the Davidic Messiah and interpreting them figuratively. With the high priestly work of Christ in glory thus resting on the *sensus plenior* of two biblical texts, the author then attaches the sacrificial theme to this work, offering a figurative interpretation of the covenant ceremony that Moses conducted at Sinai (Heb 9:19–21) and of the high priest's entry into the "holy of holies" with the blood of sacrificed animals on the Day of Atonement (Heb 9:7–14, 24–28). The author reads these various passages from the Jewish Bible consistently according to the rules of figurative interpretation, explaining them by means of a technical vocabulary that does not correspond to that of Alexandrian allegorism, which Paul uses in 1 Cor 10:6, 11 (*typos,* in one sense) and Gal 4:24 (*allēgoroumena*). Instead, the author uses a collection of technical terms to present a very elaborate typology: *typos,* meaning "model," and *antitypos,* "reproduction," with the synonyms *hypodeigma,* "imitation," and *skia,* "shadow." This is differentiated from *eikōn,* "image," which still implies a certain imitation of a reality.

This technical language is used to explain how biblical "figures" bore a resemblance in advance to the redemptive reality of Christ: the successive phases of his "sacrifice" are seen from the perspective of its culmination in his entry into glory, which is implicitly compared with the entrance of the Jewish high priest into the holy of holies in the temple. The author's figurative interpretation of these Jewish rites displays a subtlety that we may trace to his Alexandrian culture, but nevertheless he is not handling his allegory in the manner of Philo; rather, it is an original creation of his based on a parallelism between two orders of reality. The first announces the second as it prefigures it.

It would be appropriate here to offer an analogous study of the biblical quotations and allusions in the book of Revelation.[32] However, I can only sketch out briefly the general direction in which such a study would proceed to show how Revelation draws on the *sensus plenior* of biblical texts to offer a figurative rereading of redemptive history that sometimes depends on simple literary adaptation. In the book of Revelation the drama that unfolded when

---

[32] Ibid., ch. 8, "L'Agneau immolé" (= the blood of Christ in the book of Revelation).

God and his people were confronted by other nations is transposed in order to depict the confrontation between two historical realities: the community that has been renewed by the grace of the Mediator—Christ in glory, associated with God himself—and the hostile nations that oppose this community.

Jesus and the Relational Symbols in the Bible

We examined relational symbols in the preceding chapter, and this discussion can provide us with some examples for use here. Let us recall simply that the texts in which these symbols are used relate to how we enter into the life of faith. As such, they can be meditated upon endlessly; their meaning can never be exhausted. It is particularly in the Gospel of John that we hear Jesus using expressions such as "to be in," "to abide in," "to be with," and "to be near." Clearly, these local metaphors do not have a meaning that is *materially* local; rather, they suggest the intimacy of the believer's relationship with Christ and, through him, with God. This relationship is modeled on the one that Jesus, as the Son of God, has with the Father, and it involves a participation in the intimacy evident in the relationship between these "two" who are really "one" ("The Father and I are one" [John 10:30]).

To live fully in this relationship is the height of the spiritual life. Even simple believers who are—and feel—distant from it may nevertheless participate in it imperceptibly by faith. This is even more true when Jesus fulfills, through the celebration of the Lord's Supper, the promise described in Revelation: "if you hear my voice and open the door, I will come in to you and eat with you, and you with me" (Rev 3:20). As Jesus says in the Gospel of John, "the bread that I will give for the life of the world is my flesh" (John 6:51); "Those who eat my flesh and drink my blood abide in me, and I in them" (John 6:56). When this happens, what Augustine summarized in an amazing formula, which he puts in the mouth of Christ himself, takes place: *Non ego mutabor in te, sed tu mutaberis in me.* "I will not be changed into you, but you will be changed into me." This is exactly the opposite of what typically happens when we eat food. Who would not want to experience such a transformation? Though it is humanly improbable and materially impossible, Christ has become the master of the impossible, through his cross and his resurrection. Thus we need only to take him at his word. He is the one who has taken the initiative in the relationship by which he brings us not merely *toward* God, or even *to* God, but *into* God.

To understand the meaning of such a promise, we should go back to a text in the First Epistle of John that expresses it in relational terms, even as it specifies its content: "God is love, and those who abide in love abide in God, and God abides in them" (1 John 4:16). A little earlier John writes, "God's love was revealed among us in this way: God sent his only Son into the world so that we might live through him" (1 John 4:9); "Beloved, since God loves us so much, we also ought to love one another" (1 John 4:11). This is the last word of the divine revelation that has come to us in Jesus Christ. Within the Christian church the wisest spiritual teachers have always insisted on the supreme importance of this commandment to love: since "it is God who arranges all things, where there is no love, bring love, and you will gather love."[33]

---

[33] St. John of the Cross, letter no. 47, in *Oeuvres complètes* (ed. D. Poirot; Paris: Cerf, 1990), 1598

Conclusion: Biblical Truth and Theological Truths

Sacred Scripture, in its literary variety and its historical development, has fixed in writing the testimony that has been borne to the revelation of God in human history. This revelation took place in three stages. It was first affirmed progressively throughout the history of Israel by messengers whom God sent, whose witness was collected in books that God inspired (2 Pet 1:21; cf. 2 Tim 3:16). This history culminated in the coming of Jesus the Jew, who died and was raised from the dead. It was given its definitive formulation in the proclamation of the gospel by Jesus' apostles and the preservation of their teaching in the books of the New Testament. We are able to assess the contribution that each of the biblical authors—Israelite, Jewish, or Christian—personally made to the revelation of God and of his plan for human history. We are able to reconstruct what we might call the "theology" of each author, staying within the realm of objective research, and to identify what that author's individual contribution was to the total revelation. Even though what we might call the "apostolic tradition" provides no synthetic study of the entire Scriptures, we can still say confidently that the canon was closed when the apostles of Jesus Christ and those who recorded their testimony had fulfilled their providential mission. Since then, these Scriptures have been the source of the church's faith and practice.

When I speak of "practice," I have in mind that part of the apostolic legacy that is not necessarily spelled out in detail in the

texts of the New Testament, but which the local churches of the second century accepted and followed with the full awareness that they
were the being faithful to a "deposit" they had received (cf. 1 Tim
6:20; 2 Tim 1:12, 14). This is not the place to develop this point.[1] I
simply wish to observe here that from the second century onward,
local churches began to confront the cultures of the places to which
they were bringing the gospel. The leaders of these churches needed
to do so with the means that their surroundings, their own culture,
and their religious heritage provided. They needed to do more than
just repeat the words of the Scriptures they had in hand (meaning
the First Testament in two versions, Hebrew and Greek[2]) and the
words that the evangelists of the previous generation had bequeathed to them in their own writings (which became the New
Testament). Despite what all of these writings supplied to help them
remain faithful to the gospel, they still needed to engage the people
of other religious and cultural settings, who had a language of their
own. To do this, they needed to invent a special language of their
own to "speak the faith" in terms that would be accessible to those
whom they were evangelizing. If it is appropriate to speak of the
message transmitted by each author in both Testaments as that

---

[1] I have discussed this notion of the "apostolic tradition" elsewhere,
emphasizing the practical aspects of it that the first Christian generations
bequeathed to the churches of the second century. The principle *sola
Scriptura,* which has been adopted by the ecclesial communities that
emerged from the "Reformation" of the sixteenth century, considers exclusively what we have been able to deduce, and may yet be able to deduce,
from the texts. However, the continuity of the church's practical life is not
confined to the scriptural transmission of the "true faith." The apostolic
legacy also includes the structure of the churches. For a discussion of this
point see my article "La tradition apostolique: Vue general," in *La Tradition apostolique: Règle de foi et de vie pour l'église* (Théologies; Paris: Cerf,
1995), 56–97.

[2] In the early centuries of the church the Greek and Latin fathers considered the Greek version of the Bible authoritative as inspired Scripture.
Origen was nevertheless careful to present, in his *Hexapla,* the Hebrew text
and a Greek transliteration, alongside the Septuagint and several other
Greek versions. In the fourth century Greek authors refer to the translations of Aquila and Symmachus as substitutes for the Hebrew, which they
could not read directly (this is what Eusebius of Caesarea and John
Chrysostom do in their commentaries on Psalms, for example).

author's "theology," it is even more appropriate to use the term to describe the effort that this next generation of evangelists needed to make as they stood before greatly diverse audiences and defended the gospel that they were proclaiming.

Thus the theological effort that began when evangelists first brought the gospel into Jewish and pagan contexts had to be redoubled as the church moved into more and more different contexts. Expressions had to be found that suited many different requirements, both to defend the true faith against heretical innovations and to explain it to audiences of new and distinct cultures.[3] For example, from the second century on, we find Christian apologists such as the philosopher Justin using terms borrowed from popular Stoicism (e.g., the word *logos*) to express the authentic faith. Thus the gospel's engagement with culture resulted in the creation of theological vocabularies that did not simply duplicate the Bible's vocabulary (which, as we have seen, is highly symbolic, and whose symbols are chosen carefully so that they will express the experience of faith authentically). So we see various theological vocabularies developing over time as the proclamation of the gospel encounters systems of thought characterized by a diversity of philosophical systems and spiritual experiences: after Stoicism came Neoplatonism, and then came Aristotelianism—we will not make the list much longer if we wish to confine our discussion to Christian antiquity. But what happens as the gospel today confronts the thought of India, China, Japan, and Africa, and Native American spirituality? For that matter, when we seek to share the gospel with those immersed in religious systems such as Buddhism and Islam, what new languages will we have to invent, and what symbols can we draw upon, to help them understand and, even better, to help them sense the "Truth" of the Christian faith?

The symbols used in the Scriptures to "speak the faith" were not chosen at random; they are deeply rooted in the experience of this world and of the history that divine providence had in store for the "people of God." Thus they are closely connected with that people's experience of a relationship with God himself, the

---

[3] I will not offer a bibliography for this rapid survey; it would necessarily include all of the church fathers!

experience of a living faith. As the proclamation of the gospel reaches more and more people who live in different cultures, what must be done so that those cultures, and the languages that they use, can serve to express that same faith in its absolute authenticity? This enterprise necessarily creates crises, as it did in the early centuries of the church: first came the Gnostic crisis; then the crisis of Marcionism, which was hostile to the First Testament; then the crisis of a false spiritual enthusiasm that began among the Montanists in their contact with the cults in Phrygia; then the Arian crisis, which arose when certain philosophical reflections of an Aristotelian nature were carried to an extreme. These were only the beginnings of the crises that the Christian church, the guardian of the authentic gospel, had to go through over the centuries. In each of these situations the church had to do more than just repeat, with conviction, what the sacred texts said; it had to meet its opponents on their own ground and create a language capable of refuting their errors.

The inevitable result was an expansion of the church's theological vocabulary. This did not mean the generation of more symbols besides those that the sacred books contained, but rather, new ways of interpreting these symbols in popular language, and ultimately an appeal to philosophical terminology to eliminate any middle ground. Thus at the Councils of Nicea (325 C.E.) and Constantinople (381 C.E.), a "Credo" was formulated in Greek and Latin that appealed to the abstract terms *homoousios* and *consubstantialis* (= *unius substantiae*) to establish that the Father and the Son were of one nature. Then, in 451 C.E. the Council of Chalcedon, relying on the *Tome* (letter) that Pope Leo I had sent to Bishop Flavian, used the words "nature" (*physis/natura*) and "person" (*prosōpon* and *hypostasis/persona*) to define the relationship of the Son and of the Holy Spirit to the Father within the single Godhead.[4] Thus the way was opened for the elaboration of a theological vocabulary that would condense, through the use of abstract words, the doctrinal content of biblical texts that had been com-

---

[4]The creedal statements described here may be found in H. Denzinger, P. Hünermann, and H. Hoping, *Kompendium der Glaubensbekenntnisse und kirchlichen Lehrentscheidungen* (37th ed.; Freiburg im Brisgau: Herder, 1991). The Nicene Creed is no. 302.

posed from a more existential perspective, using symbolic expressions that spoke directly to the imagination. It was the Greek and
Latin church fathers who first took this direction, but not without
certain fluctuations in the way they used the new words that had
been borrowed from the vocabulary of Plato and Aristotle. In both
the Eastern church and the Western church theology then continued unabashedly in this same direction, but it never lost contact
with the language of the fundamental texts of the Bible.

We must emphasize strongly that these Scripture texts remain
the unique source of revealed "Truth." The formulations furnished
by the cultures within which reflection on the faith took place
never constituted an auxiliary language that was used to establish
the exact meaning of the particular "truths" that had to be preserved intact as they confronted new cultures, where these truths
were placed in jeopardy. The exercise was one not of carefully
examining the "theology" contained in the textual sources, but of
the church providing a necessary elaboration as the faith reached
into new cultural contexts. There was no more "truth" in the solemn definitions promulgated by ecclesiastical authorities than was
already contained in the Scripture texts themselves; it was simply a
matter of the Bible and theology clarifying one another.[5] And the
use of a most varied symbolic language, such as we found among
the biblical writers, was never abandoned, despite everything. The
sacred texts were read regularly in the church's liturgy, and so the
meaning and implications of their symbols had to be explained to
the listening believers. The psalms continued to be sung and
became the official prayers of the ecclesiastical community. To
celebrate the divine mysteries in all of their aspects, poets writing
in Latin, Greek, and Syriac frequently made use of the same kind
of symbolic and metaphorical expressions of faith that are found in
the Bible. And the truths that these symbols defined served for
each of these poets as a hedge around Christian prayer, preserving
its biblical authenticity. In our century, in all of the languages in
which God is worshiped through the mediation of Jesus Christ, the

---

[5] In this sense, we may indeed appeal to a principle of *Sola scriptura,*
relying on Thomas Aquinas himself. See F. Gaboriau, *L'Écriture seule?*
(Théologie nouvelle; Paris: FAC-éditions, 1997), 99–103. Gaboriau notes
that the formula appears nowhere in Luther's writings (pp. 73–89).

situation remains the same: the language of the Bible, with its very dense symbolism, remains the fundamental reference point for Christian faith. In the same way, official documents of the church always give the Bible the final word.

Thus it would be a mistake to think that if we can develop "catechetical" definitions of the essentials of the faith for every place and time and culture, this will make direct recourse to the sacred Scriptures unnecessary. Nevertheless, we should acknowledge that the task of "translating" the biblical texts into every culture and language will require a considerable effort if we really want the revelation of God in Christ to take root. We should expect that this will require innovations and mutations in language as well as in thought. Who would claim that the word *El/Ilu* designated the true God before the Bible gave it this meaning, or that the Greek *Theos* and the Latin *Deus* were predisposed to receive this same meaning before first Judaism and then Christianity made them take it on and excluded their prior meanings? Similar designations for the true God have had to be found or invented in each of the languages in which the gospel has been preached. Among the Christians of Rwanda and Burundi, *Imana* has become the name of the true God, just as *Tien-Djou* ("Master of Heaven") has among the Vietnamese (who borrowed the expression from the Chinese), and *Hananim* among Korean Catholics (Korean Protestants use the Chinese term). Still, all of these designations had a different meaning before they were adopted by translators of the sacred Scriptures.

The same problem exists for all of the words that appear in the original text of the Scriptures, even for those that have had a symbolic meaning right from the start, because earthly, social, historical realities do not have the same significance everywhere. What a job the translators have! And when the time comes to move on to theological reflection and bring it to diverse cultures, what an effort the preachers of the gospel once again will have to make! For the moment, however, it is enough that we have indicated the type of work that awaits them.

My task in this book has been simply to provide an overview of the symbolic language of the biblical texts, and I have discussed this language only in terms of their original composition. The rest of the work must be done by those who, throughout the world, will fulfill the responsibility of bringing the gospel to all people: "Go into all the world and proclaim the good news to the whole creation" (Mark 16:15). Through their work, the miracle of Pentecost will be reproduced: "how is it that we hear, each of us, in our own native language?" (Acts 2:8). This will happen, however, only through a sustained effort on the part of each of us who shares the good news.

Selected
Bibliography

Allègre, C. *Dieu face à la science.* Paris: Fayard, 1997.

Avril, A.-C., and D. de la Maisonneuve. *Prières juives.* Suppléments au Cahiers évangile 68. Paris: Cerf, 1989.

Barucq, A., et al. *Prières de l'ancien Orient.* Suppléments au Cahiers évangile 27. Paris: Cerf, 1979.

Briend, J. *Dieu dans l'Écriture.* Lectio divina 150. Paris: Cerf, 1992.

Bultmann, R. "Nouveau Testament et mythologie." Pages 139–83 in *L'Interprétation du Nouveau Testament.* Edited by O. Laffoucrière. Les religions 11. Paris: Aubier, 1955.

Cazelles, H., ed. *Introduction critique à l'Ancien Testament.* Rev. ed. Introduction à la Bible 2. Paris: Desclée, 1973.

———. *À la recherche de Moïse.* Études annexes de la Bible de Jérusalem. Paris: Cerf, 1979.

———. *Autour de l'Exode: Études.* Sources bibliques. Paris: Gabalda, 1987.

———. *Études d'histoire religieuse et de philologie biblique.* Sources bibliques. Paris: Gabalda, 1996.

———. "Yahwisme, ou Yahvé et son peuple." Pages 35–47 in *Études d'histoire religieuse et de philologie biblique.* Sources bibliques. Paris: Gabalda, 1996.

Dabek, T. M., and T. Jelonek, eds. *Agnus et Sponsa: Essays in Honor of A. Jankowski.* Krakow: Wydawn. Benedyktynów, 1993.

de la Potterie, I. *La Vérité dans saint Jean.* 2 vols. Analecta biblica 73, 74. Rome: Biblical Institute Press, 1977.

de Surgy, P., et al., *La résurrection du Christ et l'exégese moderne.* Lectio divina 50. Paris: Cerf, 1969.

Denzinger, H., P. Hünermann, and H. Hoping, *Kompendium der Glaubensbekenntnisse und kirchlichen Lehrentscheidungen.* 37th ed. Freiburg im Brisgau: Herder, 1991.

Dupont, J. *Pourquoi des paraboles? La méthode parabolique de Jésus.* Lire la Bible 46. Paris: Cerf, 1977.

————. *Études sur les évangiles synoptiques.* 2 vols. Bibliotheca ephemeridum theologicarum lovaniensium 70. Leuven: Leuven University Press, 1985.

Dupont-Sommer, A., et al., eds. *La Bible: Écrits intertestamentaires.* Translated by A. Caquot. Bibliothèque de la Pléiade 337. Paris: Gallimard, 1987.

Eliade, M. *Le mythe de l'éternel retour: Archétypes et repetition.* Paris: Gallimard, 1949.

Gaboriau, F. *L'Écriture seule?* Théologie nouvelle. Paris: FAC-éditions, 1997.

Grandet, P. *Hymnes de la religion d'Aton: Hymnes du XIVe siècle avant J.-C.* Sagesses 97. Paris: Seuil, 1995.

Grelot, P. "Isaïe 14, 12–15 et son arrière-plan mythologique." *Revue de l'histoire des religions* 149 (1956): 18–48.

————. "La légend d'Hénoch dans les Apocryphes et dans la Bible." *Recherches de science religieuse* 46 (1958): 5–16, 181–210.

————. *Sens chrétien de l'Ancien Testament: Esquisse d'un traité dogmatique.* Bibliothèque de théologie 1, Théologie dogmatique 3. Tournai: Desclée, 1962.

————. *La Bible, parole de Dieu: Introduction théologique à l'étude de l'Écriture sainte.* Bibliothèque de théologie 1, Théologie dogmatique 5. Paris: Desclée, 1965.

————. *Pages bibliques.* 2d ed. Paris: Belin, 1965.

————. *Documents araméens d'Égypte.* Littératures anciennes du Proche-Orient 5. Paris: Cerf, 1972.

————. *Péché originel et rédemption, examinés à partir de l'épître aux Romains: Essai théologique.* Paris: Desclée, 1973.

————. "Daniel 7:9–10 et le livre d'Hénoch." *Semitica* 28 (1978): 59–83.

————. "Étude critique de Luc 10, 19." *Recherches de science religieuse* 69 (1981): 87–100.

————. "Jésus devant le 'Monde du mal.'" Pages 131–201 in *Foi et culture à la lumière de la Bible: Actes de la session plénière 1979 de la Commission Biblique Pontificale*. Turin: Elle di Ci, 1981.

————. *Les Poèmes du Serviteur: De la lecture critique à l'herméneutique*. Lectio divina 103. Paris: Cerf, 1981.

————. "La résurrection de Jésus et l'histoire: Historicité et historalité." Pages 145–79 in J. Guillet et al., *Dieu l'a ressuscité d'entre les morts*. Les quatre fleuves 15–16. Paris: Beauchesne, 1982.

————. *Évangiles et histoire*. Introduction à la Bible 3, Le Nouveau Testament 6. Paris: Desclée, 1985.

————. "Le langage symbolique dans la Bible: Note méthodologique." Pages 43–69 in *Kecharitomene: Mélanges René Laurentin*. Paris: Desclée, 1990.

————. *Dieu, le Père de Jésus Christ*. Jésus et Jésus-Christ 60. Paris: Desclée, 1994.

————. *L'Espérance juive à l'heure de Jésus*. 11th ed. Jésus et Jésus-Christ 6. Paris: Desclée, 1994.

————. "Un examen critique du langage symbolique." Pages 56–70 in *Réponse à Eugen Drewermann*. Théologies Apologiques. Paris: Cerf, 1994.

————. *La tradition apostolique: Règle de foi et de vie pour l'église*. Théologies. Paris: Cerf, 1995.

————. "Les tentations de Jésus." *La nouvelle revue théologique* 117 (1995): 501–16.

————. *Jésus de Nazareth, Christ et Seigneur: Une lecture de l'Évangile*. 2 vols. Lectio divina 167, 170. Paris: Cerf, 1997–1998.

————. *Le mystère du Christ dans les Psaumes*. Jesus et Jesus-Christ 74. Paris: Desclée, 1998.

————. "Voir Dieu: Le ciel, l'Enfer, le Purgatoire." *Esprit et vie* 108 (1998): 241–46.

————. *Corps et sang du Christ en gloire: Enquête dogmatique*. Lectio divina 182. Paris: Cerf, 1999.

————. "L'imagerie des quatre Vivants." Pages 241–50 in *Études sémitiques et samaritaines offertes à Jean Margain*. Edited by C.-B. Amphoux, A. Ferry, and U. Schatter-Rieser. Histoire du texte biblique 4. Lausanne: Zèbre, 1999.

Grelot, P., et al. *La liturgie dans le Nouveau Testament*. Introduction à la Bible 9. Paris: Desclée, 1991.

Haudebert, P. ed. *Le Pentateuque: Débats et recherches.* Lectio divina 151. Paris: Cerf, 1992.

Jeremias, J. *Abba: Jésus et son père.* Paris: Seuil, 1972.

——. *Théologie du Nouveau Testament.* Vol. 1. Lectio divina 76. Paris: Cerf, 1973.

La Bonnardière, A.-M., ed. *Saint Augustin et la Bible.* Bible de tous les temps 3. Paris: Beauchesne, 1986.

Marchel, W. *Abba, Père! La prière de Jésus et des chrétiens: Étude exégétique sur les origines et la signification de l'invocation à la divinité comme père, avant et dans le Nouveau Testament.* Analecta biblica 19. Rome: Pontifical Biblical Institute, 1963.

Michaeli, F. *Dieu à l'image de l'homme: Etude de la notion anthropomorphique de Dieu dans l'Ancien Testament.* Bibliothèque théologique. Neuchatel: Delachaux et Niestlé, 1950.

Mondésert, C., ed. *Le monde grec ancien et la Bible.* Bible de tous les temps 1. Paris: Beauchesne, 1984.

Nodet, E., and J. Taylor, *Essai sur les origines du christianisme: Une secte éclatée.* Initiations bibliques. Paris: Cerf, 1998.

Reeves, H. *La première seconde.* Vol. 2 of *Dernières nouvelles du cosmos.* Paris: Seuil, 1995.

Riché, P., and G. Lobrichon, eds. *Le Moyen Âge et la Bible.* Bible de tous les temps 4. Paris: Beauchesne, 1984.

Ricoeur, P. *The Symbolism of Evil.* Boston: Beacon, 1969.

Schnackenburg, R. *Règne et royaume de Dieu: Essai de Théologie biblique.* Études théologiques 2. Paris: L'Orante, 1965.

Silk, J. *The Big Bang.* 3d ed. New York: Freeman, 2001.

Spicq, C. *Agapè: Prolégomènes à une etude de théologie néo-testamentaire.* Studia hellenistica 10. Louvain: E. Nauwelaerts, 1955.

——. *Agapè dans le Nouveau Testament: Analyse des textes.* 3 vols. Études bibliques. Paris: Gabalda, 1958–1959.

Strack, H. L., and G. Stemberger, *Introduction au Talmud et au Midrash.* Trans. M.-R. Hayoun. Paris: Cerf, 1986.

Vidal, J. "Mythe," Pages 1392–97 in vol. 2 of *Dictionnaire des religions.* Edited by P. Poupard. 3d ed. 2 vols. Paris: Presses Universitaires de France, 1993.

——. "Symbole." Pages 1937–42 in *Dictionnaire des religions,* vol. 2. Edited by P. Poupard. 3d ed. 2 vols. Paris: Presses Universitaires de France, 1993.

Subject Index